# CULTURES IN CONFLICT

# CULTURES IN CONFLICT

## Encounters Between European and Non-European Cultures, 1492–1800

## Urs Bitterli

*Translated by Ritchie Robertson*

Polity Press

First published 1989 by Polity Press in association with
Blackwell Publishers.
First published in paperback 1993

Editorial Office: Polity Press, 65 Bridge Street, Cambridge CB2 1UR, UK

Marketing and Production: Blackwell Publishers,
108 Cowley Road, Oxford, OX4 1JF, UK

British Library Cataloguing in Publication Data

Bitterli, Urs
Cultures in conflict: encounters between
European and non-European cultures,
1492–1800.
1. European exploration. Cultural aspects,
history
I. Title
910'.94
ISBN 0–7456–0530–3
ISBN 0–7456–1157–5 (pbk)

The publishers gratefully acknowledge the generous support of the
Pro Helvetia Foundation in the undertaking of this translation


Typeset in 10 on 12 pt Sabon
by Opus, Oxford
Printed in Great Britain by T. J. Press Ltd, Padstow

# Contents

# Introduction

## by Ritchie Robertson

Urs Bitterli, Professor of Modern History at Zurich University since 1983, is one of the foremost historians of colonialism in the German-speaking region, and one of the most original scholars in this field anywhere in the world. His method, however, does not fit the familiar moulds of political, social or economic history. He practises *Geistesgeschichte*, an untranslatable term which partly corresponds to our 'history of ideas' but also overlaps with what has recently become known as the 'history of mentalities'. Urs Bitterli has defined his approach in the preface to an earlier book, *Die Entdeckung des schwarzen Afrikaners* ('The Discovery of the Black African') dealing with West Africa in the seventeenth and eighteenth centuries:

> I am not concerned with the details of the looting of Freetown by the French, nor with the abilities displayed by a particular Governor-General in the administration of Senegal. I interpret the source-text as the evidence of a personal standpoint, capable of acquiring a lasting significance from the individuality of the author and the uniqueness of the historical situation. The principal subject of my account is not the historical reality of events and states of affairs to which a particular source-text may refer; what appeals to me is the reality of the mental activity manifested in the travel narratives and scientific treatises of the time.[1]

In all his books Bitterli's focus is on encounters between cultures. This subject has two main aspects. Firstly, there is what may be called the phenomenology of the encounter: the experience that can be reconstructed from contemporary documents, within the indispensable framework of political, economic and social history. Secondly, there is intellectual reflection on the encounter, given written form not only in travel narratives but also in ethnographic, scientific treatises, historiography and literature. His project means also that, to a greater extent than most historians, he is concerned with the status of his sources as written texts. His works include a densely packed essay, *Schriftsteller und Kolonialismus* ('Writers and Colonialism'), examining the critical treatments of imperialism in Conrad, Malraux, Graham Greene and the German dramatist Peter Weiss.[2]

It may be to Bitterli's advantage that he is Swiss. The peaceful coexistence of different national groups has long since been achieved in Switzerland, and the country lacks the burden of an imperialist past. At the same time, Swiss national identity is hard to define, since it cannot be equated with a single language or culture. The theme of national identity is present in Urs Bitterli's first book, based on his doctoral thesis: a study of Thomas Mann's political writings on National Socialism.[3] Many of these writings date from Mann's exile in Switzerland between 1933 and 1938. As Bitterli points out, Mann felt himself to be intensely German, yet the nature of this identity was a problem he never solved. His commitment to German culture and to liberal democracy made it impossible for him to support the nationalist movements which travestied the one and destroyed the other. Hence, Mann found Switzerland a tolerable refuge. In eastern Switzerland, where he settled, he was able to live in an atmosphere of German culture without culture being used to enforce political homogeneity. Bitterli cites his description of Switzerland as 'a country where refreshingly un-German things can be said in German.'[4]

Bitterli's next book, *Die Entdeckung des schwarzen Afrikaners*, deals with relations between Europeans and Africans on a section of the West African coast corresponding to present-day Gambia, Senegal and Sierra Leone, from the viewpoint of intellectual history. In both subject and approach, its most obvious precursor is Philip Curtin's *The Image of Africa* (London, 1965), in which a factual account of trade and exploration is interwoven with an account of the changing image of the African recorded in travellers' reports and in literary and scientific texts. In the preface to his own book, Bitterli pays generous tribute to Curtin's work and thanks him personally for help and stimulus. Bitterli, however, deals with an earlier period and places the emphasis more strongly on the encounter between Europeans and Africans. He shows that early European accounts are predominantly moralistic and ethnocentric. Visiting traders condemn the Africans' seemingly shiftless and unproductive way of life: when, however, the Africans show themselves to be cautious and calculating trading partners, the Europeans change their tune and call the Africans cunning and vengeful. In the eighteenth century the image of the 'noble savage' is applied to the

Africans, and a demand arises firstly for the humane treatment of African slaves, then for the abolition of the slave trade altogether. Bitterli also gives ample space to theological and scientific debates about the African's place in creation, culminating in the classification of physical races by the ethnologist Blumenbach in 1798.

*Die Entdeckung des schwarzen Afrikaners* ends with the first great exploration of the West African interior: the journey made by the Scotsman Mungo Park in 1795–7 to establish the direction of the Niger, and recorded in his *Travels in the Interior Districts of Africa* (1799). Bitterli underlines the epoch-making character of Park's journey. Firstly, its object was disinterested enquiry instead of commercial profit. Secondly, and even more importantly, Park was forced into a direct encounter with Africa. He was robbed and imprisoned; he travelled long distances alone, tormented by hunger and thirst; rescued by well-disposed Africans, he lived among them and shared their life for several months before regaining contact with Europeans. 'The absoluteness of his personal commitment and the difficulties of his enterprise', concludes Bitterli, 'allow Park to enter into an unmediated, inescapable relationship with the native Africans.'[5] It is perhaps not too bold to suggest that this concept of direct encounter with the other underlies all Bitterli's work and that it is existentialist in origin. It may be no coincidence that while working on Thomas Mann, Bitterli attended seminars on Herder given by the literary critic Emil Staiger, whose approach to literature was deeply indebted to existentialism and phenomenology.[6]

Having examined relations with the Guinea Coast through the lens of intellectual history, Bitterli, in his next and most important book, extended this approach to the whole of the early modern world. *Die 'Wilden' und die 'Zivilisierten'* ('The "Savage" and the "Civilized"') is too large and rich a book to be summarized easily.[7] Political and economic history serve as the framework for a study in intellectual history and cultural encounter. Bitterli gives due attention to the literary forms in which explorations were recorded, such as the factual journals kept by individual voyagers and the celebratory narratives composed by official chroniclers, and those in which knowledge was collected, from the encyclopaedic cosmographies of the late Middle Ages to the scientific treatises and compendia of the Enlightenment. Much space is given to changing views of non-Europeans, in science and literature, including the controversy between monogenists and polygenists, the origins of physical ethnology, and the literary image of the 'noble savage'. He concludes with a close examination of three Enlightenment works in which 'noble savages' are used by the authors to question the values of European civilization: Voltaire's *L'Ingénu*, Diderot's *Supplément au voyage de Bougainville*, and the lesser-known *Voyages dans l'Amérique septen-*

*trionale* by Baron La Hontan. At the end of Bitterli's narrative, therefore, knowledge of other cultures becomes self-knowledge. Encounters with other cultures enable Europeans to relativize their own culture by seeing it as one among others.

Both in *Die 'Wilden' und die 'Zivilisierten'* and in the present book, though with slight changes of terminology, Bitterli classifies encounters between Europeans and non-Europeans under three headings. Firstly, there is more or less fleeting and superficial contact, as when voyagers touch at Pacific islands in order to take in fresh supplies. Secondly, there is a more sustained relationship, illustrated by the slave trade and by missions to the heathen – both strikingly ethnocentric enterprises. Thirdly, there is collision, in which the weaker partner is swept aside, suffering at worst genocide, at best the absorption of its survivors into the civilization of the conquerors.

*Cultures in Conflict* takes this scheme, illustrating it with an extraordinary range of detail, and uses it as the framework for a number of case studies. The opening chapter sets out the economic and social context. Material history also figures largely in some of the studies, particularly that dealing with the Portuguese trading empire. The main emphasis, however, is on intellectual history in the broad sense. Thus, we hear about the debates among Spanish jurists on the legal status of the native Americans; about William Penn's resolve to practise the Quaker principle of religious toleration in his dealings with the Indians; and about the eighteenth-century tendency for voyages of discovery to turn into scientific expeditions, planned and sometimes accompanied by botanists and zoologists. However, different varieties of history – economic, social and intellectual – are so deftly interwoven that they cannot be separated. The whole book illustrates Bitterli's contribution to historiography: the transformation of colonial history into cultural history.

Bitterli stands out among historians by his explicit (though not overstated) interest in the epistemological and moral problems arising from encounters and clashes between cultures. Epistemological problems, the difficulties of recognizing and evaluating other cultures, take their most dramatic form during the phase of initial contact. As Bitterli shows, members of non-European cultures, especially the high civilizations of Mesoamerica and Peru, often reacted to the first appearance of Europeans by assuming that the newcomers must be gods. There was no other way in which such a novel event as contact with a different civilization could be fitted into their world pictures. For the Europeans, these initial contacts evoked images of paradise and the golden age. Closer acquaintance, however, soon disabused both sides of such mythopoeic fantasies. The non-Europeans always discovered sooner or later that the newcomers were intent on dispossessing them and eroding their traditional culture. The newcomers turned out to be far from godlike, not only because of their brutality and greed, but also because experience proved that they could be killed. Meanwhile the Europeans found that the newly discovered peoples, thanks to their ineffectual weaponry or their good-natured compliance, could be used as an almost inexhaustible supply of forced labour or sexual gratification. Initial contact developed all too often into cultural collision. Bitterli shows how blind the Europeans were to the nature of this process. Desperate counter-attacks such as the Virginia massacre of 1622 (described below, p. 30) might have been expected, but Europeans persistently described them as 'treachery', 'conspiracies' or 'rebellions'. Bitterli provides numerous historical counterparts to the naïve attitudes of the Europeans in Conrad's *Heart of Darkness*, for whom 'natives' being futilely bombarded from the sea are 'enemies' and the heads on posts around Kurtz's compound are those of 'rebels'.[8] However, the Europeans' blindness was of course largely wilful. It was in their interest to overlook the specific character of the cultures they encountered. As Bitterli shows, nomadic tribes were thought to be uncivilized because they did not have settlements, and to have no right to land that they did not cultivate. In Chapter 3 Bitterli describes the more sophisticated justification for exploitation employed by the Spanish jurists who adopted Aristotle's definition of 'barbaric' peoples as natural slaves.[9]

Here the epistemological problems shade into moral ones. 'The conquest of the earth', says Conrad's Marlow, 'which mostly means the taking it away from those who have a different complexion or slightly flatter noses from ourselves, is not a pretty thing when you look into it too much.'[10] Few nowadays would disagree. The really intriguing moral problems arise over cultural relationships that might seem beneficial to non-European peoples. Such relationships include commercial and missionary activity. As Bitterli shows in Chapter 4, it was in the Europeans' interest to maintain good relations with the Canadian Indians who supplied them with beaver pelts. Europeans, however, ignored the deleterious effects of the fur trade on Indian society. Indians altered their traditional way of life to specialize in trapping beaver. When the beaver became rare in eastern Canada, the Indians lost their new livelihood and no longer had their traditional occupations to fall back on.[11]

Discussing missionary activity, Bitterli pays ample tribute to the selflessness of the Jesuits who ventured among the Indian tribes of Canada. He notes that their mission settlements staved off the harmful effects of contact with Europe for several decades. He also acknowledges, however, that the appalling privations suffered by the missionaries were largely futile. The Indians did not want Christianity. Life in the settlements meant submitting to an uncongenial discipline, especially at school, from which Indians often ran away. Similar problems arise with the Jesuit 'reductions' in Brazil and Paraguay. These preserved Indian tribes from the barbarities of slave-raiders, but the Indians who lived there had to sacrifice their traditional culture and submit to a discipline which was much milder, but no less inimical to their habitual way of life, than the monotonous work-discipline imposed in the slave plantations. The missionaries wanted to destroy Indian culture while saving the Indians from ill-treatment: a noble but deeply ethnocentric aim.

Chapters 5 and 6 explore possibilities of peaceful coexistence between European and other cultures. High civilizations like China and Japan had little need for European commerce, kept firm control over such trade as did develop, and thus set severe limits to the productive interaction of cultures. (The Opium Wars of the nineteenth century were to confirm the wisdom of keeping Europeans at arm's length.) In seventeenth-century Pennsylvania a serious attempt was made to establish a European colony without detriment to the Indians. However, as Bitterli demonstrates in his most thought-provoking chapter, this attempt rested on a concealed ethnocentrism. Ignoring the nomadic character of Indian society, it assumed that the Indians shared the European view of land as a possession which could be assigned by contractual agreements; and it took for granted that in the event of conflict the settlers' interests would override those of the Indians. When the inevitable happened, William Penn's 'Holy Experiment' ended in tragic failure.

Bitterli is not alone, of course, in his interest in European contact with other cultures. The dissolution of the European colonial empires and the weakening of Western hegemony over the Third World – a process whose reality was forcefully brought home by the world oil crisis of 1973 – have shaken the ethnocentric arrogance of the West. Accordingly, a whole series of studies has recently examined relations between Western and other cultures from a variety of viewpoints. It may be useful to glance at some of these approaches and the problems they raise, in order to suggest how Bitterli's work is related to other studies of cultural contact.

Encounters between different cultures are instances of a more extensive problem which has received considerable attention recently: that of relating to whatever group one's society defines as other than oneself. Most societies define women as other than men; many define children as other than adults; while medical, ethnological, sexual and religious classifications produce such groups as 'madmen', 'blacks', 'homosexuals' and 'heretics'. This classifying process gives us a map of our society and provides us with stereotypes in terms of which we approach other individuals.[12] Given the pervasiveness of stereotyping, one might ask sceptically whether it is possible to understand another culture at all. This scepticism is prominent in the important book *Orientalism* by Edward Said. Said undercuts his polemic against Western misrepresentations of the Orient by maintaining that the distinction between a true and false representation is merely one of degree, because 'all representations, because they *are* representations, are embedded firstly in the language and then in the culture, institutions and political ambience of the representer.'[13] One can accept this truism without yielding to outright scepticism. Perception, understanding and representation are all obliged to use stereotypes. Stereotypes are not falsehoods, but simplified models which are necessary if we are to cope with the multiplicity of experience. The error lies not in using stereotypes, but in supposing that stereotypes are fully adequate representations. In addition, it is an error to which the self takes refuge when threatened, creating crude oppositions of them vs. us, black vs. white. However, it is possible, though difficult, to use stereotypes in a critical and tentative manner, as frames within which the reality of the Other can be perceived and described with precision. By such methods another culture can be accurately understood and represented; but this can only be done from an observer's specific historical standpoint, and within the conventions of representation that the observer employs. As E. H. Gombrich says of the 'correct portrait', the result will be 'an end product on a long road through schema and correction', 'not a faithful record of a visual experience but the faithful construction of a relational model'.[14]

Bitterli's work reminds us that genuine encounters with other cultures are rare, while ways of avoiding such encounters are manifold. The commonest mode of evasion is to deny the otherness of other peoples by classifying them as an imperfect version of oneself. The concept of the 'primitive', for example, defines other societies as crude and simple anticipations of one's own. This device appealed especially to eighteenth-century believers in the perfectibility of humanity. Thus, Schiller, in his inaugural lecture as professor of history at Jena, listed the barbarous qualities imputed to 'primitive' peoples by recent travellers – their ignorance of useful arts, of marriage and property, their warfare, cannibalism, drunkenness and idolatry – and concluded: '*We* were like that. Caesar and Tacitus, eighteen centuries ago, found us to be little better.'[15] In saying this, Schiller was uttering a commonplace. The social theorists of the Scottish Enlightenment had constructed an evolutionary scheme in which society advanced through four stages, each defined by the dominant mode of subsistence. The most primitive stage, that of hunting, was followed by herding, then by agriculture, and finally by commerce.[16] The 'four stages theory' survived into the nineteenth century and helped to ensure that early anthropology rested firmly on evolutionary assumptions. It underpinned James Mill's *History of British India* (1817), which argued that Hindu society was a stagnating and primitive society which it was the duty of the British gradually to bring up to date; and it contributed to Frazer's well-known description of magic as primitive science.[17] To discern evolutionary categories in present-day anthropology is less easy, but their presence has recently been powerfully argued by Johannes Fabian: 'As distancing devices, categorizations of this kind are used, for instance, when we are told that certain elements in our culture are "neolithic" or "archaic"; or when certain living societies are said to practise "stone age economics"; or when certain styles of thought are identified as "savage" or "primitive".'[18]

The 'primitive', of course, is only one of many concepts that can be used to categorize other cultures. In the period discussed by Bitterli, the most popular such concept was that of the 'pagan'. Newly discovered peoples were fitted into the Christocentric world view by being classified as pagans in need of conversion; resemblances were sought between their religions and those of the Greeks and Romans.[19] The centrality of this category helps to explain the massive efforts at conversion made by Christian missions. However, other peoples were sometimes also seen as 'wise pagans' who had anticipated the truths of Christianity. Many Renaissance scholars believed in an ancient theology which could be excavated from such sources as Platonism, the Jewish Cabbala, and the doctrines ascribed to Orpheus, Hermes Trismegistus and the ancient Egyptians. The Chinese were often seen in this way. Leibniz thought that the *I Ching* might be part of an ancient theology, while the Jesuit Joachim Bouvet declared in 1704 that the Chinese classics contained 'a mysterious and prophetic summary of all the principles and of the whole economy of the Christian religion and nothing else'.[20] Thus, the beliefs of another people could be simultaneously praised and ignored, by being misrepresented as simply an anticipation of one's own.

Responses to other cultures often take the form of extravagant value-judgements. The others may be beatified as noble savages or demonized as barbarians; in neither case are they seen matter-of-factly as people living by social rules and values of their own. The *topoi* of the golden age and the noble savage are familiar, and are abundantly documented by Bitterli and other writers.[21] Most remarkable, perhaps, is the double-think that often accompanies such notions: thus, Columbus, as Bitterli tells us in Chapter 3, regarded the Tainos of Hispaniola as living in the golden age, yet had no scruples about proposing to turn them into slaves. It is probably commoner to demonize other peoples by ascribing barbarous vices to them, especially those vices which are repressed and tabooed in one's own society. Hence, other peoples have constantly been accused of cannibalism and incest, on the flimsiest of evidence. Strabo described the ancient inhabitants of Ireland as cannibals; in medieval Europe Jews were accused of devouring Christian children; and it has recently been argued that the ascription of cannibalism to 'primitive' peoples is equally unjustified, since no trustworthy record exists of cannibalism actually being performed. Cannibalism always turns out to have been suppressed shortly before the observer's arrival, or is imputed by his informants to *other* people. Thus, an enquirer early in this century was told by the Baganda, who live on the shores of Lake Victoria, that they were not cannibals, but that the Sese, who lived on islands in the lake, ate human flesh: the Sese denied it but insisted that another tribe, on the far shore of the lake, were cannibals.[22] Cannibalism, in short, is a way of defining other people by locating them in a system of values which is an inversion of one's own.

Two further, complementary ways of denying the separate existence of other peoples deserve mention. One is to represent them, not as a society with its own values, but as exotic and wondrous, and hence too peculiar to make one question one's own values. In classical and medieval times, the remote corners of the globe were supposed to be peopled with marvellous beings, such as giants, pygmies, headless men and dog-headed men. These were not entirely imaginary. The pygmies and the giants had obvious prototypes among Central African tribes, while the Amyctyrae, who were said to project their upper lip so far that it could serve as a parasol, might have been suggested by the lip-stretching customs of the Ubangi.[23] In the thirteenth century, Marco Polo claimed to have seen dog-headed men on the Andaman Islands. In his more sober passages, traditional marvels of the East served as models against which he defined the curious things he actually had seen. Thus, he calls the rhinoceros a unicorn, but adds that it does not correspond to the European conception of the unicorn.[24] Contact with Islam did not, as one would have expected, encourage a more sober apprehension of other cultures. Despite the Crusades, medieval writers seem incurious about Islamic culture. Muslims are demonized as idolatrous worshippers of 'Mahound'. The Mongols were equated, equally absurdly, with the legendary Christian monarch, Prester John.[25]

Besides representing other peoples as exotic, it is possible to make the complementary error of ignoring their otherness altogether. Columbus says in his diary that he will take some Indians to Spain so that they may 'learn to talk', as though they had no language of their own.[26] At other times he seems to think that they are speaking bad Spanish. Thus, when they utter the word 'Cariba', Columbus hears it as 'Caniba' and concludes that he must be near the territories of the Great Khan; but he also misinterprets them as saying that their neighbours have dogs' heads (from the Italian *cane*, 'dog').[27] Worse still, the administrators who caused the *Requerimiento* to be read aloud to the Indians, taking formal possession of their lands, seem to have assumed that there was no language barrier between the Indians and themselves. Again, Columbus shows his Christocentrism by asserting that the Indians 'have no creed'.[28] A literary example of comparable arrogance is Robinson Crusoe's assumption that his black companion has no name: 'I made him know his name should be Friday, which was the day I saved his life.' This gratuitous christening locates Friday not only within the English language but within the European calendar, one of Crusoe's most important links with the civilization from which he has come.[29]

All these forms of misperception of other peoples could be multiplied over and over again for the early modern period. J. H. Elliott has observed how slowly Renaissance Europe reacted to the discovery of America. Maps showing the traditional division of the world into the three land masses, Europe, Asia and Africa, continued to be used in schools until late in the sixteenth century. References to America in sixteenth-century literature are surprisingly few and stereotyped.[30] In addition to the obvious difficulties of assimilating new discoveries, to which Elliott refers, one might suggest that early modern Europe was a society ill qualified to encounter other peoples. Xenophobia seems to have been widespread and intense, directed against stereotypes of the bloodthirsty Turk, the usurious and child-killing Jew, and the devil-worshipping witch. 'Hatred of outsiders', it has been suggested, 'was so common as to make one wonder whether most ordinary people of the period were not what psychologists sometimes call "authoritarian personalities", combining submissiveness to authority with aggressive-ness towards people outside their group.'[31] This society was forced to confront 'otherness' in its midst by the Reformation, which split Europe into two warring camps and created new stereotypes, the impious Protestant and the wicked 'Papist'. It is possible that this internecine bitterness was displaced on to groups of 'others' already available in society – Jews and women – and on to the 'pagan' inhabitants of the New World. This would help to explain why massive expulsions of the Jews from Germany, Switzerland and much of Italy coincided with the Reformation and Counter-Reformation.[32] It also helps to explain why over three-quarters of victims in the great European witch-hunt were female. Judeo-Christian tradition represented women as prone to sensuality and malice, and as a potential source of social disorder. They provided ready-made scapegoats for people rendered insecure and aggressive by the religious conflicts, as well as by the economic and social disorder, of the period.[33] Such an epoch was hardly favourable to the dispassionate investigation of other cultures.

The rediscovery of classical learning supplied one potential model for the study of other cultures: the *Histories* of Herodotus, which describe soberly the manners and customs of the Egyptians, Persians, Scythians and other peoples surrounding the Greek world. Although modern research has largely confirmed the accuracy of Herodotus' reports, his veracity was questioned in classical times by Cicero and Plutarch. Partly for this reason, it was not Herodotus but Thucydides, with his insistence on the primacy of political history and the use of first-hand evidence, who set the pattern for subsequent historiography.[34] Herodotus' approach to history was revived in the Renaissance by Italian and Spanish writers who wanted to provide accounts of the newly discovered territories and were partly or wholly dependent on hearsay evidence. Their work raised Herodotus' standing; but few writers seem actually to have taken Herodotus as a model in their accounts of newly discovered peoples. One who did was Olfert Dapper, who translated Herodotus into Dutch and was probably inspired by his example in compiling detailed descriptions of Africa and Asia, based on travellers' reports and rich in ethnographic information.[35] On the whole, however, it is in the eighteenth century that we find other cultures described without ethnocentric moralizing and with appreciation for their diversity. The three writers whom I want to single out in this connection are Lafitau, Vico and Herder.

The Jesuit Joseph-François Lafitau (1681–1746) was a successor to the priests described in Chapter 4 below as a missionary to the Hurons and Iroquois of Canada. His account of them, *Mœurs des sauvages américains comparées aux mœurs des premiers temps* (1724), remained the best source of ethnographic information on these peoples until the work of Lewis Henry Morgan in the later nineteenth century. In some ways Lafitau is a backward-looking writer. Like earlier scholars, he wants to fit the American Indians into history by relating them to classical antiquity, and he argues that the Hurons and Iroquois are descended from the peoples of Asiatic Thrace who spread into the Persian Empire and thence passed through 'Tartary' into America via a land-bridge or narrow strait. His method of arguing, however, is more forward-looking, for it is based on comparative ethnography. He notes that certain customs among the American Indians, such as the *couvade* or the transvestism of some men, have parallels in classical sources. More generally, he compares the customs of the Indians to those of the early stages of Greek and Roman civilization. Their tribal self-government reminds him of the self-governing village republics of the ancient Lycians; their councils of war are compared with those of the early

Roman republic; their wars, in which numerous nations form confeder-
acies, are compared to the Trojan War; and after a gruesome description
of the tortures inflicted by Indians on their prisoners of war, Lafitau,
instead of moralizing like his seventeenth-century predecessors, remarks:
'In fact, what do they do more than the Greeks and Romans used to do
formerly? What more inhumane than the heroes of the Iliad?'[36] Here we
have the beginnings of cultural relativism. Lafitau's account gains
freshness, too, from his realization that primitive tribes like those
recorded in ancient sources still exist at the present day. It is as though
the Homeric heroes had come to life.[37]

Lafitau's book was published almost simultaneously with the first
edition (1725) of the *New Science* of Giambattista Vico (1668–1744), a
professor of rhetoric at Naples. Though fascinated by primitive man,
Vico is no primitivist. He believes neither in a golden age nor in an
ancient theology. Nor does he share the common Enlightenment
assumption that human nature is basically uniform. For him, human
nature is a process, in which people gradually deepen their understanding
of the world and themselves, and realize the capacities latent in them.
This process takes place throughout a variety of languages and cultures,
each of which is to be understood on its own terms. Vico proclaims the
'great truth' that linguistic diversity is an aspect of the diversity of
humanity: 'by virtue of the aforesaid diversity of their natures they have
regarded the same utilities or necessities of human life from different
points of view, and there have thus arisen so many national customs, for
the most part differing from one another and at times contrary to one
another; so and not otherwise there have arisen as many different
languages as there are nations.'[38] Despite their diversity, other cultures
are intelligible because they are products of the same capacities that
present-day people possess. Hence, we have the imaginative resources to
understand primitive people, though Vico acknowledges the difficulty of
the task. Vico assumes that primitive people had not yet learned abstract
thinking but expressed themselves in vivid and concrete images, as the
peasants of southern Italy still did in Vico's own day. Thus, the
'primitive' is not confined to the remote past: for Vico, as for Lafitau, it
still exists. Moreover, educated people are linked with 'primitives' by
their capacity for metaphor, an artificial technique but one based on the
same concrete thinking that characterizes the primitive mentality.

Neither Lafitau nor Vico exercised as much influence as Johann
Gottfried Herder (1744–1803), a Lutheran clergyman who lived from
1776 onwards at Weimar, in contact with Goethe and other great figures
of German literature. An important event in Herder's life was his voyage
from Riga to Nantes in the summer of 1769. This may sound tame

compared to the voyages that Cook and Bougainville were making at that time in the Pacific. As Herder's *Journal of my Voyage* shows, however, it seemed to bring him into contact with primitive culture. The strict subordination required aboard ship reminded him of the primitive despotisms described in Homer; the sailors' yarns seemed to be the raw materials of mythology; and their superstitions helped him to understand the origins of religion. Thus, though he had not yet read Vico, Herder applied Vico's method of understanding other cultures through exercising one's own imaginative resources. Also, ancient times were reanimated for him, as for Lafitau, by contact with present-day people who were in some respects primitive. However, Herder is anxious not to dismiss earlier cultures as merely primitive anticipations of the present. He constructs a philosophy of historical development in which each period is seen as valuable in its own right. Each culture, he maintains, is animated by its own spirit, which finds expression primarily through language. Though we cannot restore past cultures, we can learn from them, and Herder thinks his over-civilized contemporaries need to regain something of the vigour of primitive peoples. Otherwise he foresees an aridly uniform future in which all people become 'philanthropic citizens of the world', a prospect which inspires his ironic disgust. 'The princes speak French, and soon everybody will follow their example; and then, behold, perfect bliss: the golden age, when all the world will speak one tongue, one universal language, is dawning again! There will be one flock and one shepherd! National cultures, where are you?'[39]

Herder stands at an intellectual watershed. The Enlightenment's humane interest in other cultures, documented in Chapter 7 below, was the basis for Herder's more inward appreciation of the spirit of another culture. His influence encouraged Romantics all over Europe to explore, revive and invent national traditions.[40] It also helped to impel the rise of modern nationalism. Arguably, nationalism is a defence against the homogenizing tendencies of modern civilization which Herder deplored; it also provides a sense of identity to compensate for the enforced transformation of people's lives by industrialization.[41] However, nationalists too often assert the supreme value of their own culture and misrepresent, disparage and attack those of other nations. Nationalism has generated an array of hostile stereotypes fully comparable with those that flourished in the Renaissance.

It should be apparent by now that the encounter with other cultures must be in large part a problem of representing these cultures, and the modes of representation the historian attends to will most often be written ones. Experiences of direct encounter are only available as recorded: Mungo Park's experiences in West Africa are accessible only by reading and interpreting his subsequent narrative. How, therefore, does one write about other cultures? How can one write about the unfamiliar when all the words at one's disposal already refer to familiar objects?

This is a problem both for anthropologists, who encounter other cultures in the field and subsequently write up their notes into scholarly treatises, and for intellectual historians interpreting the written records of such encounters. The literary devices employed to render the unfamiliar accessible have been investigated by François Hartog in his study of Herodotus and by Michel de Certeau in essays on Montaigne and Jean de Léry, who visited the Brazilian Indians in the 1550s. Elaborate strategies are often required. In order to describe Scythian nomadism, something unknown to the Greeks, Herodotus employs an implicit homology with the Athenians' seafaring. When attacked by the Persians, he points out, the Scythians retreated to the steppes, just as the Athenians took to their ships. Thus, Scythians and Athenians, as mobile or potentially mobile peoples, are temporarily equated and both are contrasted with the settled Persians. Léry makes sense of Tupinambá festivals, including their alleged cannibalism, by calling their ceremonies a 'sabbat' and thus invoking a comparison with the supposed witch-cult of Europe.[42] Meanwhile, anthropologists have recently become more conscious of the problems of writing. Alongside the scholarly literature we now have a growing genre of autobiographical narratives in which anthropologists write with qualified frankness about their experiences among other cultures. Sometimes the same writer practises both genres, as though the encounter between cultures could not be fully rendered in any single literary form.[43] Further, even in the scholarly literature we find *topoi* which link it to the travel narratives of earlier periods. The *topos* of approaching a tropical island at dawn, which Bitterli illustrates from Columbus and Forster, recurs in 1936 in Raymond Firth's account of his arrival in Tikopia.[44]

These examples illustrate the difficulties that Westerners have in writing about other cultures, and one might wish that other cultures could speak directly for themselves. For obvious reasons, however, this is rarely possible. Some cultures discovered by Europeans are now extinct, like the Hurons and the Tupinambá. Most have been pre-literate. Oral tradition is a doubtful means of reconstructing historical events, since it tends to preserve the immediate past of first- or second-hand experience, and the remote past of legend, but little in between. Even where ample written records exist, as in China, few Westerners have the linguistic skills to read them and to surmount the problems of translation. Bitterli gives due attention to the recorded or conjectured reactions of the Tainos to Columbus, of the Hurons to the Jesuit missionaries, and of the Chinese to the intrusive Portuguese traders. However, the surviving documentation is overwhelmingly Western, and the historian, however critical, has to rely principally on the testimony of the victors.

In recent years, however, historians have increasingly sought to write colonial history from the viewpoint of its victims. Deservedly successful books by Dee Brown and John Hemming have recounted the fate of the Indians of North and South America so far as possible through their eyes. Eugene Genovese has reconstructed the lives of black American slaves, while Jacques Gernet has shown us what the Chinese thought of the missionaries who appeared in their midst.[45] I want to end by drawing attention to two recent books which break new ground in using scholarship and imagination to reconstruct the experience of colonized peoples: Nathan Wachtel's *The Vision of the Vanquished* and Marshall Sahlins's *Islands of History*.[46]

Wachtel's study examines the effects of the Spanish conquest of Peru on the lives of its inhabitants. The material consequences were of course devastating. War, epidemics and ill-treatment reduced the population from about eight million in 1530, on the eve of the conquest, to about 1.3 million in 1590. The economic structure of the Inca state broke down and the Peruvian Indians were compelled to submit to an alien and oppressive money economy. Expropriation and exploitation weakened the village community as a social unit and created a large mobile proletariat which relied on employment in mines and in domestic service. These forms of economic and social destructuration concern Wachtel, however, as the framework to the destruction of the Incas' symbolic universe. Before the Conquest, the Emperor was regarded as the Son of the Sun and as the reference point which guaranteed the meaning and harmony of the universe. The death of Atahuallpa, the last Emperor, plunged the universe into chaos. Cuzco, formerly the centre of the Inca world, became merely a staging-post between the mines of Potosí and the port of Lima. Missionary activity was half-hearted. On the whole, the Indians lost their own culture, except for fragmentary survivals, but were not admitted to the culture of their conquerors. The Conquest, Wachtel argues, meant a painful break with the past and left an unresolved trauma in the Indians' collective mind which finds expression in the ritual dramas performed at the present day.

In one of the essays in *Islands of History*, Sahlins focuses on a single event, the death of Captain Cook (discussed briefly below, p. 175), and uses his expert knowledge of Pacific anthropology to interpret its meaning for the Hawaiians. He argues that Cook was unwittingly playing a part in a religious ritual, and was killed when he deviated from the script. According to Sahlins's reconstruction, the Hawaiians represented the seasonal cycle as a conflict between two gods, Kū and Lono. At the end of winter, the image of Lono was carried round the island of

Hawaii, and when the circuit was completed, a symbolic combat took place between the King and the followers of Lono. The King's victory brought the spring and confirmed his sovereignty for that year. Cook arrived at Hawaii in January 1779, after circumnavigating the island in the same direction as the image of Lono. He landed at Kealakekua, where the image normally ended its circuit, and was welcomed by a joyful crowd of 10,000 islanders. A priest draped Cook in a red cloth and led him to the temple where a sacrifice was performed. The Hawaiians, that is, chose to regard Cook as an incarnation of Lono.

Cook departed the following month, but a week later he was obliged to return to Kealakekua to make repairs to his ship. Hawaiian religion had no room for the return of the god after the annual ceremony. The islanders kept asking the British why they had come back; the British could not understand why the islanders had suddenly become hostile. Assuming that Cook was issuing an unprecedented challenge to the sovereignty of the King, the islanders, Sahlins suggests, assigned a close relative of the King the task of killing Cook; and as soon as Cook went ashore, this was done. Thus, Sahlins has reconstructed the meaning which the event had for the Hawaiians. What seemed wanton murder to the British was for the Hawaiians a necessary response to a blasphemous threat.

These examples should demonstrate that the study of contacts between cultures is currently producing a wide variety of imaginative historical writing. This is an area where conversation among historians, anthropologists and literary scholars is both possible and necessary. Urs Bitterli is one of the most learned and original participants in that conversation. His work is outstanding in its encyclopaedic range of reference, its focus on the diverse forms of encounter and its emphasis on the irresolvable and often tragic conflicts they generated. It is high time for his voice to be heard in English.

NOTES TO INTRODUCTION

1   *Die Entdeckung des schwarzen Afrikaners: Versuch einer Geistesgeschichte der europäisch-afrikanischen Beziehungen an der Guineaküste im 17. und 18. Jahrhundert* (Zürich, 1970), p. 8.
2   *Schriftsteller und Kolonialismus: Malraux, Conrad, Greene, Weiß* (Zürich, 1973).
3   *Thomas Manns politische Schriften zum Nationalsozialismus 1918–1939* (Aarau, 1964).
4   T. Mann, 'Die Entstehung des *Doktor Faustus*', in *Gesammelte Werke*, 12 vols (Frankfurt, 1960), vol. XI, p. 201; quoted in Bitterli, *Thomas Mann*, p. 85.
5   *Die Entdeckung des schwarzen Afrikaners*, p. 202.

6   See E. Staiger, *Grundbegriffe der Poetik* (Zürich, 1946); also R. R. Magliola, *Phenomenology and Literature* (West Lafayette, Ind., 1977).
7   *Die 'Wilden' und die 'Zivilisierten': Grundzüge einer Geistes- und Kulturgeschichte der europäisch überseeischen Begegnung* (Munich, 1976). Since then Bitterli has edited a collection of primary texts on exploration: *Die Entdeckung und Eroberung der Welt* (Munich, 1981).
8   *Heart of Darkness* in *The Works of Joseph Conrad*, vol. VI (London, 1925), pp. 62, 132.
9   See pp. 80–6 below. An important recent account of these debates is A. Pagden, *The Fall of Natural Man*, 2nd edn (Cambridge, 1986).
10  *Heart of Darkness*, pp. 50–1.
11  On this and other aspects of economic influence on non-European cultures, see E. R. Wolf, *Europe and the People without History* (Berkeley, 1982).
12  On the varieties of 'otherness', see S. L. Gilman, *Difference and Pathology: Stereotypes of Sexuality, Race, and Madness* (Ithaca, NY, 1985).
13  E. Said, *Orientalism* (London, 1978), p. 272.
14  E. H. Gombrich, *Art and Illusion* (Oxford, 1960), p. 78. See also P. Mitter, 'Can we ever understand alien cultures? Some epistemological concerns relating to the perception and understanding of the Other', *Comparative Criticism*, 9 (1987), pp. 3–34.
15  F. Schiller, 'Was heißt und zu welchem Ende studiert man Universalgeschichte?', in *Werke*, ed. G. Fricke and H. G. Göpfert, 3 vols (Munich, 1966), vol. II, p. 14 (italics in original). There is an English translation in *History and Theory*, 11 (1972), pp. 321–34.
16  See R. L. Meek, *Social Science and the Ignoble Savage* (Cambridge, 1976).
17  See J. W. Burrow, *Evolution and Society* (Cambridge, 1966).
18  J. Fabian, *Time and the Other* (New York, 1983), p. 30.
19  See M. T. Ryan, 'Assimilating new worlds in the sixteenth and seventeenth centuries', *Comparative Studies in Society and History*, 23 (1981), pp. 519–38.
20  Quoted in D. P. Walker, *The Ancient Theology* (London, 1972), p. 225. See also Bitterli, *Die 'Wilden' und die 'Zivilisierten'*, p. 64.
21  See H. Baudet, *Paradise on Earth: some thoughts on European images of non-European man* (New Haven, 1965); K.-H Kohl, *Entzauberter Blick: Das Bild vom Guten Wilden und die Erfahrung der Zivilisation* (Berlin, 1981). Cf. Shakespeare, *The Tempest*, II.i.137–62.
22  W. Arens, *The Man-Eating Myth* (New York, 1979). See also E. E. Evans-Pritchard, 'Zande Cannibalism', in his *The Position of Women in Primitive Society and Other Essays in Social Anthropology* (London, 1965), pp. 133–64; P. Hulme, *Colonial Encounters: Europe and the native Caribbean, 1492–1797* (London, 1986), pp. 78–87.
23  J. B. Friedman, *The Monstrous Races in Medieval Art and Thought* (Cambridge, Mass., 1981), p. 24.
24  R. Wittkower, *Allegory and the Migration of Symbols* (London, 1977), p. 77.
25  See R. W. Southern, *Western Views of Islam in the Middle Ages* (Cambridge, Mass., 1962).

26   *The Journal of Christopher Columbus*, tr. C. Jane, revised by L. A. Vigneras (London, 1960), p. 24.

27   T. Todorov, *The Conquest of America: the question of the Other* (New York, 1984), p. 30. See also S. J. Greenblatt, 'Learning to curse: aspects of linguistic colonialism in the sixteenth century', in *First Images of America*, vol. II, ed. F. Chiappelli (Berkeley, 1976), pp. 561–80. There are thought-provoking essays on Elizabethan encounters with other cultures in Greenblatt's *Renaissance Self-Fashioning* (Berkeley, 1980) and *Shakespearean Negotiations* (Oxford, 1988).

28   *The Journal of Christopher Columbus*, p. 58.

29   D. Defoe, *Robinson Crusoe*, ed. A. Ross (Harmondsworth, 1965), p. 209. For comment on this episode, see I. Watt, *The Rise of the Novel* (London, 1957), p. 69; Hulme, *Colonial Encounters*, p. 206.

30   J. H. Elliott, *The Old World and the New, 1492–1650* (Cambridge, 1970).

31   P. Burke, *Popular Culture in Early Modern Europe* (London, 1978), p. 169.

32   J. Israel, *European Jewry in the Age of Mercantilism, 1550–1750* (Oxford, 1985), pp. 10–23.

33   See C. Larner, *Enemies of God: the witch-hunt in Scotland* (London, 1981), pp. 89–94; B. P. Levack, *The Witch-Hunt in Early Modern Europe* (London, 1987). pp. 123–31.

34   See A. Momigliano, 'The place of Herodotus in the history of historiography', in his *Studies in Historiography* (London, 1966), pp. 127–42.

35   See Bitterli, *Die Entdeckung des schwarzen Afrikaners*, pp. 53–6.

36   J.-F. Lafitau, *Customs of the American Indians Compared with the Customs of Primitive Times*, vol. II, ed. and tr. W. N. Fenton and E. L Moore (Toronto, 1974), p. 161.

37   On the importance of Homer in eighteenth-century primitivism, see K. Simonsuuri, *Homer's Original Genius* (Cambridge, 1979).

38   *The New Science of Giambattista Vico*, ed. and tr. T. G. Bergin and M. H. Fisch (Ithaca, NY, 1984), p. 148. On Vico, see I. Berlin, *Vico and Herder* (London, 1976); on his intellectual context, P. Burke, *Vico* (Oxford, 1985).

39   *J. G. Herder on Social and Political Culture*, ed. and tr. F. M. Barnard (Cambridge, 1969), p. 209. On Herder's social and intellectual context, see W. H. Bruford, *Culture and Society in Classical Weimar, 1775–1806* (Cambridge, 1962); P. H. Reill, *The German Enlightenment and the Rise of Historicism* (Berkeley, 1975), esp. Chapter 8.

40   For an introduction, see R. Porter and M. Teich (eds), *Romanticism in National Context* (Cambridge, 1988).

41   See H. Seton-Watson, *Nations and States* (London, 1977); B. Anderson, *Imagined Communities* (London, 1983); on the intellectual history of nationalism, E. Kedourie, *Nationalism*, 3rd edn (London, 1966).

42   M. de Certeau, *L'Écriture de l'histoire* (Paris, 1975), p. 243; F. Hartog, *Le Miroir d'Hérodote* (Paris, 1980), p. 218. An English translation is now available: *The Mirror of Herodotus* (Berkeley, 1988). See also de Certeau, 'Montaigne's "Of Cannibals": The Savage "I"', in his *Heterologies* (Manchester, 1986), pp. 67–79.

43   Cf., for example, N. Barley, *Symbolic Structures: an exploration of the*

*culture of the Dowayos* (Cambridge, 1983) and *The Innocent Anthropologist: notes from a mud hut* (London, 1983). The genre of anthropological autobiography may be traced back to B. Malinowski, *A Diary in the Strict Sense of the Term* (London, 1967).

44  See M. L. Pratt, 'Fieldwork in common places', in J. Clifford and G. E. Marcus, *Writing Culture: the poetics and politics of ethnography* (Berkeley, 1986), pp. 35–6.

45  D. Brown, *Bury My Heart at Wounded Knee: an Indian history of the American West* (London, 1970); J. Hemming, *Red Gold: the conquest of the Brazilian Indians* (London, 1978); E. D. Genovese, *Roll, Jordan, Roll: the world the slaves made* (New York, 1974); J. Gernet, *China and the Christian Impact* (Cambridge, 1985).

46  N. Wachtel, *The Vision of the Vanquished* (Hassocks, 1977); M. Sahlins, *Islands of History* (Chicago, 1985).

# 1

# Types of Cultural Encounter
## *Contacts, Collisions and Relationships*

In this introductory chapter the encounters between European and non-European cultures are reduced to three basic types: contacts, collisions and relationships. History, of course, never reveals these basic types in a pure state. They mingle and interpenetrate, displaying peculiarities and complexities that result both from the variations of time and place and from the differing mental structures of the participants in the encounter. Nor does any one of these types lead necessarily to any other. Contact between cultures may lead to a relationship between them, but need not; a relationship can dwindle into mere contact; collision is not the inevitable outcome and need not mean the end of contact between cultures. Moreover, this typology is intended to apply only to the pre-industrial period of European expansion overseas, with which this book deals. For the mixed-race colonial societies which arose here and there in the nineteenth and twentieth centuries, one would need to introduce an additional type, such as cultural intermingling.

By cultural contact is meant an initial, short-lived or intermittent encounter between a group of Europeans and members of a non-European culture. The early voyages of exploration derived their character largely from contacts of this sort. Examples might include the casual contacts with the native population made by the Portuguese in the fifteenth century during their voyages along the west coast of Africa and round the Cape of Good Hope, or the first ventures of the Spaniards in the Caribbean, the French in Canada and the English on the north-east coast of America. Similar contacts occurred later during the exploration of the Pacific in the late eighteenth century, and again during the great expeditions into the interior of Africa and Asia which laid the groundwork for the age of imperialism. Such contacts are characterized not only by their casualness and limited duration, but also by the rudimentary forms of communication between the representatives of the cultures concerned. Communication did take place, but through sign language and pantomime instead of dialogue; presents were exchanged, but only to help bring the two groups together, not to create the kind of mutuality required for a trading relationship. As a rule, European travel narratives give brief and sketchy accounts of such contacts, with insufficient understanding of the context and the historical implications of the event.

For both sides, cultural contact had the attraction, but also the peril, of novelty. A typical description of such contact comes from Giovanni da Verrazzano, who in 1524 explored the coast of Newfoundland on the orders of François I of France:

> We reached another land [ . . . ] where we found an excellent harbour; before entering it, we saw about XX [*sic*] boats full of people who came around the ship uttering various cries of wonderment. They did not come nearer than fifty paces, but stopped to look at the structure of our ship, our persons, and our clothes; then all together they raised a loud cry which meant that they were joyful. We reassured them somewhat by imitating their gestures, and they came near enough for us to throw them a few little bells and mirrors and many trinkets, which they took and looked at, laughing, and then they confidently came on board ship.[1]

The initial contact described in this report follows a pattern which occurs repeatedly in reports from other parts of the world. The natives on shore see the ships approaching: never having dreamt of vessels equipped with sails and guided by a rudder, they are astounded by the sight of these 'floating houses' and 'hovering clouds' which move by incomprehensible means. They gather on the beach and point out the spectacle to one another; they climb hills in order to see and be seen more clearly; they jump into boats in order to inspect the sailing-ships at close quarters. The main concern of the European seafarers, in this phase of cultural contact, is to lose no time in establishing peaceful relations with the natives, on whom they depend for provisions and geographical directions. They make overtures to the natives by handing, or rather throwing, small presents to them, without as yet wishing to engage in barter. These presents are mostly cheap baubles, the allure of which has already been tested on previous voyages in other regions. By these means the natives' confidence is often quickly gained. Recounting his first contact with inhabitants of the New World in October 1492, Columbus writes:

> I, in order that they might feel great amity towards us, because I knew that they were a people to be delivered and converted to our holy faith rather by love than by force, gave to some among them some red caps and some glass beads, which they hung round their necks, and many other things of little

value. At this they were greatly pleased and became so entirely our friends
that it was a wonder to see. Afterwards they came swimming to the ships'
boats, where we were, and brought us parrots and cotton thread in balls,
and spears and many other things [ . . . ][2]

These contacts almost always took place in an atmosphere of mutual
goodwill, though a rich spectrum of variants can be observed – from the
extreme timidity which Columbus encountered in some Caribbean
islanders, to the overwhelming displays of friendship with which
eighteenth-century voyagers were welcomed in Polynesia. Very rarely did
the natives behave with spontaneous hostility; so rarely, in fact, that one
wonders whether in such instances the supposed 'initial encounter' had
been preceded by other, unrecorded contacts in which the natives had
already suffered at the hands of the newcomers. This may, for example,
have been the case in New England, where the devout Puritan settlers
who arrived after 1620 met with a surprisingly hostile reception: several
decades earlier this particular stretch of coast had been visited by
fishermen and fur-traders, about whose impact we know virtually
nothing.[3] The remarkable absence of conflict from the early stages of
most cultural contacts has led some to the conclusion that hunters and
gatherers are essentially peaceable, partly because they are not concerned
to defend personal claims to land and property. Such an interpretation is
belied, however, by the frequency of inter-tribal conflicts, many of which
were observed, and exploited for political ends, by the earliest European
explorers.[4]

On first making contact with non-European peoples, the Europeans
generally refrained from aggressive behaviour. There is, however, no
denying that on some occasions they fired at the natives without pro-
vocation or even treated them with an unrestrained violence that suggests
sadistic motives. This occurred, for example, in most of the twenty or so
cultural contacts during Fernando Magellan's voyage round the world in
1520. Antonio Pigafetta, the ship's chronicler, reports a succession of
encounters which, despite friendly approaches from the natives, ended in
blood-baths, pillage and destruction. When he reached the island of Cebu
in the Philippines, this reckless and tactically indefensible conduct was to
cost Magellan his life.[5] The Spaniard Luis Báez de Torres, who in 1606
discovered the north-eastern Australian straits which now bear his name,
did not hesitate to open fire on natives who were rowing towards him
with peaceful intentions off the coast of New Guinea. 'On reaching
them', says his narrative, 'we saluted them with our arquebuses and
killed some, and when any fell dead they gave them blows with their
clubs to make them get up, thinking that they were not dead.'[6] This must
have been an initial encounter, for the natives obviously had no idea of
the fatal effect of European weapons at a distance.

There is no doubt – and the Europeans themselves soon came to realize it – that such a brutal demeanour at the very outset of cultural contact was counter-productive. The terrified natives fled into the forests, warned the neighbouring tribes, and often remained inaccessible for decades. Only a handful of cases is recorded in which such intimidation produced momentary advantages. One such instance occurred off the coast of Virginia at the beginning of the seventeenth century. Captain John Smith, a hardened campaigner with no regard for human life, bombarded the native Indians and reduced their dwellings to ashes. Thereupon, we are told, they agreed to share all their possessions with the English: 'they desired we would make no more spoyle, and they would give us halfe they had.'[7] The case of Virginia was to demonstrate that such ruthless behaviour at the outset contained the seeds of the subsequent collision. Indeed, even in the sixteenth century, the instructions given to explorers when they set out showed an awareness of the futility of such wilful conflicts by recommending a restrained and peaceable approach to the natives, though at the same time the explorers were urged to be well armed and on their guard.[8]

Although the Europeans mostly behaved peacefully at the beginning of their contacts with non-European peoples, they had not relinquished their claim to supremacy. On the contrary, everything the Europeans did upon arriving on a strange coast was intended to demonstrate that their presence had brought a new and final authority. Even while landing on a strange coast they took care to maintain a certain ceremonial. This was to signalize the importance of the discovery, which, thanks to the law of sovereignty, amounted to conquest; it was also meant to leave a lasting impression on the natives and ensure their respect. Salutes were fired and flags hoisted, and the most important persons on board, magnificently attired, formed a cortège and were the first to land. The arrival of Christopher Columbus on the island of San Salvador has been made famous by the engraver Theodor de Bry, who later gave an artist's impression of it. Here we see the admiral in great splendour, the other captains and the officers with the banners of their Catholic Majesties Isabella and Ferdinand, a guard of heavily armed and armoured mercenaries, and the notary with paper and ink, ready to record the event on the spot.[9] The sources constantly attest the Spaniards' unquestionable mastery of ceremonial. We need only recall how, when Vasco Núñez de Balboa first set eyes on the Pacific Ocean in 1513, his sense of his own importance was powerfully enhanced by making his escort kneel down and sing a 'Te Deum'.[10] These acts of virtual conquest culminated in the grotesque solemnity of reading the *Requerimiento*, which exhorted the natives, with hints of menace, to submit as loyal subjects of the Crown. Even though, at a later stage, interpreters were occasionally employed, none of the natives had the faintest notion what this ritual meant, and their ignorance made it yet more awe-inspiring.

However, it was not only the Spaniards who behaved in this way. The Portuguese, French and English adopted a similar demeanour. An account of the voyage of John Cabot, who visited Newfoundland in 1497, reveals with naïve frankness that during such ceremonies the Europeans were already thinking of the solid profits to be made from dealings with the natives. 'They disembarked there with a crucifix', we are told, 'and raised banners with the arms of the Holy Father and those of the King of England, my master; and they found tall trees of the kind masts are made [of].'[11]

Scenes of the kind described involved a ritual display which could sometimes be interpreted as a direct threat; at other times it was intended to imply the possession of supernatural powers. The best way of achieving the latter purpose was to fire off heavy artillery, which sowed panic among many non-European peoples and was of crucial importance in Cortés's conquest of Mexico. According to Sahagún's account, which describes this episode from the Aztecs' viewpoint:

> it was as if one had lost one's breath; it was as if for the time being there was stupefaction, as if one were affected by mushrooms. [ . . . ] Fear prevailed. It was as if everyone had swallowed his heart. Even before it had grown dark, there was terror, there was astonishment, there was apprehension, there was a stunning of the people.[12]

The Spaniards achieved a similar effect in Central and South America by displaying their horses. These animals aroused fear and trembling among the Indians, who had never seen them before. The Europeans also made an impression by their technological superiority. They often evoked awe and admiration by setting off fireworks, interpreting meteorological phenomena, or healing the sick. By closely observing the effects they produced, they managed to prolong both the terror and the admiration. Thus, Cabeza de Vaca, around 1530, managed to save his skin from what seemed certain death, and to roam the southern regions of North America for many years thereafter, by advertising himself as a miraculous healer, with the result that the Indians honoured him and recommended him to one another.[13]

We know little about how the non-Europeans judged the demeanour of the Europeans and tried to fit them into their conceptions of the world. The sources are too fragmentary to permit a generalization covering all the cultural contacts of the fifteenth and sixteenth centuries. Often, though certainly not always, the newcomers were seen as gods or godlike beings, at any rate in the first phase of contact when they were not yet known to be mortal. Their divinity or quasi-divinity was deduced both from the supposed miracles mentioned above and from the wholly unfamiliar appearance of the Europeans, with their white skin, their beards, and sometimes their bald pates.

Time and time again, as contemporary travel narratives testify a hundredfold, the alien appearance and behaviour of the Europeans gave rise to incredulous amazement and amazed credulity. The Venetian Cadamosto, who visited West Africa about 1450 in the service of Portugal, writes:

> These negroes, men and women, crowded to see me as though I were a marvel. It seemed to be a new experience to them to see Christians, whom they had not previously seen. They marvelled no less at my clothing than at my white skin. My clothes were after the Spanish fashion, a doublet of black damask, with a short cloak of grey wool over it. They examined the woollen cloth, which was new to them, and the doublet with much amazement: some touched my hands and limbs, and rubbed me with their spittle to discover whether my whiteness were dye or flesh.[14]

Three hundred years later, when Captain James Cook became the first European to land on Hawaii, the islanders regarded him as a supernatural being. Wherever the English landed, crowds of islanders gathered and pressed close to the newcomers, in order to touch them and be touched by them: the throng was so great that the whites saw no alternative but to clear a path by gunfire.[15] There is a revealing account of the Europeans' arrival as seen by American Indians in the notes made by the Jesuit priest Le Jeune. Father Le Jeune had managed to interrogate an Indian who could remember hearing the event recounted by his grandmother. This Indian described the boundless astonishment with which his forebears had perceived living creatures aboard the approaching 'floating islands'. He told how the women had promptly begun preparing accommodation for the unexpected guests, and how spies had been sent out to discover what kind of people the newcomers were. The spies had found that they were 'prodigious and horrible' people, who dressed in iron, ate bones and drank blood; for they had seen them wearing their breastplates while eating ship's biscuit and drinking wine.[16]

Such was the impression created, at least on archaic cultures, by the first appearance of Europeans in the rest of the world. Need one be surprised, therefore, that as soon as these alien visitors amused themselves by shooting a parrot down from a tree, showing the natives a conjuring trick, or letting them look in a mirror, they were transformed into supernatural beings? The feeling that moved the natives on first seeing the Europeans may best be understood, perhaps, by borrowing Rudolf Otto's concept of a *mysterium tremendum*, a sensation of trembling awe, which is present in all acts of divine worship.[17]

The European newcomers were often seen as gods, as Indian

documents from Central America reveal with particular clarity. We know from Aztec sources that when Cortés and his companions landed on the east coast of Mexico in 1519, Motecuhzoma saw in them the god Quetzalcoatl and his attendants, whose return had been foretold by prophecies.[18] He sent ambassadors with presents and sacrificial gifts to meet the Spaniards, and was appalled to learn that the 'gods' had rejected this honour with contempt. Motecuhzoma was further horrified by descriptions of the Europeans' appearance and the effect of their cannon.[19] When the Aztec ruler had become almost convinced that the Spaniards must be 'evil spirits', he sent medicine-men to render them harmless by casting spells on them, but without success. The Aztec sources make it strikingly clear that Motecuhzoma and those around him were paralysed by terror, and that their paralysis helped the kingdom to collapse with such startling rapidity: 'No longer had he strength; no longer was there any use; no longer had he energy. [ . . . ] [Motecuhzoma] only awaited [the Spaniards]; he made himself resolute; he put forth great effort; he quieted, he controlled his heart; he submitted himself entirely to whatsoever he was to see, at what he was to marvel.'[20]

Much the same happened in Peru, where the Spaniards' arrival was likewise preceded by ominous portents, and where the return of a god was also expected. In 1526, when Pizarro appeared on the scene, a civil war was raging between Huascar and Atahualpa, the two pretenders to the throne, and each party hoped for support from the 'gods' or 'divine emissaries'. When the Incas saw how brutally the Spaniards behaved, their attitude changed. A native chronicler, whose words have been preserved by an Augustinian monk, wrote:

> I thought they were kindly beings sent (as they claimed) by Tecsi Viracocha, that is to say, by God; but it seems to me that all has turned out the very opposite from what I believed: for let me tell you, brothers, from proofs they have given me since their arrival in our country, they are the sons not of Viracocha, but of the Devil.[21]

Like other sources, this one reveals that the Europeans were skilful in fostering the natives' expectations, while the massive culture-shock to which the natives were exposed made it imperative for them to assimilate the incident by locating it within their horizon of expectation. And they did this by extracting from their own mythology allusions to an imminent visit from the gods and seeking omens and prophecies to support this interpretation.

Similar methods were adopted in other cultures: for example, after encountering whites and their black slaves in the seventeenth century, the Cherokee Indians devised a remarkable creation legend. This legend tells how God created man with the help of an oven in which he baked three pieces of dough, moulded in human shape. His impatience made God remove the first man from the fire prematurely. Being undercooked, this man was repulsively pale in colour; from him are descended the white men. The second figure, nicely browned, became the ancestor of the Indians. His delight at this masterpiece made God forget to remove the third figure from the oven; when he at last remembered to do so, he found only a black, charred creature – the negro.[22] This Indian creation myth, which has counterparts in African tradition, has basically the same function as the prophecy of the return of the gods, mentioned earlier. It enables an archaic culture to perform the mental reorientation which is required to cope with the arrival of the European.

In this respect the Europeans had a considerably easier task. For one thing, the non-Europeans they encountered possessed no inexplicable powers, and were inferior in military terms; and besides, encounters with other cultures, such as Islam, were an important part of their historical experience and tradition. The official colonial doctrine of Spain and Portugal defined the inhabitants of other continents as people who had had the misfortune not to share the Christian revelation: by promising to convert them, one gained the right to conquer their territories.[23] No one ever thought of regarding the natives as gods, a heretical idea which would promptly have brought one before the Inquisition, though it was suggested very early on that these 'savages' might have stayed close to prelapsarian innocence.[24] It is remarkable how seldom European travel narratives compare the natives to animals, with reference, for example, to the cannibal practices ascribed to them. In popular accounts, of course, this comparison is developed with the aid of illustrations, drawing on older legends about monsters, giants and pygmies.[25] The European explorers and conquistadors, however, knew full well that the members of archaic cultures were human beings. It is impossible to absolve them of the charge that they subsequently treated these people worse than animals.

Even though the eventual conflict was generally implicit in the Europeans' first appearance, it can be stated not only that cultural contact was generally marked by peaceable behaviour on both sides, but also that in this phase the two sides began getting to know one another. For all those involved this experience could provide excitement, diversion and, indeed, delight. The initial impossibility of verbal communication did not significantly impede personal contact; besides, gifted linguists on both sides soon came forward as interpreters. Of course there were continual misunderstandings, but in retrospect some of these gave rise to hilarity. When Giovanni da Verrazzano arrived at the mouth of the St Lawrence River in 1525, a sailor fell overboard and was washed ashore by the current. The crew watched in horror as their comrade was surrounded by Indians who began lighting a fire. Their relief was great when the Indians did nothing more than dry the Frenchman's clothes and give him something to eat: 'With the greatest kindness, they accompanied him to the sea, holding him close and embracing him; and then to reassure him, they withdrew to a high hill and stood watching him until he was in the boat.'[26]

The Europeans were astonished to learn how easily the language of expression and gesture could overcome cultural barriers, and how universal is the semiotic system with which people can express sympathy and hostility, affirmation and denial, joy and sorrow. An early English narrative from Virginia tells how 'the Captain called to them in signe of friendship, but they were at first very timersome, until they saw the Captain lay his hand on his heart.'[27] And the German Georg Forster, who accompanied Cook on his second voyage, describes how the Tahitian population welcomed the visitors: 'They waved a large green leaf in the air, and accosted us with the repeated exclamation of *tayo!* which even without the help of vocabularies, we could easily translate into the expression of proffered friendship.'[28]

Since the Pacific region was free from military rivalry in the eighteenth century, we can observe here the various stages in which the two sides became acquainted. There was a stage of teasing advance and withdrawal, followed by one in which information was freely exchanged, and one which saw the development of mutual trust and the accompanying obligations. The two groups visited each other, joined in everyday activities, and discovered that both shared the same elementary human needs; the natives often spent the night aboard ship. Sometimes, though not very often, the more open-minded European travellers managed to make use of the favourable atmosphere during this period of contact in order to obtain insights into native society. This was certainly the case with the French Huguenot Jean de Léry, who lived among the Tupí Indians of Brazil around 1550. Between the lines of Léry's report we can discern, time and again, his pleasure and interest in meeting members of the alien culture, while they were not lacking in warmth and devotion: 'I have observed that they prefer cheerful, merry and generous people, while on the other hand they hate taciturn, mean and melancholy people so much that I can state this with certainty: spiteful, moody, quarrelsome, and self-centred characters will not be welcome among our Tupinambaults: for their nature makes them detest such people.'[29]

How long such contacts might last was dependent on the home country's commitment to colonizing, the distance and accessibility of coasts and territories, and the activities of rival maritime powers. The nature of these contacts was such that they could last only a few years. After that, given luck, a *modus vivendi* based on peaceful interchange might be worked out. This was a cultural relationship, based on mutual dependence and mutual adjustment. It was commoner, unfortunately, for the initial contact to turn into collision, in which the weaker partner, in military and political terms, was threatened with the loss of cultural identity, while even its physical existence was jeopardized and sometimes annihilated altogether. Collisions occurred in every part of the world where the white man appeared, but they followed many different patterns and ended in diverse ways. Their course was crucially determined by the geographical situation and the discrepancy in power between the partners. On islands, collision often resulted in the complete liquidation of the original population, while on the mainland, which offered victims somewhere to escape, their fate was the superficially milder one of forcible displacement. Advanced cultures with adequate military equipment, or those that were in a position to take defensive measures in good time, managed to evade or localize collision, or freeze it in the form of 'cold war'. We should regard the slave trade and the slave economy as a special form of collision, in which part of the defeated population survived, albeit in circumstances which largely precluded the survival of their culture.

The transformation of contact into collision can be observed very early, in the wake of Columbus's first voyages. On Christmas Day, 1492, with willing help from the Indians, Columbus had built the fort *La Navidad* on Santo Domingo, where some forty colonists were to await their captain's return with additional men and material from Spain. When Columbus returned to Santo Domingo the following November, however, he found the fortification destroyed, the garrison killed, and the Indians fearful and unfriendly.[30] The same thing happened to the Dutch colonists who set out in 1631 for the recently established settlement of Swanendael in Delaware, only to find the fort destroyed and the settlers and cattle killed.[31] The Dutch were no more fortunate in their attempt, about 1610, to extort from a local Muslim potentate the right to build a fort on the spice island of Ternate. A German eye-witness who accompanied the colonists recounts: 'The Moors had chopped off the heads of the Admiral and of Mynheer Grunwegen van Delft, and taken the heads away with them.'[32] To cite a final example, world-wide indignation was aroused by the murder of Captain Cook at the hands of the people of Hawaii in 1779. From the inadequate and inconsistent sources it will never be possible to establish the precise circumstances of this incident;[33] but here, too, the collision of cultures took the Europeans by surprise.

No doubt the reasons for the transformation of contact into collision must often have been complex: they can seldom be reconstructed precisely from European accounts, which are strongly partisan in such matters. Basically, however, there were two main reasons for conflict:

either the members of the alien culture sensed a threat to their property and their accustomed way of life; or they had ceased to respect and trust the Europeans. The entirely ethnocentric manner in which the Europeans interpreted their encounters with other cultures is apparent from their failure to judge the consequences of their appearance or to realize how fragile the natives' respect and trust generally were. This explains why the chroniclers of these voyages were almost always surprised by collision and stigmatized it as treachery.

In order to clarify the process that could lead from peace to war, from contact to collision, let us choose a representative instance – the Virginia massacre of 1622. The first group of English settlers had arrived in Virginia in May 1607, and had cut down trees and built a fort. The Indians, though timid and fawning at first, soon made the settlers welcome. The early days of the settlement were hard, and it could not have survived without food supplied by the natives. Despite occasional clashes, the English succeeded in forming friendly relations with the powerful chief Powhatan, who intended thereby to strengthen his own position in the federation of Indian tribes. It was hoped that the marriage of the chief's daughter, Pocahontas, to a settler would confirm the friendship between the Indians and the English. The colonial situation was consolidated by growing tobacco, allocating land for cultivation by individuals, introducing English law, and importing marriageable women. In March 1622, however, one of the Indian tribes, led by Opechancanough, attacked the scattered inland settlements and killed over 300 colonists, a quarter of the total European population, in a particularly cruel fashion. A chronicler writes: 'They fell again upon the dead bodies, making as well as they could a fresh murder, defacing, drugging, and mangling their dead carkases into many peeces, and carrying some parts away in derision, with base and brutish triumph.'[34]

In European accounts an attempt was subsequently made to present this massacre as a wholly unexpected and unprovoked attack, and to emphasize the peacefulness of previous dealings with the Indians, as well as the child-like trustfulness of the colonists. Such an interpretation, however, will not stand up to scrutiny. Here, as in innumerable other cases, the truth is rather that the conflict was already implicit in the nature of the relations which the Europeans established with the natives at the outset. Although the first settlers had of course sought peace when they were still weak, their principal aim was not to maintain peace but to increase their own power. In addition, although they had been flexible and conciliatory in their dealings with the Indians, they had never taken any trouble to ascertain whether their allies really understood their intentions. In America, Asia and Africa, misunderstandings frequently arose from the fact that the Europeans who wished to acquire land did not understand, and did not want to understand, the cultural conditions governing such transactions. Noticing that, by European standards, the natives did not cultivate their land at all intensively, the colonists assumed that the natives had more land than they knew what to do with and lacked any definite concept of ownership. The natives, on the other hand, had never entertained the notion that land could be handed over to people of alien origin, and in concluding agreements and treaties with the white men they thought they were only temporarily transferring the right of cultivation. When they saw the Europeans transforming the landscape by clearing forests and putting up permanent dwellings and fortifications, they felt outraged and deceived.[35] At times the Europeans realized quite clearly that the natives were astounded by what seemed to them shameless presumption. Thus, one of the first settlers in Virginia wrote: 'The people vsed our men well vntill they found they begann to plant & fortefye.'[36] Yet the underlying reasons for this reaction were hardly ever understood.

While the main source of conflict was the seizure of land by Europeans, there were numerous others which can be mentioned here only briefly. The Europeans frequently intervened in internal disputes among the natives, and managed, usually by supplying weapons, to alter the balance of power to their own advantage or to destroy the equilibrium that had existed previously. This happened on several occasions in West Africa. In the early fifteenth century, for example, the commercial and missionary activities of the Portuguese in the Congo served only to provoke internal disturbances; while later the slave trade unilaterally enhanced the power of the coastal population.[37] Nor was it uncommon for Europeans to attempt to influence power relations within native tribes. Sometimes they did this unintentionally, by negotiating with partners who lacked the necessary competence. At other times they did it deliberately, by supporting tribal leaders whom they favoured. In both cases, however, the Europeans were inadequately informed about the structure of the tribe and its rules of hierarchy. In Muslim Asia, where disputes about succession were traditional in any case, the Europeans were willing to intervene, and it can well be imagined that they did not exercise a restraining influence.[38] Often, too, conflicts originated in connection with trade, the new needs it had aroused, and the exhaustion of resources. All along the North American coast, for example, continual strife arose from the supply of grain to the early colonists, furnished by tribes who could scarcely support themselves and laid up no reserves.[39] Finally, there were repeated violent clashes everywhere, often under the influence of alcohol, between individual members of two different cultures, and such incidents could easily make smouldering tensions blaze up into open warfare. It must, unfortunately, be emphasized that these individual conflicts were largely due to the widespread discrimination practised by the Europeans, who attached less value to the lives of members of alien cultures and regarded murder, assault and rape as venial sins.

It is certainly true that many archaic peoples, especially the American Indians, liked to begin hostilities with surprise attacks, though one must also realize that the surprise was heightened by the Europeans' deficient understanding of the problems of cultural encounters. In dealings between more highly developed cultures, it was commoner to issue advance warnings and formal declarations of war. Thus, the conflicts with Japan and China were generally preceded by diplomatic activity.[40] However, the view repeatedly expressed by European contemporaries, that the 'savages' conducted warfare in a particularly cruel manner unknown to civilized nations, is false and can be refuted from the sources. Most archaic peoples were certainly familiar with torture, sometimes in ingeniously sadistic forms; but such tortures were also practised in Europe during the wars of religion, though with a somewhat different function. It was certainly customary for Red Indian youths to be sent on scalping expeditions to prove their manhood, but it was also as proof of manhood that the sons of the Portuguese aristocracy fought against North African Moors and were subsequently knighted. And as for scalping, it is known that the Europeans also took part in it, though there is no basis to the claim occasionally put forward by the American Indian Movement that this custom was introduced by the whites.[41] Nor can the natives fairly be accused of bloodthirstiness and vengefulness, for there are many examples of prisoners' lives being spared and conflicts being settled peacefully. Finally, there is no doubt that wars among the natives were generally carried on less stubbornly and with smaller loss of life than wars among Europeans, though this is partly due to the natives' less effective weaponry.[42]

'Surprise attacks and massacres of the kind described generally provided European colonists with a pretext for opening systematic hostilities against the indigenous peoples. After the Virginia massacre, the English responded with deliberate anti-guerrilla tactics. The settlers were enjoined to 'pursue and follow them, surprisinge them in their habitations, intercepting them in theire hunting, burninge theire Townes, demolishing theire Temples, destroyinge theire Canoes, plucking upp theire weares, carrying away theire Corne, and depriving them of whatsoever may yeeld them succo$^r$ or relief.'[43] This procedure proved highly effective. Around 1650, after a further desperate uprising, Opechancanough's tribe was finally defeated and compelled to evacuate its territories; and these events were associated with a remarkable change in the Europeans' image of the natives. The massacre had confirmed their subliminal prejudices and exposed the Indians' barbarity and perfidy; now that nothing more was to be feared from them, the conception of the 'noble savage' once more gained ground in travel literature, and Europeans grew melancholy in contemplating the fate which they themselves had imposed on the Indians.[44]

Soon afterwards the Puritan settlers in New England were to behave in an analogous fashion. In 1675 they were faced with an uprising of the Wampanoag Indians, who massacred the frontier settlers. Hundreds of whites lost their lives within a few days. Here, too, the English carried through their retaliation and expulsion without a trace of mercy. Within a short time some 5,000 Indians were killed and the remainder forced into the interior. Modest attempts at peaceful co-existence and missionary work were brought to an abrupt end.[45]

The English settlers were naturally not alone in reacting with such extreme harshness to surprise attacks by the natives. The Spaniards had already behaved in much the same way in Central and South America, often in response to acts of desperation by the Indians, which were answered with 'pacification strategies'. Georg Friederici has stated clearly what the conquistadors meant by the term *pacificación*: the resolve 'to overrun, plunder, and appropriate a territory which had previously been independent, whether it was familiar or wholly unknown, whether it opposed the Europeans or remained completely inoffensive.'[46] Moreover, right up to the age of imperialism, 'pacification' always involved an insinuation that the nation receiving this treatment was already in a state of internecine war and could only lead a decent existence with the help of military intervention by its European 'protector'.

Although war and subsequent punitive action formed the keynote of the early history of cultural encounters, and have been studied in particular detail by historians, other types of collision exacted still greater sacrifices among alien populations. They were menaced by the introduction and transmission of such previously unknown diseases as smallpox, tuberculosis and syphilis, to which the natives had been unable to build up any resistance. There is no doubt that, especially in North and Central America, such epidemics wrought more havoc than direct military operations. Given the absence of relevant statistics for this period and the necessity of relying on estimates, it is of course very difficult to quantify precisely the diminution in the indigenous population caused by disease. The most recent studies, however, agree that during the century after the Europeans' arrival, the native population of North and Central America which had encountered them was reduced by 80–90 per cent of its total numbers. Military conflicts did not contribute significantly to this loss. Epidemics spread repeatedly, sometimes after only the briefest of contacts. In Central America and in the Andean region, even before Pizarro's campaign, thousands of Indios, among them the Inca ruler Huaina Capac, were carried off by the ravages of a previously unknown disease. In Mexico, whose Indian population had been reduced by illness and warfare from an estimated 25 million in 1519 to 2.6 million in 1568, there were recurrent epidemics, especially in 1519, 1524, 1529, 1557 and 1576.[47] North America presents a similar picture. Thus, it has been calculated that some 3,000 Indians were settled on Martha's Vineyard, an island off Rhode Island whose terrain could easily be surveyed, when the Europeans arrived in 1642; 100 years later, without hostilities of any kind, this number had shrunk to 300.[48] An expert on the native population of North America, John Heckewelder, who spent the early years of the nineteenth century living among the Lenni Lenape south of New Jersey, stated: 'What the numbers of this nation were when the Europeans first came into this country is difficult to tell; all I can say is, that so early as 1760, their oldest men would say that they were not then as many hundreds as they had been thousands. They have considerably decreased since that period.'[49]

It has already been mentioned that illnesses were transmitted even during contacts preceding colonization. We know that even before the arrival of the *Mayflower* in 1620 there were serious epidemics among the Cape Cod Indians, who attributed them to European fishermen; hence, no doubt, the unfriendly reception met with by the Pilgrim Fathers. Numerous statements by colonists record the rapid drop in the native population, mostly without regret. As early as 1590 Thomas Hariot reports from Virginia that 'the people began to die very fast, and many in short space', and about 1700 a settler in Carolina reports that the Indian population around his farm has been reduced within fifty years to less than one-sixth of its original strength.[50] There were no known remedies against the diseases introduced by Europeans: the medicine-men were powerless, and the risk of infection was increased by the custom prevalent in many tribes of assembling at the bedside of the dying person. Children and young men were the most frequent victims of epidemics, but the old, who performed important functions in the tribal federation, were not spared either, so that the tribe's structure and its capacity for military resistance were damaged practically beyond repair. The advancing colonists were well aware of what they owed to these diseases. Sometimes, like the New England Puritans, they saw them as a sign of divine providence: Governor John Winthrop thanks God for 'sweeping away great multitudes of the natives [ . . . ] that he might make room for us there.'[51]

Collision in the form of transmission of foreign diseases had its most devastating effects in America, where it has also been most thoroughly studied. Comparable events occurred, however, in other parts of the world, especially when Europeans encountered populations which had previously lived in relative isolation. The rapid spread of venereal disease in the Pacific islands may serve as an example.[52] Conversely, it was quite possible for Europeans overseas to fall victim to diseases that they had scarcely known before. The west coast of Africa is a notorious instance. Roughly half the white traders there died of malaria, yellow fever and other tropical diseases after only one year's residence, while the survivors became increasingly immune and often lived to a ripe old age.[53] The high mortality rate among Europeans was the main reason why collision between cultures in this part of the globe often modulated into a stable relationship, and why large-scale colonization was deferred until the age of imperialism, after the discovery of quinine and other remedies.

It was not only war and epidemics that had disastrous effects on alien cultures; they suffered equally from the reduction of large parts of their population to slavery and forced labour. At an early stage the Spaniards, in their anxiety to attain wealth rapidly through others' efforts, had begun employing Indian labour, first on the islands, later on the mainland. On the initiative of the governor of Santo Domingo, Nicolás de Ovando, the natives' obligation to labour was first legally defined in 1503 by an edict of Queen Isabella. The reason given was that no workers other than Indians could be found to provide the Spaniards with the necessities of life and to help them to obtain the gold present on the island.[54] This decree did indeed provide explicitly that the natives should be regarded not as serfs but as free individuals, and that they should receive suitable payment and be instructed in the doctrines of Christianity; but across the Atlantic such provisions were observed very negligently, and were difficult for the authorities in Spain to enforce. The allocation of Indian labour among the settlers in the system known as *repartimiento* had grave and lasting consequences for the native population, quite apart from the frequent deaths resulting from violence, draconian punishment and infectious disease. Although similar forms of compulsory labour had existed in many places even in pre-Columbian times and were thus not unknown to the Indians, the more intensive *repartimiento* system, with its focus on new products and modes of production, frequently led to the disintegration and dissolution of native society. Since detachments of young and vigorous men were required to spend part of the year doing forced labour, they were unable to help with the harvest in their villages, and the agricultural yield in their districts declined. The effects of their absence on female fertility, and the demographic consequences, seem to have varied in different regions and are hard to quantify. It is certain, however, that family life and the traditional social order and moral values suffered severely as a result.

Many Indians never returned and instead scraped a meagre living as petty traders and craftsmen on white men's estates and in their mines. It is impossible here to give a full account of the *repartimientos* and the *encomiendas*, based largely on tributary payments, which finally replaced them, especially as these systems assumed different forms according to local requirements.[55] It is, however, beyond dispute that all these methods of imposing servitude on the Indians estranged the latter from their inherited society without integrating them into colonial society. Even when the Indian labourer remained alive, he led a lamentable existence, cut off from his cultural roots and his moral inhibitions.

Since the *repartimiento* system soon had to be abandoned because of the declining Indian population, it was of less historical significance than the plantation economy using imported African slaves. In many parts of Latin America – particularly in the Caribbean and Brazil, but also in Mexico and Venezuela – the Africans had to replace the missing Indian labour force; this 'solution' is said to have been demanded by humane critics who could no longer bear to see the Indians' sufferings.[56] Even before Columbus's first voyage, slavery had been known and practised in Portugal, Spain and other Mediterranean countries, but it was introduced into the New World in 1505, when a cargo of Africans was shipped from Seville to Santo Domingo. Soon afterwards black slaves made their appearance in Brazil, where, as in the Caribbean, they were used chiefly on sugar plantations. The English possessions in the south of North America, where Indian forced labour was not used, received their first Africans in 1619. They were used initially on tobacco plantations, and later, on a larger scale, on cotton plantations. Towards the end of the eighteenth century, in which the slave trade and the slave economy had experienced a final upsurge, slavery came under fire from critics, while the development of the world economy, as well as the declarations of egalitarian principles in the American and French revolutions, also helped to spread abolitionist views. In 1807 the slave trade was abolished by the British Parliament, and the Congress of Vienna in 1815 extended this advance to other countries.

In retrospect, the Atlantic slave trade is among the most monstrous and brutal projects undertaken by humankind to subjugate fellow human beings in the entire course of history. Its effects on the ethnic character of the population of the Western hemisphere are manifest at the present day. Various totals are assigned for the number of Africans shipped across the ocean, while there are also widely differing estimates of the mortality rate during the crossing and during the hardest phase of adaptation, immediately after arrival in America. Recent studies suggest a total of approximately 9,800,000 slaves transported to the New World: 3.1 per cent in the period up to 1600, 16 per cent between then and 1700, and 52.4 per cent in the eighteenth century. Even in the nineteenth century, in defiance of international agreements, approximately three million more were transported to America. The largest group among these slaves, some four million, found its way to the Caribbean islands; Brazil accounted for some 3,800,000, and North America, before the War of Independence, for about 427,000. The number of slaves taken from West Africa between the sixteenth and nineteenth centuries should be put considerably higher, since one must assume that 10–20 per cent died on the crossing; and to this must be added the number of those who died on the way from their homes to the West African coast. Present-day estimates of the decline in the West African population resulting directly from the slave trade vary between totals of 11,700,000 and 15,500,000.[57]

A detailed investigation of the slave trade and the slave economy would fall outside the limits of the present study. There is room only for a few brief remarks on the forms taken by collision on the transatlantic plantations. Despite the regional differences which are currently the subject of vigorous scholarly debate, it can be assumed that the slave was everywhere used as the 'living tool' within a mercantilist world-system aimed at exploiting the colonies' raw materials and natural products, especially sugar.[58] By being shipped overseas the Africans were severed from their cultural roots more thoroughly than in any other known case of international migration. The blacks had no say whatever in choosing their destination or type of work, and if they survived the rigours of the crossing, they found themselves placed in an alien environment and in a wholly novel system of labour. To minimize the risk of conspiracies and rebellions, the plantation owners ensured that slaves belonging to the same family or tribe were separated immediately on arrival. The development of a new and authentic cultural life was precluded by the monotonous regularity of the daily routine on the plantation, the prevailing atmosphere of violence and terror, and the slaves' scanty leisure time.[59] Conversely, the gradual integration of the African into the settler community was ruled out by the sharp social divide between white masters and black slaves. It is certainly true that closer contact between whites and slaves was occasionally unavoidable, and we know that in Brazil and the Southern States the household servants, often mulattos, were sometimes regarded as part of the family. However, although there is reasonable documentary support for the often-quoted instances of black nursemaids, cooks and domestic servants who were treated familiarly by their paternalist masters and began to share or imitate their manners and their sense of social superiority, these instances remain exceptional.[60] The general rule was that slave status was defined by the whites precisely and rigidly and maintained by all possible means. Even when slaves were freed, which was everywhere possible and in Brazil not uncommon, slavery as such was never challenged. Such measures, taken only when no ill effects were anticipated, were generally individual gestures of gratitude.

We need not wonder that such a despotic system often gravely deformed the characters of both masters and slaves, made all human relationships insecure, and undermined the sense of responsibility. On the slave farm the collision of cultures occurred within the narrowest compass. In such seclusion, most of the forms of moral and mental corruption which likewise hindered the co-existence of races elsewhere were cultivated in extreme intensity. Denied the chance to develop freely, the African's natural loyalty and warmth were perverted into fawning servility, hypocrisy, surreptitious malice and listless apathy. 'When such a master is a tyrant', writes a black plantation worker in his memoirs, 'the slaves often become cringing, treacherous, false, and thieving.'[61] An impressive study by a recent American historian, Stanley Elkins, enquires how far the loss of freedom and the terror reigning on the plantation can help to produce a specific 'black mentality' which he finds represented by the child-like, docile, but unreliable 'Sambo type'.[62] Admittedly, Elkins goes too far in equating concentration camps and slave plantations: he seems to forget that it was in the owners' interest to keep their slaves healthy and fit for work for as long as possible, a motive not shared by those Nazis responsible for the 'final solution'.

The need to maintain the slaves' capacity for work meant that in some regions, particularly the Southern States, they gradually acquired more personal freedom. They were encouraged to raise large families, and instead of being compelled to work by force, they were urged on by deliberate relaxations of pressure and by special rewards. Hence, the abolition of slavery did not in itself cause the traditional system to disintegrate. Numerous historical works, especially the brilliant studies by Herbert G. Gutman, have shown how the slave family remained largely intact and supplied the basis for an authentic 'culture of poverty', which continued to flourish after the Civil War and the abolition of slavery and is now an integral part of the United States' social and cultural life.[63]

While based on the slave family, this cultural innovation derived its inner credibility and its social anchorage from Christian religious feeling. Until the end of the eighteenth century the plantation owners had mostly discouraged missionary activity and Christian teaching, fearing that these might promote emancipation. After 1830, however, it was widely held that Christian doctrines were well adapted to keep the slave humble and docile and to legitimize the masters' rule as a form of paternalistic guardianship. We need not decide whether this was true, but the religious instruction pioneered by Baptists and Methodists undoubtedly helped the slaves to develop a genuine culture of their own.[64] In the case of the plantation economy, collision therefore did not result in the disappearance of the traditional culture, but led to a new form of culture, in which remnants of tradition entered into a remarkable synthesis with new materials to produce a unique outcome. The most impressive example of this process, and the one most frequently studied, is Black American music. Fascinating cases of acculturation are to be found here. In the Christian Negro Spiritual, for example, the River Jordan retained an archaic significance through being equated with the West African rivers which, according to inherited cultural traditions, the spirits of the dead had to cross on their way to the next world. Similar phenomena can be observed in Central and South America. In Haiti, for instance, Catholic saints and African divinities were sometimes joined in surprising personal unions which lent religious ceremonies a syncretistic yet original character.

In extreme cases the slaves refused to adapt to the degrading situation in which they found themselves. Instead, they reacted individually by running away and collectively by rebelling. Slave revolts were particularly common on the islands of the Caribbean, where working conditions were extremely harsh and the white population was numerically tiny. The instruction which the black leaders of these rebellions had received from the plantation owners sometimes equipped them with a mastery of rhetoric and an intensely religious belief in their mission. Nat Turner's rebellion in Virginia in 1831 illustrates what overwhelming charismatic power such people could exercise.

Slaves were continually escaping, though their chances of remaining at large were slight, and those who were recaptured received merciless punishment. The *cimarrones* or 'maroons', as the runaway blacks were known in Spanish and English respectively, attempted either to disappear from sight in the towns along the coast or to found new settlements in inaccessible regions: sometimes they joined Indian tribes or took service in the navy or on pirate ships. The settlements established by these fugitives, which were known in Brazil as *quilombos*, seldom lasted for more than a few years. It would be wrong to regard the *quilombos* as an alternative society to the plantations, for they were ruled by familiar methods, with strict laws and penalties; nor did they abolish slavery, though there were frequent changes of master. On the other hand, these isolated, virtually all-male communities developed a luxuriant variety of social forms, and it has rightly been said that the *quilombos* 'were not merely a protest against the regime of slavery. They also represent the resistance of a civilization unwilling to die.'[65] In the African communities around Bahia, Islam played a similar role, encouraging people to recollect the past and serving as the vehicle for a new experience of unity. In a comparable fashion, certain ethnic groups among the North American Indians responded to the cultural pressure of the frontier situation by taking refuge in fantastic-sounding rituals. These modes of recollection sometimes verged on the pathological in their exaggeration of archaic cultural forms. Even in the nineteenth century the collision of cultures still provoked similar 'fundamentalist' reactions. The Mahdi rebellion, which gripped the Sudan in 1883 and severely shook English and Egyptian dominance, could be interpreted as a comparable response, though one of military aggression instead of resignation.

Of all the ways in which political underdogs reacted to cultural collisions, the most desperate can here be mentioned only briefly — suicide. Wherever cultural contact turned into collision, a marked increase in the number of suicides can be established. The occupation of Santo Domingo was followed by veritable epidemics of suicide, and much the same occurred soon afterwards in Mexico and Peru. The custom laid down in the European code of honour, whereby someone defeated in combat takes his own life sooner than fall into his opponents' hands, is attested both among the American Indians and throughout Asia. However, there is no doubt that the propensity to suicide, and occasionally also to self-mutilation and abortion, was particularly apparent within slave society. Even before being transported from the African coast, the blacks tried to kill themselves by eating earth; once at sea, they leapt overboard; in America they were found hanged in their wretched quarters. To mention at least one figure, out of thirty-three suicides recorded in the province of Bahia in 1848, twenty-six were slaves.[66] It is significant that their fellow-sufferers did not regard their suicide as a criminal act, but celebrated it in legends.[67]

There can be no doubt that from the fifteenth century to the eighteenth the commonest form of encounter between European and non-European peoples was collision in its manifold variations. In certain circumstances, however, contact could develop into a relationship; much less often, a relationship could result from collision. The remainder of this chapter will deal with relationships. By a cultural relationship we mean a prolonged series of reciprocal contacts on the basis of political equilibrium or stalemate. Relationships depended on supply and demand, and were sustained on the European side by traders and missionaries. It must be remarked that what the missionaries had to offer was seldom really in demand. However, dealings with representatives of the Church offered not only eternal life but more solid advantages such as political prestige and technical know-how.

A lasting and largely peaceful relationship was established on the west coast of Africa, where, until the nineteenth century, there was no serious threat to the balance of power between the Europeans who dominated the sea and the native peoples who ruled the land. The inhospitable climate, the barren soil, the presence of powerful feudal organizations among the natives, and (after 1590) rivalries among the Europeans themselves, made it impossible for the latter to exploit their military and technical superiority by conquering territory. The Portuguese had been the first to discover that it was counter-productive to attack coastal settlements and raid the interior in search of slaves, since the supply of gold, ivory and slaves required an appropriate infrastructure, including groups of intermediaries on the coast, which had to remain intact. Subsequently, therefore, the Portuguese, Dutch, English and French confined themselves to installing fortified bases along the coast. The defensive and offensive equipment of these bases was aimed at unwelcome European competitors rather than the African population. The legality of this way of acquiring land always remained dubious, and was never brought into the open. Believing in its legality, the Europeans asserted that the 'customs' paid at regular intervals to native princes were voluntary gifts, while the princes, who were probably not competent to dispose of land, regarded these 'customs' as rent or tribute confirming their supremacy.[68] The Africans disliked these forts and would have preferred to deal directly with the ships, but they had to admit that in the last resort their interests, too, were better served by bases of this kind. The Europeans did not feel quite at ease either, since they knew that they were largely dependent on the Africans for water and provisions and that in a real conflict the Africans would ultimately have the upper hand. Thus, since the disagreeable aspects were outweighed by the interests of both parties, they managed to work out a *modus vivendi* permitting reciprocal dealings.

The beginnings were not always easy, and since the west coast has few suitable inlets and landing-places, there were many stretches of coast where for a long time only casual contacts were possible. Encounters between Europeans and Africans were initially limited to silent trade, in which goods were exchanged without speech or any other attempt at communication. As late as 1640 the Frenchman Jannequin recounted a visit to the Guinea coast as follows:

> These barbarous people, who I dare say judge all other nations by themselves, would not venture close to us in order to exchange their fish and water for our tobacco and ship's biscuit. They behaved rather as we behave towards victims of the plague: our people were obliged to take the goods which they wanted to exchange for fish some distance from the ship and then turn back. After the natives had observed this, they approached, took what had been brought to them, put their fish in the same place, and returned to their huts.[69]

Nevertheless, wherever the Europeans established trading posts, from the Ivory Coast to Angola, the two cultures soon devised means of carrying on commerce. Not only did each side want the other's goods, but both were equal in business acumen. In 1550 an early visitor to Guinea, John Lok, praised the black merchants: 'They use weights and measures, and are very circumspect in occupying the same. They that shall have to doe with them, must use them gently; for they will not trafique or bring in any wares, if they be evill used.'[70] The Africans were also quick to realize the advantages that might accrue to them from competition between Europeans, and anticipated the economists of the Enlightenment in asserting the principle of free trade. They had little interest in exclusive treaties of any duration and always sought the most profitable offer in the short term. Moreover, their diplomacy was sophisticated and astute enough to maintain contacts simultaneously on different levels and with different aims in view, and they were generally better informed than the Europeans. The newcomers soon realized that there was nothing to be achieved by a brutal or menacing demeanour. Time and again, officials at trading posts found themselves compelled to remind their fellow countrymen or the directors of their company at home of the necessity of friendly behaviour. John Snow writes to the directors of the Royal African Company in 1705: 'Great care should be taken here at home what persons are entertained into your service that they should have an experience of mankind as well of their yeares as their conversation, such qualityes being extreamly wanting on the Coast to gain the affection of the negroes.'[71]

The relationship between the European governor, or commandant of the fortress, and the local African princes and their entourage, developed in a solemn and ritualized manner that went well beyond what, in the case of cultural contact, we have termed ritual display. Both sides in such encounters were pursuing political as well as commercial objectives. On the one hand they wanted to ensure the continuity of their reciprocal relationship: this was not always easy, since sickness and death caused frequent changes in the European personnel, and it was made harder by the Africans' preference for taking decisions on the basis not of traditional loyalties but of a cool assessment of the current state of the market. In addition, both partners used such encounters to convey their own supremacy; this gave rise to awkward disputes over protocol – who should take off his hat to whom, who should visit whom, what sort of escort was appropriate, and so on. The French seem to have been past masters in the art of maintaining contacts solemnly at certain times, informally at others; this enabled them, both in West Africa and in North America, to strengthen their position even when they were numerically inferior to their European rivals.

To illustrate the pattern followed by such an encounter, we may cite the traveller Jean-Baptiste Labat, who visited Senegal in the early eighteenth century. Labat describes the meeting between the governor André Brue and the 'Siratick', the local Fulbe prince:

> The prince was resting upon a small bed, surrounded by some of his wives and daughters lying on mats. He rose as soon as the General appeared, raised his cap as soon as the General had put his hand to his hat, took a few steps forward, held out his hand several times to the General and invited the latter to sit down beside him. An interpreter had come forward. The General told the king that he had come to renew the immemorial friendship between the Royal Africa Company and his Majesty; that the Company had as its protector the most powerful king in the world [Louis XIV], who valued the friendship between himself and the 'Siratick' so highly that he was much more anxious to maintain this friendship and exchange tokens of esteem than to consider the advantages of trade. [...][72]

If a relationship based on trade was to run smoothly, it required a group of Africans and half-castes to serve as negotiators, boatmen, interpreters or craftsmen. These intermediaries, who were midway between the cultures and employed a pidgin language, could sometimes assume such importance as to jeopardize the interests both of the white traders and of the local native government. Inhabiting the no-man's-land between two social and cultural orders, these *lançados*, as the Portuguese called them, developed polished manners and great mercantile skill, along with an easy-going morality which often offended moralistic travellers and helped to confirm the contemptuous stereotype, widespread on the African coast in the seventeenth century, of the lazy and cunning negro.

Since the early days of contact between Europeans and Africans it had been common for Europeans, mostly seamen and marines who had deserted, to seek obscurity in the mixed society of the coastal stations, to become assimilated rapidly as cultural renegades, and to make a tolerable living thanks to their knowledge of both cultures. In European accounts such behaviour was always stigmatized as singularly reprehensible. This was not only because at sea and on land everybody's help was urgently needed, but also because by abandoning civilization and 'going native' they revealed the fascination of the alien culture. In Africa and elsewhere people retailed horrifying rumours of how such deserters had adopted pagan customs and taken part in cannibal feasts.[73] In the Enlightenment and in the Romantic period, it was also possible to regard the fates of these renegades with secret or even open envy. That was the case, for example, with the French-Canadian *coureurs de bois*, whose untrammelled way of life is recorded in the colonists' songs. A large part of European colonial literature, from Lahontan to Pierre Loti and Joseph

Conrad, derives its seductive exoticism from the description of lives like these.[74]

The process described here with reference to West Africa occurred, *mutatis mutandis*, in other parts of the world where cultures were prepared to enter into a longer or shorter relationship. It was probably in dealing with the peoples of India and the Far East that European overtures met with the greatest obstacles: for here, at the extreme periphery of their non-European sphere of influence, a relatively small number of Europeans came upon powerful and advanced cultures whose self-awareness was strongly ethnocentric. These cultures had developed court ceremonial and the art of international diplomacy to such a degree of magnificence and subtlety that European visitors could not restrain their astonishment. The Englishman Thomas Roe, who visited the court of the Great Mogul in India at the beginning of the seventeenth century, compared the scenery that met his eye to 'a great stage', and one of his countrymen, who was living in India at the same time, gives the following description of an encounter with a provincial governor: 'The five and twentieth in the morning, the Nabob came downe with a very great traine, and six elephants [ . . . ] I purposed to go unto him (as a sonne to his father) in my doublet and hose, without any armes or great traines according to custome, thereby to show my trust and confidence that I reposed in him.'[75]

No less impressive were the receptions given to Europeans at the courts of Peking and Yedo (Tokyo). After being made to learn the humiliating formalities of courtly behaviour, the Europeans were permitted at regular intervals to pay their most obedient respects as embassies bearing tribute. The visitors were only too painfully aware that the Oriental despots' display of magnificence had the ulterior purpose of showing in whose hands absolute sovereignty lay.[76] In these parts of the earth the Europeans were tolerated inferiors, rather than partners in a reciprocal relationship. The Eastern potentates repeatedly made it clear to the Europeans that basically they did not need to trade with Europe, and for a long time they were powerful enough to confine commercial exchanges within sharply defined limits. With regard to these encounters we might speak of a 'controlled relationship', in which the members of the alien culture decided on the location of trade, the number of traders, and the type and character of the goods, while exports and imports were determined by monopolistic trade agreements and appropriate customs arrangements. Eastern civilizations were deliberately selective in their acceptance of European influences. They welcomed the strangers when these appeared as astronomers, map-makers, cannon-founders or physicians, but they rejected the way of life which the strangers represented.

Intermediaries also played an important part in the relationship with such high cultures. Once again, they were often half-castes; the Portuguese quite deliberately promoted the formation of a Eurasian mixed-race society, doubtless with commercial objectives in mind. About 1640 the English traveller Peter Mundy found in Indian Cochin 'few Portugalls of quallity, most Mestizoes', and about the same time the German Mandelslo estimated the population of Achin in Sumatra at 12,000 souls, of whom only 300 were Portuguese, and the rest half-breeds.[77] Important functions within a cultural relationship could also be performed by Europeans who had spent a long time in the Orient and become largely integrated. One need only think of British consular officials in remote regions of Arabia, or of the important mediating role played by the Jesuits in trade with China.

In describing such commercial relationships as peaceful, one must nevertheless bear two things in mind. Firstly, they generally remained peaceful only as long as the supply of goods continued, along with the demand for them. Secondly, a relationship that had a pacifying effect on one region could produce collisions of the worst kind in the immediate neighbourhood. West Africa once again offers a striking example of the latter situation. Since the slaves were mostly captives taken in tribal wars, the increasing need for these 'goods' heightened the competition among the ethnic groups supplying them and intensified tribal warfare in general. Tribal conflict acquired a particularly devastating character once the coastal peoples were equipped with superior weapons, so that the traditional balance of power was often destroyed. Much the same could be said with reference to the fur trade in North America, where rivalries among the suppliers were further heightened by the marked hostility between the British and the French. Towards the end of the seventeenth century, when beaver skins were becoming rare in the coastal districts, the Europeans showed little interest either in continuing their peaceful relations with the local inhabitants or in exploring new forms of trade and production. The coastal Indians, who had become increasingly dependent on goods imported from Europe and whose own crafts had been ruined, were left to their own devices. Being wholly unfamiliar with the methods of capital accumulation, they had failed to derive any lasting benefit from commerce. As the British advanced inland, tribes living in remoter areas were drawn into the same development. The peaceful and prosperous relationship founded on commerce, therefore, remained for the most part a localized and short-term phenomenon.

Peaceful relationships like those made possible by commerce were also sought, and sometimes achieved for long periods, by missionaries.[78] The Portuguese and Spaniards had described the propagation of the Christian faith among the heathen as an objective which justified colonization in terms of international law; with this aim in mind it had also been approved by the Curia, *auctoritate Apostolica*. Since the Crusades the Muslims had been considered incorrigible infidels who could only be dealt with by the sword; but the members of other alien cultures, especially archaic ones, were seen as human beings who, owing to the inscrutable decrees of Providence, had either not yet attained the knowledge of the Gospel or attained such knowledge only to lose it, but in either case were capable of receiving Christianity. The question of how the heathen were to be converted, whether by force or through persuasive arguments and exemplary conduct, was hotly debated by Iberian churchmen and royal jurists at the beginning of the sixteenth century, and the final decision was in favour of non-violence. Whatever one's personal view of such activities may be, there is no doubt that missionaries of all denominations sincerely tried to ensure that their encounters with other cultures remained peaceful. This happened in two ways. On the one hand, the missionaries realized that conversions could only be credible in an atmosphere of mutual trust, and endeavoured to create such an atmosphere. On the other, they recognized the importance of reducing the tensions arising from the relation between the indigenous population and the colonists, and were often successful in doing so. Nevertheless, the relationship cultivated by the missionaries was a highly problematic undertaking: for while missionaries differed from the trader and the colonist in endeavouring to approach the natives sympathetically, they still remained at bottom exponents of European culture and ultimately dependent on material support from ecclesiastical institutions and from the colonial administration.

As a rule missionaries sought out members of the alien culture in their own territories and entered into contact with them directly: interpreters were occasionally employed, but rarely proved suitable for this task. The missionaries' sphere of action discouraged the formation of an intermediary group of half-castes, since the Catholic clergy were celibate, while the Protestant clergy were mostly married and worked in close association with their wives. It is true that missionaries under the first colonial powers, as well as later ones, tried to remove young Africans and Indians from their traditional society, educate them as Christians and later employ them in the mission; but this procedure showed no significant results until the nineteenth century. In attempting a direct encounter, the missionaries were obliged to adjust their social behaviour to that of the natives. They lived in the natives' dwellings, ate their food, sometimes adopted their clothing; above all, however laborious it proved to be, they learnt the natives' language. This assimilation resulted in part from simple necessity, and fitted the ascetic life-style enjoined by the religious orders to which the missionaries belonged. In part, however, it arose also from the reflection that integration into the native society, at least in outward matters, would make it possible to conduct a mission 'from within'. There can be no doubt that, thanks to what may be called their intimate relationship with other cultures, the missionaries became the professional group which, in every case of contact, possessed the fullest information about the alien culture. Since they were ordered to send in reports, they also provided the most detailed ethnographic accounts until the beginning of anthropological fieldwork in the later nineteenth century.

These concessions in social behaviour made no difference – how could they? – to the fact that the Christian message everywhere in the world remained one and the same. The Jesuits might put on Buddhist robes in China, appear as members of a superior caste in India, or take part in the Hurons' hunting expeditions in Canada, but the purity of their teaching had to remain unalloyed. If this rule were transgressed, all deviations, real and suspected, would promptly be reported to Europe by rival orders, and the Church had no hesitation about taking drastic measures, as it did over the 'rites controversy' in China.[79]

The missionaries remained inseparably attached not only to their teaching but to a certain colonial infrastructure. While putting the utmost possible distance between themselves and the European settlements in order to seek out natives who were not yet corrupted by alcohol, firearms and other innovations, they still could not do without communications and supplies. In many ways the missionaries behaved like the European traders, for they too were providing goods, the difference being that in exchange they received not raw materials and slaves but, as their opponents spitefully remarked, souls. It is beyond question that the welcome extended to missionaries by non-European peoples was due not to their teaching but to their presents and technical skills; this applies to high cultures like China and Japan as well as to all archaic cultures. There is disagreement as to how far the missionaries operated a sideline as profit-oriented traders: no doubt it varied from place to place. In the earlier seventeenth century, for example, the Jesuit missionaries in China performed important services as intermediaries, and certainly did not do this for nothing. One critic reviled them on the grounds that their church in Macao had direct access to the commercial sector. Yet in Canada at the same period they avoided dealings with *coureurs de bois* and fur traders, and abstained from any personal enrichment.[80] At times the missionaries worked on behalf of, or at least in close contact with, the political authorities. After 1790, for example, as part of George Washington's enlightened policy towards the Indians, the missionaries were supposed to guide the Cherokees towards happiness by training them in civilized arts and crafts.[81] These manifold cultural and structural links with the colonial power, sometimes glossed over in missionary reports, were not weakened by the missionaries' frequent sharp and responsible criticisms of colonialism. It is significant that their criticism was generally aimed at inhumane treatment of the non-European peoples, while failing to question the assumptions that made such treatment possible. Thus, it was a very long time before forced labour for Indians, or the slave trade and the slave economy, were challenged and systematically opposed by either Catholic or Calvinist missionaries.[82]

Until the end of the eighteenth century, missionary activity did manage to delay collision here and there, but it nowhere achieved any lasting success. Some socio-cultural forms of behaviour which were central to the alien culture were diametrically opposed to any acceptance of the Christian message: not only shamanism and other forms of religion, but also polygamy, promiscuity and nomadism. Every alien culture certainly contained groups such as children, sick people, half-castes and oppressed minorities, which at times were more receptive to Christian missions. Any more broadly based success, however, would have required the dissolution of the alien culture and its system of ethical values. We need not be surprised, therefore, if missionaries were able to register partial successes mainly in places where they found the alien culture already in crisis. This was the case in Japan between 1560 and 1587, when social disintegration within the Japanese ruling class combined with the desire for increased European imports to encourage missionary activity. Similarly, in China, the political and intellectual crisis during the decline of the Ming dynasty was probably the reason for the increasing influence of the Jesuit missionaries in the early seventeenth century. In both Japan and China, however, the homogeneity of the alien culture was unimpaired and its ethnic identity remained intact, so that missionary work had no real chance of success, even though the missionaries continued to send home euphemistic reports.[83] It was in Paraguay that the Jesuit mission attained its most spectacular success by establishing missionary settlements, or *reducciones*, between 1630 and 1700; but here, too, one principal reason lay in the demoralization of the Guaraní Indians by earlier attacks from Portuguese colonists and slave-hunters.[84] In the islands of the Pacific, in the early nineteenth century, English and American missionary societies were able to make such rapid progress only because the religious beliefs of the inhabitants had been shattered by the seafarers' military superiority and their value system had been undermined by alcoholism.[85]

The early history of Christian missions offers the paradox that in the very places where the missionaries sought to help the non-European population by taking advantage of their simple, unspoilt way of life, they contributed to the decline of the indigenous culture. Thus, without the participants realizing what was happening, it was possible for the relationship guaranteed by the missionaries to culminate in collision, not unlike the collision that we have observed in connection with the slave economy. Certain alien cultures responded to the encounter in pathologically exaggerated form, through fundamentalist religious movements based on apocalyptic visions, and these would not have been possible without the arrival of the missionaries.[86]

When relationships lasted for some time, they encouraged processes of acculturation which have as yet received insufficient attention from historians of colonialism. Acculturation makes its appearance in so many forms and on so many levels that the historian needs the help of anthropologists and sociologists in order to interpret it. The American anthropologist Herskovits offers the following definition of acculturation: 'Acculturation comprehends those phenomena which result when groups of individuals having different cultures come into continuous first-hand contact, with subsequent changes in the original cultural patterns of either or both groups.'[87] Although colonial mixed-race societies like that of Brazil are rare and developed (if at all) only in the nineteenth century, specific forms of acculturation are nevertheless to be met with at every turn, even in the earliest period of colonialism. A few brief references may serve to conclude this introductory chapter.

In general it can be firmly stated that in the course of colonial history European culture was never adopted as a seamless whole; instead, its individual components met with very different degrees of receptivity. This does not apply only to the high cultures of the Orient which conducted a 'controlled relationship' by cautiously and deliberately filtering European and later North American influences. Most archaic peoples also responded selectively, even though they were rarely guided by rational considerations of economic or political expediency and their selection could easily damage their own culture. Thus, the Plains Indians of North America lost no time in taking over the horse from the white settlers. They rode and bred horses with incomparable skill and put them to good use in hunting bison, though relations among the Indians were placed under considerable strain by the rapid spread of horse-stealing. In cultivating the soil, on the other hand, the Plains Indians generally refrained from employing European tools and practices: their unshakable traditionalism kept them attached to their accustomed forms of agriculture, so that they remained fatally dependent on the produce of their hunting-grounds, while their use of horses led to the extermination of the bison they hunted.[88] Again and again we see that not all the persons and institutions composing an alien culture react similarly to the importation of new techniques and ideas. The younger people often responded more favourably both to technical innovations and to missionary work than did the older, more conservative members of a tribal organization. Hence, the process of assimilation produced complicated displacements and overlaps, known as 'cultural lags',[89] which often instigated tumults verging on civil war. We have also seen that single items of European civilization, like firearms and alcohol, could bring about the disintegration of many alien cultures. It seems, too, that isolated communities, governed by rigid tradition and seldom exposed to the enlivening 'challenge and response' of encounters with other cultures, are in particular danger of dissolution.[90]

A component of one culture, by being transmitted to another, changes its character, acquiring new functions and new meanings. This can be observed with particular clarity in the area where Europe was most conscious of its civilizing task: in the mission to the heathen. It was common for Christian concepts and rituals to be laden with alien meanings, or for a traditional religion to have alien notions of salvation foisted upon it. The resulting syncretistic forms of religious culture have already been mentioned in connection with Negro Spirituals. This phenomenon of reinterpretation can cause members of the culture affected to feel alienated and spiritually homeless. In a study of the urban population of twentieth-century West Africa, the sociologist Georges Balandier has shown how the African city-dweller, when faced with any one of innumerable everyday decisions, is uncertain whether to follow traditional or adopted principles, and how he or she is compelled to play in different registers.[91] Such alienation can be scientifically demonstrated. Thus, the anthropologist Roger Bastide has established that contact with classical ballet has not only taught African dancers new forms of bodily movement, but has also changed their 'rhythmic sensibility'.[92] Likewise, the dances which Africans perform for European tourists reveal commercial and erotic motives which were originally alien to them. Observations like this have led Bastide to distinguish between 'formal' and 'material' acculturation and thus to contrast the external acquisition of aspects of another culture from fundamental modifications of one's mentality.

It goes without saying, finally, that acculturation affects everyone concerned, even when the technically superior culture appears dominant and its effects on the 'inferior' partner are more obvious. Colonial history records innumerable examples of European traders, settlers, soldiers, and even missionaries becoming so integrated into a non-European culture that fellow-countrymen, meeting them subsequently, reported in alarm that they had completely adopted an alien life-style and that communication with them was scarcely possible. Such 'cultural renegades' have already been mentioned, and will reappear occasionally in the pages that follow. It is also well known that conspicuous aspects of the mentality of a settler community could develop a long way from their origins, as in the United States of America, where the 'frontier experience' has been shown to play a determining role, though here it was contact with a new environment that was crucial, rather than the collision with Indian cultures.[93] It is remarkable how seldom the components of an alien culture adopted by white colonial society had the destructive effects that were so frequently observable in the converse case. This reveals one of the strengths of Western culture which, in the long run, was perhaps more important than military and economic superiority: the fact that in the course of an extremely varied history, Western culture has absorbed, transformed and rejected so many alien influences that it has acquired an astonishing capacity for change and renewal.

# 2

# The System of Limited Contacts
## *The Portuguese in Africa and Asia*

In any discussion of the Portuguese Empire, the first question must be: how was it possible? Within scarcely more than a century, between 1415 and 1515, how did one of the smallest countries in Europe manage to secure its access to the most important trading centres of two continents? What material conditions made this possible? What motives drove people on? How did they set about it? And how did they manage to hold on to what they had attained?

Towards the end of the fourteenth century, Portugal numbered one million inhabitants. Lisbon, the largest city in the kingdom, had a population of 40,000. As usual at that time, the soil was cultivated by primitive methods requiring a disproportionate amount of land.[1] Wheat and millet were grown, as were vines, olives and fruit; cattle-breeding was poorly developed; there was fishing along the coast. The vast majority of agricultural workers owned no land themselves, but were tenants or day-labourers in the service of lay or ecclesiastical landlords. The peasants handed over the greater part of their produce to their feudal lords, and they could also be summoned by the Crown and the great landowners to perform compulsory labour (socage) or military service. Only in the late fourteenth century, when long-standing border conflicts with Castile had been resolved and a treaty of mutual trade and friendship had been concluded with England, did it become possible to make a decent living from agriculture. This applied chiefly to the northern provinces; in the less fertile south, the Alentejo, peasants continued to migrate to the ports. Those who could do so sought their fortunes in urban commerce and crafts, and tried every possible means, whether string-pulling, marriage or education, to escape from the arduous lot of the rural worker. This desire to avoid agricultural labour helped to shape the character of Portugal's expansion overseas.

Portugal's thrust into the non-European world started from its harbours – Lisbon, of course, but also Oporto in the north and Lagos in the south. Since the beginning of the fourteenth century, these cities had maintained trading relations with leading Mediterranean ports like Genoa and Venice as well as with Flanders and England; they were also in contact with North Africa, the Canary Islands and Madeira. The granting of royal privileges enabled Lisbon to attract members of the most diverse nationalities and professions, including merchants and diplomats as well as experts in navigation, cartography and shipbuilding. The Portuguese nobility and clergy were financially involved in Mediterranean and Northern European business, and some middle-class families rapidly attained wealth and political influence. The ports had a motley population. In their alleys the royal and municipal officials rubbed shoulders with craftsmen and traders who were directly or indirectly dependent on maritime trade, whether as carpenters, sail-makers or ship-caulkers, or in the fabrication and sale of imported goods. There was a large Jewish minority, working with textiles and precious metals. The Moors no longer had any political importance, but in previous centuries many of them had mingled with the native population, and numerous physiognomies bore witness to this contact. The influence of Islam could still be felt in many areas, such as arithmetic and medicine, as well as in the arts. One could also encounter black Africans who had made their way here long before the departure of the Portuguese caravels for the Guinea coast.[2]

The achievement of showing the Portuguese the way to the oceans has been repeatedly assigned by historians to Prince Henry, known as 'the Navigator'.[3] According to a carefully nurtured tradition, Henry planned and co-ordinated the overseas voyages from Sagres, the south-western tip of Portugal. Being notable for his curiosity, initiative and determination, he made extensive geographical and astronomical studies and attracted a team of scholars who assessed the results of the voyages, enlarged the maps, and added to the equipment of the ships. Very little of this tradition can be found in contemporary sources, at least in those still extant since the Lisbon earthquake of 1755. It is quite possible that Henry the Navigator – who hardly ever set foot on shipboard – knew a great deal about seamanship; but so did others. It is true, too, that the Prince did his utmost to encourage shipbuilding, with considerable aid from his own purse; but he did not invent the caravel – it existed before him, and would have been further developed even without his assistance. Finally, it is also correct that the rocky extremity of the Sagres peninsula was well suited for a research station; but the historical documents say nothing whatever about the existence of a 'School of Navigation'. The present state of knowledge, therefore, entitles one to say that although Henry the Navigator was not the trail-blazing pioneer of genius that is often depicted, he was undoubtedly a character who knew how to seize and exploit the opportunities offered by the age in which he lived.

As for the motives that may have impelled the Crown Prince, we are informed about these by his court chronicler Gomes Eanes de Azurara. Several motives stand out: scientific curiosity and the prospect of commercial gain; the desire to spread Christianity among the heathen; rivalry with Portugal's Spanish neighbours.[4]

Scientific and commercial motives were intertwined. It is not easy to establish just what the Portuguese knew about the non-European world at the end of the fourteenth century.[5] Many sources of information may have dried up in the mean time, and much knowledge may have been lost. Moreover, people's knowledge of the outside world varied according to whether they lived inland or on the coast and according to their social class. Many people read the narrative of the Venetian Marco Polo, who had lived in China in the late thirteenth century and vividly described the riches of the Far East. Also popular were the *Travels* of the Englishman John Mandeville, which became available to Portuguese readers in the fourteenth century, and which likewise spoke of the unimaginable treasures of the Great Khan and praised the spices of the Malay Archipelago and the precious stones of India. The Portuguese also derived a good deal of geographical and scientific information from their contacts with North Africa, where they encountered travellers who themselves were linked with Egypt and the Near East by the caravan trade. The Muslims possessed outstanding geographers who were enlarging the heritage of the Greeks by exploring remote regions of the globe. About the year 1350 one of these scholars, Ibn Battuta, visited large parts of Africa, the Near East and India. His account of his travels brought news of the gold and ivory of the regions south of the Sahara and the richly embroidered silk fabrics of Asia. From the fourteenth century onwards, such information was recorded by Spanish and Italian cartographers in their atlases, which are also important works of art: a famous example is the Catalan Atlas of 1375, whose author, Abraham Cresques, was later summoned to the court of Henry the Navigator. The Portuguese could not help being more and more tempted to make an empirical test of the accuracy of what they learnt from books, maps and oral accounts. Accordingly, Azurara writes: 'And because the said Lord Infant wished to know the truth of this, [ . . . ] and seeing also that no other prince took any pains in this matter, he sent out his own ships against these parts, to have manifest certainty of them all.'[6]

Azurara leaves us in no doubt that such curiosity was far from disinterested. A nation already accustomed to trading with the Mediterranean and Northern Europe could not refuse the chance of bypassing its Muslim intermediaries and moving directly into the regions of Africa and Asia whose products were becoming increasingly popular. In their colonial trade, as Azurara tells us, the Portuguese had no competitors to worry about; they also hoped to export their own goods to the non-European world.[7]

Alongside scientific and commercial motives we find the equally clear urge to propagate Christianity through missionary activity. Within Christian culture the missionary tradition can be traced back to the New Testament, where Jesus addresses the following words to his disciples: 'All power is given unto me in heaven and earth. Go ye therefore, and teach all nations, baptizing them in the name of the Father, and of the Son, and of the Holy Ghost: teaching them to observe all things what-soever I have commanded you: and, lo, I am with you alway, even unto the end of the world.'[8] Ever since the activities of the Apostles in the Mediterranean region, Western people, on crossing the boundaries of their culture and coming upon peoples regarded as 'different', 'alien', 'barbarian', have repeatedly shown the urge to convert these peoples to their own faith. Hence, Christian missions have remained closely linked with colonialism, whether as its purpose or its pretext, right down to our own century. Moreover, in the twelfth century Portugal had been involved in the Crusades: Christian knights from England had halted here on their way to the Holy Land, and many of them had helped Portuguese princes to fight against the Moors, who still occupied parts of the country. Even after the expulsion of the Muslims in 1249 the crusading spirit remained alive in Portugal and became closely linked with the idea of the Christian mission; indeed, it was in a sense the latter's heroic and military counterpart.

As a rule the population of non-Christian cultures was divided into two groups: heretics and heathens. The heretics, among whom the Moors were included, were thought to be stubbornly and incorrigibly attached to their erroneous beliefs. Instruction and persuasion alike were wasted on them: the only language they understood was that of the sword, and combat with them was regarded by Christian noblemen, and by those who aspired to such status, as a divinely sanctioned test of virtue. By contrast, the heathen, such as the Africans and the Brazilian Indians, were generally judged more indulgently. It was argued that some inexplicable mishap had deprived them of Christian enlightenment, leaving them in the blindness of idolatry. Fundamentally, however, they were thought to be ready and willing to accept the true faith, if the Europeans could only manage to dispel the infernal forces that had taken possession of their souls. The conversion of the heathen benefited them by saving them from eternal damnation, while the agents of conversion thus ensured their own salvation; 'for,' writes Azurara, 'if God promised to return one hundred goods for one, we may justly believe that for such great benefits, that is to say for so many souls as were saved by the efforts of this Lord, he will have so many hundreds of guerdons in the kingdom of God.'[9]

Besides the mission and the crusade, the Portuguese had yet another religious motive: the search for Prester John. There were in circulation numerous accounts of distant regions, including the one by Mandeville, which mentioned a powerful priest-king residing somewhere in Africa or India. The twelfth-century German chronicler Otto of Freising had associated him with the dark-skinned Caspar, one of the Three Kings from the East. Another rumour claimed that Pope Alexander III and the Emperor of Byzantium had corresponded with him, though nobody had ever met him. It may be that the legend of Prester John was reinforced by an Ethiopian embassy that arrived in Venice about the year 1400. At any rate, this figure was thought to be a potential ally against Islam, and provided a major stimulus for Portuguese expansion overseas. His name still crops up even in reports from the mid-sixteenth century.[10]

Besides these scientific, commercial and religious impulses, we must finally mention the competition between Spain and Portugal. Since Portugal had attained national independence in the twelfth century, rivalries and border conflicts with its neighbour Castile had flared up repeatedly. This opposition was also apparent in trade with North Africa, but Castile was too much weakened by succession disputes and too preoccupied with the expulsion of the Moors to be a dangerous rival outside Europe. The biographies of two leading explorers, Columbus and Magellan, serve to reveal the tensions in the two countries' relationship. Both seafarers, one Italian and the other Portuguese by birth, had their projects and demands rejected by the Portuguese crown. Disappointed, they turned instead to Spain; and in both cases this behaviour was subsequently interpreted as treason. In 1494, soon after Columbus's discovery of America, the two countries signed the Treaty of Tordesillas which separated their extra-European spheres of influence. A line of demarcation running through the western Atlantic from pole to pole assigned Central and South America, with the exception of Brazil, to Spain. After Magellan's circumnavigation of the globe the Treaty of Saragossa (1529) extended this line beyond the poles. Both treaties, and a large number of similarly worded agreements, were concluded under the supervision of the Pope: this shows to what extent international law in the Middle Ages embodied the notion of a single Christian world, the *Orbis Christianus*.[11]

The first step in Portugal's overseas expansion was the capture of the North African port of Ceuta in 1415. Situated on the straits of Gibraltar, Ceuta was of considerable strategic importance. It controlled the straits, and its possession seemed to give access to the trade routes of the Sahara.

This last expectation, however, was not fulfilled, for the Islamic positions were not to be taken by a frontal assault. The Portuguese decided instead to outflank the Arabs by a grandiose maritime manoeuvre southwards along the coast of Morocco. In 1434, after several tentative probes, they passed Cape Bojador for the first time; a decade later the first caravels returned from Cape Verde with black slaves and gold-dust; and about the middle of the century they reached the mouth of the River Gambia, and established the first base for trade in slaves and commodities at Arguim, south of Cap Blanc. About the year 1480 they crossed the Equator and founded another trading post, Elmina, in the Bight of Benin; a little later Diego Cão reached the mouth of the Congo, and soon afterwards Bartolomeo Diaz sailed round the Cape of Good Hope. Finally, the journey on which Vasco da Gama embarked in 1497 with four ships was no longer a matter of pressing forward and trusting to luck, as these previous enterprises had been: it was a well-organized expedition, whose planning virtually ensured its success. Since earlier voyages had collected ample and precise details about the course of the West African coastline and its tides and wind conditions, Vasco da Gama and his captains were able to follow a new route on the high seas, which had been calculated with masterly skill: hence they succeeded in passing the Cape of Good Hope and reaching India with no significant difficulty. On 20 May 1498 Gama dropped anchor before the town of Calicut, on the Malabar coast. Only two years later, King Manuel sent out a full-scale fleet of thirteen ships with over 1,000 men on board: by sailing in a long westward curve, its commander, Pedro Cabral, discovered Brazil, and then arrived in India in September 1500.[12]

The instrument that made these voyages possible was the sailing-ship commonly known as the caravel, though this name does not denote a single, uniform type of ship.[13] In comparison with the galley, which retained its importance in Mediterranean navigation until the eighteenth century, the caravel possessed two decisive advantages. Having sails, it was no longer dependent on the strength of the oarsmen; and its robust construction, with raised hull and prominent superstructures at bows and stern, was well suited to withstand the powerful seas in the Atlantic. Caravels generally had three masts, two of which were equipped with square sails and the third with a triangular sail, known as the lateen sail. For lengthy voyages it was necessary to calculate the precise relation among interdependent factors like the size of the crews, the storage area and the ships themselves. A hundred-ton caravel, with a crew of fifty and the necessary stores, could only take about five tons of goods for trade. Living conditions on board were bad. The crew were meagerly fed, and the hygiene defied description. When the weather permitted, the sailors slept on deck; in bad weather they sought refuge in the damp interior of the hold. These conditions were not improved until the hammock was taken over from the Central American Indians. Illness was frequent, and it was not until the eighteenth century that effective precautions were taken against scurvy, a disease caused by vitamin deficiency. Most of the crew had 'chosen' their professions as sailors and soldiers under the pressure of material hardship. Even the ship's officers were often unable to read or write, and it is clear that only a few of the people who actually made the voyages were inspired by the scientific curiosity often spoken of in royal documents. Camoens's famous epic *Os Lusiadas* tells us about the gloomy – and often justified – forebodings with which the Portuguese put out to sea.[14]

It was thanks to their ships' armaments that the Portuguese succeeded in defeating Arab naval forces in the Indian Ocean. Who first thought of taking artillery on board is not known: it may have been the Venetians during their conflict with the Genoese in the early fourteenth century. Even the earliest Portuguese caravels to leave for Africa had small cannon on their forecastles and sterncastles. Later, the artillery was placed on either side of the deck and fired over the bulwarks, and early in the sixteenth century battery decks and gun-ports were installed, making it possible to deliver highly effective broadsides. This revolutionary innovation linked seamanship to fire-power, and left Portugal without serious competition for a long time.[15]

An important asset for the Portuguese voyagers was their charts. The oldest surviving sea charts date from the first half of the fourteenth century. Known as portolan charts, they can be recognized by the rhumb-lines and direction lines which helped the captain to determine his course from one harbour to the next. Such portolans seem first to have been produced in Venice and Genoa, and also on Majorca and in Barcelona; only a few Portuguese copies from before 1500 have survived. The charts are drawn in several colours on tanned animal hide and generally depict the course of the coastlines and good anchorages; many are decorated with a variety of shapes, sea-monsters and grotesque figures. Though often astonishingly precise in detail, early cartography made considerable errors in representing larger areas, as in maps of the world, since the longitude could not be determined exactly until the eighteenth century, and it was a long time before anyone worked out how to allow for the curvature of the earth.[16]

Further indispensable aids were the compass, the astrolabe and the log. In the twelfth century the Chinese knew how to exploit the phenomenon of magnetic attraction by the compass, and so, shortly afterwards, did the Arab navigators in the Indian Ocean: it was probably another 100 years before this instrument came into general use in the Mediterranean. The astrolabe, recommended by the late fifteenth-century German geographer Martin Behaim as a means of establishing the latitude in mid-ocean, was likewise previously known to the Arabs, who used it to ensure that they faced Mecca when praying. Finally, the log had been used since ancient times to measure the speed of the ship. We know that the helmsmen of the caravels in Lisbon were able to attend a training course in nautical sciences, and there was also a series of textbooks on these subjects.[17]

As we have seen, the African continent was not the goal of Portuguese efforts, but rather, especially in the early period, an unwelcome obstacle on the way to the treasures of Asia. The few bases established on the east and west coasts in the second half of the fifteenth century were thinly manned and served only as staging-posts for seafarers bound for India. Their existence depended on the goodwill of the local rulers. Exploration and conquest, such as the Spaniards had undertaken in Central and South America, were ruled out by the unfavourable climate, the inaccessibility of the interior, and the tropical diseases which drastically reduced the life expectancy of the European settlers. Among the native population on the coast, an intermediary group of black and mixed-race boatmen, interpreters, traders and craftsmen rapidly developed, and played an important part in initiating contacts, sustaining relations, and settling such conflicts as happened to arise. The Portuguese possessed only a strip of coastal territory or an offshore island, where they erected a fort containing their stocks of goods and accommodation for the military garrison, the commercial employees and the slaves. Among the most important 'factories' (*feitorias*) of this kind were Arguim, Axim and Elmina on the Guinea coast, and Sofala, Mozambique and Malindi on the east coast.

During the sixteenth century Portugal's Africa trade came to concentrate more and more on slaves, while the importance of gold, ivory, spices, ebony, ostrich feathers, gum arabic and leather varied from one region to another. In exchange for these the Portuguese offered textiles, glass beads, metal goods, brandy and firearms from Portugal itself, and from other parts of their colonial empire mussel-shells and coral beads, which were accepted as currency.[18] The first shipments of black slaves from Africa reached Portugal in the mid-fifteenth century.[19] After slave raids on the coast had proved counter-productive, the Portuguese relied on the help of local princes, who were in contact with tribes in the African interior. The black Africans could be enslaved under the following circumstances: if they had broken the laws and taboos of their community; if they had been taken prisoner in combat; and if a native prince was obliged by economic pressure to offer his subject to a neighbouring people in exchange for corn. The slave trade in the interior of Africa was well established: in pre-colonial times the export of slaves from the Sudan to Egypt, the Near East and India had been particularly important. The West African trade was conducted by black slave-dealers, who brought their 'goods' – mostly men aged between fifteen and thirty, but also women and children – over long distances to the coast. There, sometimes after prolonged haggling, the slaves passed from the hands of the native princes into those of the Portuguese.

At first the Africans were almost all dispatched to Portugal, where they became household slaves in the service of well-to-do families. Black servants soon became fashionable: about the year 1550 the population of Lisbon, 100,000 in all, included no less than 9,500 slaves, some of whom were of Moorish origin.[20] After the introduction of sugar cane in the late fifteenth century, first in Madeira and on the Cape Verde Islands, later on the islands of Principe and São Tomé in the Gulf of Guinea, slaves were increasingly employed on the plantations. Around 1530, when the Portuguese began colonizing Brazil, more and more Africans were shipped across the South Atlantic, and Angola became the principal supplier of slaves. It is estimated that in the late sixteenth century some 15,000 blacks arrived in Brazil every year, and most were set to work on sugar plantations in the Pernambuco and Bahia regions. According to further estimates, Portuguese Brazil in 1584 had a population of about 57,000: 25,000 whites, 18,000 domesticated Indians and 14,000 black slaves.[21] Since the Indians were incapable of the heavy exertions demanded by slave labour, they were increasingly replaced by blacks.

One cannot but be surprised that scarcely any Portuguese criticized the slave trade and the slave economy, while they had more sympathy for the situation of the Brazilian Indians. The main reason for their tolerance of the trade in African slaves may be that the Portuguese had long been familiar with slavery in the interior of Africa and in the Mediterranean region. In addition, the fact that it was the blacks themselves who delivered their fellows into slavery may have helped the Portuguese to displace any feelings of guilt on to others.

Although slavery devastated its victims spiritually, as well as physically, the missionaries were illogically determined to save the Africans' souls.[22] As early as 1490 a missionary expedition, manned principally by Franciscan monks, was sent into what is now northern Angola, with instructions to visit the 'Manikongo', the most powerful ruler in the Kingdom of the Kongo, and to reconnoitre routes leading to India and the realm of Prester John. The welcome they received from the native population seemed to justify the most ambitious hopes: the king and the principal notables of the country were baptized, and the building of a church was begun. Subsequently the Portuguese managed to place an African ally, the Christian convert Alfons I, on the throne of the Kongo, and the European sources are warm in their praise of this unique figure.

One missionary reported: 'So delighted is he with the reading of the Scripture, that he is as if beside himself. When he gives audience or when he dispenses justice, his words are inspired by God and by the examples of the saints.'[23] A correspondence between the King of Portugal and his African feudatory got under way; Alfons's example led to mass conversions in his realm; young men were sent to Europe for their advanced education. After Alfons's death, however, it became apparent that the Church had been building on shaky ground. Portugal failed to provide a sufficient number of trained missionaries who were properly aware of their responsibilities, and the various orders – Franciscans, Dominicans, Jesuits, Capuchins – stultified one another's efforts through their rivalries. Since clerics too often tolerated and justified the slave trade, indeed sometimes engaged in it themselves, relations between the two cultures were marred by an atmosphere of distrust which damaged the very heart of the traditional order of native society. The few missionaries left in northern Angola by the end of the eighteenth century told of violent family disputes between the African ruling houses, in which Europeans surreptitiously intervened. The hopes of a victory for Christianity, which had been aroused in 1500, were disappointed.

It was not in Africa, however, but in India, that Portugal established its most substantial presence overseas. The Portuguese arrived in this part of the world at a peculiarly fortunate moment, inasmuch as the sub-continent around 1500 was unable to muster any united defence. India was divided into regions of Hindu and Muslim rule, and within each of these cultures there was a multitude of dynasties and ethnic groups which often neutralized one another politically by their constant feuding.[24] Since the eleventh century the Muslims had been pushing southwards from Afghanistan. When Vasco da Gama landed in Calicut, large tracts of North India were ruled by Muslim sultans, particularly Gujarat in the west, Bengal in the east, and Delhi. Several such sultanates had also grown up in the Dekkan, where they were at war both with one another and with the Hindu dynasty of Vijayanagar to the south. Since the Indians were preoccupied by these internal divisions, which were partially reconciled only with the rise of the powerful Mogul Empire in the late seventeenth century, they regarded the arrival of the Portuguese on the west coast as a comparatively trivial occurrence. Indeed, it is doubtful whether they had any notion of the political implications of this event, which, from a Western viewpoint, seems a turning-point in world history. As Portugal could not found settlements in India, its presence was rarely considered a threat. Besides, the Portuguese were supple in adapting to circumstances and sensitive in their response to alien cultures. Admittedly, like the Spanish conquistadors across the Atlantic, they sometimes displayed the crusader's militant fervour and the pioneer's tendency to unrestrained brutality; nevertheless, in Asia these attitudes were less prominent than the readiness to enter into dialogue with their new partners and to investigate the scope for mutual enrichment through trade. Since there was less opportunity here for the easy and rapid acquisition of precious metals, the Portuguese did not show the feverish hysteria which determined the rhythm of cultural encounters in America.

The first serious resistance encountered by the Portuguese arose from the presence of an Arab fleet in the Indian Ocean. At the time when the Portuguese first passed the Cape of Good Hope, the Muslims maintained a series of naval bases in East Africa, on the Red Sea, on the Persian Gulf and on the coast of Gujarat, and from there carried on a flourishing trade with South-East Asia and even China. In these ports goods from India and the Far East were transferred to camel caravans serving Cairo, North Africa and the Levant; and from there the goods found their way, usually by ship, to Istanbul and Venice. The Arab merchants were prompt to recognize the historic implications of the Portuguese intrusion into their maritime domain. When Vasco da Gama's sailors arrived in Calicut, two Tunisian traders who lived there and spoke Spanish are said to have exclaimed: 'May the Devil take you!'[25] The Portuguese, for their part, saw clearly that their Asian trade had no chance of prospering unless they could smash the Arabs' power. It does not seem to have occurred to them that they might give up seeking a trading monopoly and enter into commercial competition with the Arabs. Once more, collision with Islam was inevitable.

The task of leading the struggle against the Arabs' maritime power was assigned to the first 'Viceroy of India' appointed by King Manuel, Francesco de Almeida, and to his successor Afonso de Albuquerque. In 1509, with the united Portuguese naval forces of some twenty ships, Almeida attacked the entire fleet that plied between Egypt and India, then lying in the harbour of Diu. The fight, in which both sides displayed equal courage and cruelty, ended in complete victory for the aggressors. Although the Arab fleet, especially when reinforced by Ottoman ships, was to make several further attempts to threaten the Portuguese, the battle of Diu proved decisive. The power of the Portuguese Crown in the Indian Ocean remained secure for a whole century, and was to be threatened only by another European naval power, the Dutch East India fleet, which had learned from the Portuguese example. Albuquerque set to work single-mindedly to consolidate Almeida's victory. The port of Goa was conquered in 1510, and soon afterwards Malacca, Hormuz and Aden came into Portuguese hands. In 1513 they reached the bay of Canton, where they established a small base, Macao, in 1556. At the same time they advanced to the spice islands of the Malay Archipelago, and visited Japan, the last great Portuguese discovery, in 1543. Such stupendous achievements in so short a time testify not only to the bravery and enterprise of this small seafaring nation, but also, as mentioned earlier, to their navigational skills and their technical and military progress.

The system of bases which the Portuguese established in Asia did not differ fundamentally from its African counterpart. At first they confined themselves so far as possible to a spectacular demonstration of power in order to induce the local ruler, the Sultan or Rajah, to give them a small territory with a harbour. For the rest, they did their utmost to avoid becoming embroiled in the internal affairs of the alien country, except when they employed diplomatic means to exploit rivalries among the natives. In Asia, as in Africa, the trading-post included a fort, dwelling-houses and stores, sometimes a wharf, and often a church as well; though in Asia, where commercial profits were higher, the buildings tended accordingly to be more elaborate and often luxuriously appointed. The native population was usually left in undisturbed possession of its territories and retained its previous hierarchy and laws. More prominent than in Africa was the intermediary group of half-breeds who smoothed trading contacts – not with slave-hunters this time but with the farmers and spice producers of the interior. In the enormous areas extending from the coast of East Africa to that of China there were probably never more than between 12,000 and 14,000 Portuguese actively employed, half of them as sailors and soldiers, the rest as administrators, traders and missionaries.[26] This 'thalassocratic'[27] or sea-based form of colonial empire-building seems to have had no adverse effect on the demographic vitality of Portugal itself, though people went overseas at the age of maximum fertility. It is more likely that eastern expansion provided a safety-valve, drawing off the turbulent and adventurous characters and thus strengthening the stability of Portuguese society. The extreme periphery of the colonial sphere provided these soldiers of fortune with a welcome field of activity, especially in the Philippines, where they sometimes came into conflict with the Spaniards operating from Mexico. In China and Japan, admittedly, very tight restrictions were placed on individual initiative and endeavour. There, at the extreme edge of their far-flung empire, the Portuguese came upon alien cultures whose ethnocentric attitudes were solidly based on long historical traditions. After their first brush with Europeans, both China and Japan did their utmost to keep the strangers at arm's length. The thousand or so Portuguese who established themselves in Macao after 1557 lived in strict seclusion and communicated with the native population through a small group of intermediaries, chiefly customs officials, while the Chinese made no secret of their condescending attitude to the Europeans. Much the same was true of the Portuguese base in Japan; this was on the artificial island of Deshima, which could easily be cut off from the mainland. While on the east and west coasts of India fraternization helped to reduce the distance between cultures, this happened far less in the Far East; and while the Portuguese in India, realizing the limits on their power, found a happy *modus vivendi* for reciprocal dealings, further east it was the Chinese and Japanese who determined the relatively chilly style of their 'controlled contact'. The encounters between the Portuguese and the Chinese will be discussed later in a separate chapter.

The centre of the Portuguese trading empire in the East was India, or more precisely Goa.[28] The city was on a well-protected and easily defensible island, some distance from the sea, in the estuary of two rivers. Its population can only be guessed at. One document says that in 1635 it contained 3,000 households, 800 of them Portuguese; but we cannot tell how many people were thought to constitute a household.[29] There is no doubt that the Portuguese were distinctly in the minority: a chronicler writes that in wartime only a few hundred soldiers could be recruited.[30] In contrast with the smaller trading-posts, the colonial domain in Goa extended beyond the harbour region and included an ever-increasing number of natives, especially those whose Christianity bore witness to the success of missionary activity.

Even by the shortest route, Goa was 10,000 miles distant from Lisbon, and from Goa it was another 4,000 miles to Macao. The journey to Europe and back was reckoned to take eighteen months, and the Viceroy of India, who resided in Goa and held his post for three years, had only one or two opportunities during that time to receive direct orders. During the sixteenth and seventeenth centuries Portugal sent out twenty ships a year, with a total of some 15,000 voyagers on board, including no more than a couple of dozen women.[31] Mortality was high: it was common for one-third of those making the *Carreira da India*, as the voyage to India was called, to die during the journey. The most frequent causes of death were scurvy, tropical fever, syphilis and consumption. One ship in every ten leaving Portugal was wrecked, while losses resulting from enemy action remained slight after the first decisive clashes, but could never be ruled out. It has been estimated that on a two-year voyage some 25 per cent of the seamen and colonists on board would die.[32]

On the return journey to Europe the Portuguese voyagers brought chiefly spices and textiles. The most important among their goods was pepper, which was imported in great quantities from the Malabar coast and Indonesia. Around the year 1520 some 6,000 tons of pepper are thought to have been shipped annually from Asia to Portugal.[33] The best cinnamon came from Ceylon. Nutmegs, mace and cloves came from the

Moluccas. Horses were imported from Persia and Arabia; from the east coast of India came a great variety of printed textiles; and China and Japan supplied silk, porcelain and precious metals. In contrast with Africa, where cheap manufactured goods served as currency, the East disappointed hopes of a similarly lucrative barter trade, for there the native traders demanded payment in hard currency. Since the Portuguese treasury had insufficient reserves of bullion, gold and silver were acquired from the Spanish colonial empire and made into coin in the mints established in Goa and Cochin. The Crown claimed the monopoly of overseas trade, demanding that all dealings should be conducted or checked by state officials, and punishing infractions of this rule. Official salaries, however, were so low that Portuguese living in Africa and Asia were virtually compelled to supplement their incomes with business dealings on the side, sometimes of a highly dubious character.

Goa was the residence of the highest official in the Portuguese seaborne empire, the Viceroy of India. Like the governors of smaller settlements, he came of a noble family and generally held his office for three years. As old engravings show, the viceroy's public appearances were most magnificent, not least because it was tactically essential to impress the local rulers. Even in the early days of colonial expansion, the viceroy maintained a staff of advisers; after 1563 a council of state was set up, including the officials in charge of finance, justice and military matters. From 1516 onwards, the affairs of Goa were dealt with by a municipal council, chosen by remarkably democratic methods and able to take decisions without reference to the viceroy and his chief officials. There can be no doubt that in such a colonial government, remote from metropolitan control and obliged to respond flexibly to novel circumstances, many things could be done contrary to Portuguese law and to natural justice. Indeed, a detailed study of the sources has led the German colonial historian Georg Friederici to a devastating verdict on Portuguese administration in India:

> The royal officials were unreliable, negligent, ignorant of commerce, and incapable of efficiently conducting the business entrusted to them, because they were constantly seeking to feather their own nests. The officers and officials were irresponsible, loose-mouthed, disloyal, dishonest, corrupt, mendacious and given to back-biting. Not only were they insatiably greedy, but all of them, the captains at sea and the officers and officials on land, disregarded orders to the point of insubordination. They illustrated the collapse of moral standards by their maladministration of justice and their violence culminating in murder. The universal corruption of all officers and officials, right up to the viceroy, and the dishonourable and unchivalrous impulses of most of them, ensured that serving and retired soldiers were cheated of their well-earned pay and pensions, and that the natives' wives and daughters were forcibly robbed of their virtue.[34]

In the later sixteenth century this state of affairs seems to have worsened and finally to have been partly responsible for the rapid capitulation of the Portuguese when faced by competition from Dutch traders. A chronicler in Goa wrote in 1610, eight years after the founding of the *Oostindische Compagnie*: 'There is no health left in India; all is rotten and ulcerous and wellnigh covered with a foul tetter; and if a limb be not cut off, the whole body will sicken and decay.'[35]

Goa was also the seat of the archbishop, and was proud to be called the Rome of *Asia christiana*. Pastoral and missionary activity were so prominent that one cannot question the sincerity of the religious motive behind colonization. Although the missionaries upheld the crusading tradition in their vehement antipathy to Islam, they sometimes went so far as to consider Hinduism a religion related to their own, and they began to direct their efforts systematically at the Hindus. The propagation of the faith was undertaken chiefly by Jesuits, who arrived in Asia in 1542 and whose zeal was spurred on by the Inquisition and the Counter-Reformation. The church council of Goa, admittedly, maintained in principle that the mission should avoid force or pressure in dealing with potential converts. Reality, however, often showed a different face. In order to prevent what was condescendingly called 'idolatry', the missionaries did not hesitate to destroy alien places of worship, and the Portuguese in India did this as readily as the Spaniards in Central and South America. Missionary zeal was enhanced by the promise of social privileges: indeed, the tenure of certain offices was made subject to the adoption of Christianity. A disturbing phenomenon was the Church's arrogation of the right to bring up orphans, including those who still had one parent living. Yet there is no doubt that the Portuguese mission in India, supported by the charisma of an extra-European episcopal see, could point to a greater and more lasting achievement than its counterpart in Africa. In the late sixteenth century Goa and the surrounding district are thought to have contained some 60,000 Christians, and even in 1961, when the colony was absorbed by India, almost two-fifths of the native population were Roman Catholics. The Jesuit priest Francis Xavier, a friend of Ignatius Loyola, left Goa for China and Japan because he found that the most demanding work in India had already been done and wanted to open up virgin territory for the Christian faith.[36]

In sixteenth-century Goa, different population groups lived together in a confined space and in a community of interests, while the clergy encouraged racial mixing provided that both parties had been baptized. Appropriately, it is in Goa that we find the first works of art produced outside Europe that show the influence of diverse cultures. These are chiefly objects used in the households of the viceroy, leading clerics and local rulers: furniture with delicate intarsias made of precious woods, ivory and mother-of-pearl; reliquaries and caskets in enchanting gold and silver filigree work; ivory carvings with motifs from legends and chivalric romances; blankets, carpets and chasubles with the finest weaving and embroidery. Such objects of art often combine motif and ornament, form and technique, with no stylistic incongruity, in a successful syncretism of Eastern and Western traditions.[37]

Whether one considers its origin or the solidity of its far-flung structure, the Portuguese trading empire, as it appears on early seventeenth-century maps of the world, was an achievement unparalleled in history. Earlier historians have emphasized the pioneering drive of the Portuguese explorers, the high level of their scientific and navigational knowledge, and the aggressive vitality of the crusading idea. Modern commentators tend to focus on the functioning and the comparative stability of this version of colonial rule, for the Portuguese achievement was not only daring and reckless; contradictory as this may seem, it also demonstrates an astonishingly sure judgement of where to stop. Portugal was of course a small country, with natural limits to its scope for action. How many temptations the Portuguese had to resist on their long route to the East! After the capture of Ceuta they could have worn themselves out in fruitless skirmishes with the Barbary states; in West Africa they could have been seduced by greed for gold into undertaking fatal expeditions into the interior; from the Persian Gulf they could have tried to obtain the legendary wealth of the Shah or to advance to the Holy Places of the Near East. However, they did none of these things. They adhered to their original plan of by-passing Islam and using the best sea routes in order to secure their access to the East and its coveted products, thereby continuing on a global scale the mediating role which they had previously performed between the Mediterranean and the North Atlantic. They had to operate within the existing economic, political, technical, geographical and cultural frameworks provided by the system of monopoly capitalism exercised by the Crown; by the caravel and its further development; and by the distances, currents and winds, as well as by the topography of remote coastlines and the mentalities of their inhabitants. Within these constraints they had to develop a variety of talents and skills, which in turn demanded many qualities that might seem mutually incompatible: courage and calculation, toughness and flexibility, endurance and the capacity to improvise, the ability both to get their own way and to empathize with others.

From a present-day viewpoint, the most impressive achievement of the Portuguese is perhaps their frequent and rapid success in arriving at a mutually satisfactory relationship with the many and various peoples they encountered on their way to the Far East. To ask how they managed this is to touch on the mystery of the Portuguese mentality. It is clear that the Portuguese were markedly superior to the Spaniards, and incomparably superior to the Dutch and English, in their capacity for an unprejudiced and adaptable response to influences from alien cultures. Though it is easy to recognize this as a historical fact, the tangle of interdependent causes makes it very hard to offer a final explanation. Here we can do no more than sketch the phenomenon.[38] We may confine ourselves to the astonishingly positive Portuguese attitude to the intermixing of races. Even in Africa and Asia this was clearly apparent, and in Brazil it was finally to have important social consequences. The lack of European women is not an adequate explanation, for other colonial powers felt the same lack yet abstained almost entirely from racial mixing. This attitude results rather from the facts of Portuguese history. The Portuguese were themselves a mixed race, having absorbed Phoenician, Jewish, Roman, African, Arab and Moorish blood over the centuries, and had thus been unable to develop racial awareness or racial prejudice. Moreover, neither in Portugal itself nor overseas was the intermixing confined to particular social classes: even the clergy did not always exercise self-denial in this respect. In general, Catholicism seems to have assisted racial integration through its tendency to see the non-European as a potential Christian, in stark contrast with Calvinism with its concept of the elect. Economic considerations also promoted racial mixing: in Brazil the young white master could add to his property by impregnating slave women, while in India the loyalty of half-breeds to the Europeans could be of great importance for the politics of trade. The sociologist Gilberto Freyre has drawn attention to the very marked sexual preference for exotic women shown by the Portuguese and has shown to what extent, even within the family, physical relationships have encouraged the easy transfer of cultural elements.[39] There is no doubt that this readiness for intermixing defused potential conflicts, or at least displaced them to less conspicuous areas of cultural contact, though modern Brazil shows that it did not resolve social problems.

The long strides taken by the Portuguese eastwards round the Cape of Good Hope had many implications for Europe, especially for Mediterranean trade and for Venice, which had been trying ever since the Crusades to maintain its links with the Near East. Just after the return of Bartolomeo Diaz, a Venetian merchant living in Lisbon sent a warning letter to the Signoria: 'Therefore, now that this new voyage of Portugal is found, this King of Portugal will bring all the spices to Lisbon. And there is no doubt that the Hungarians, Germans, Flemish and French, and those beyond the mountains, who formerly came to Venice to buy spices with their money, will all turn towards Lisbon.'[40] However, the decline of Venice, hastened by its conflict with the Ottoman Empire, was only one aspect of an economic and historical process that affected the entire planet. The eastward advance of the Portuguese resembles one wing of a diptych, the other being Spain's expansion in the west. Each process assisted the other. The vast wealth drawn by the Spaniards from the gold and silver mines of Mexico and Peru passed via the slave trade to the Portuguese in Asia, who thus paid for goods imported into Europe. In Europe itself economic dominance shifted to the west, where the union of Portugal and Spain in 1580 and the rise of the Habsburg Empire under Maximilian I and Charles V formed a powerful economic region. Once the Turkish threat had been rebuffed by the battle of Lepanto in 1571, and Spain under Philip II had assumed a leading role in combating the Reformation, there was good reason to speak of a 'golden century', a *siglo de oro*.[41]

The Dutch became the dominant power in the African and Asian area after attaining their independence in 1581 and after the defeat of the Spanish Armada in 1588. They largely copied the system of bases developed by the Portuguese, but transferred its centre to Batavia (now Jakarta) in Indonesia. Portugal had no reserves with which to combat the economic dynamism of the Dutch East India Company, founded in 1602 and supported by the urban merchants of an independent republic. After 1615, when England became active in this area, the Portuguese colonial empire in the East led only a shadowy existence. Its former importance was inherited by Brazil, which after decades of stagnation managed to fend off the attacks of European rivals and in the seventeenth century developed a distinctive variety of European colonization.[42]

# 3

# Cultural Collision
## *The Spaniards on Hispaniola*

---

The European intrusion into the transatlantic world can best be understood, along with its implications, by taking the island of Hispaniola, which now comprises Haiti and the Dominican Republic, as a model. As Pierre Chaunu has said, Hispaniola is a 'microcosm of the entire history of America'.[1] It was the original setting for the sequence of events which was later to be repeated in Mexico, Peru and Chile. Thanks to favourable currents and winds, sailing-ships had easy access to the island. It occupies a key position in the curve formed by the Greater Antilles, and its pleasantly warm climate encourages luxuriant tropical vegetation and permits the cultivation of useful crops. All these factors gave Hispaniola considerable strategic and economic importance until the end of the eighteenth century.

On 6 December 1492 Christopher Columbus became the first European to reach the island, arriving at its north-west coast. Two months earlier, his flotilla had touched on American territory for the first time, at the island of San Salvador in the Bahamas, which its Arawak inhabitants called Guanahani. Hoping and believing that he was near the Chinese mainland and within reach of the Far Eastern treasures celebrated by Marco Polo, Columbus had then followed the northern coastline of Cuba. On reaching Hispaniola, he gave it this name in order to emphasize a certain resemblance to Spain and, more importantly, to underline the importance of his discovery. He identified Hispaniola with Japan, and this conjecture seemed to be supported by the fact that part of the island was called 'Cibao', which sounded not unlike Marco Polo's 'Zipangu'.[2]

At this time Hispaniola was inhabited by an Arawak tribe, the Tainos. This ethnic group led the settled existence of an early planting and hunting culture, far less advanced than the high cultures of the Mexican mainland.[3] These Indians – a term of Spanish origin which, as is well known, perpetuates Columbus's mistake – had left the north coast of the South American mainland a few centuries before Columbus's arrival, perhaps driven out by the military superiority of the Caribs. They lived chiefly on manioc, sweet potatoes and maize, fished with nets, lines and spears, and practised hunting on a more modest scale. They had no domestic animals except a species of dog. The islanders had no conception of clothing as such; only the women, after puberty, wore a kind of loincloth. Both sexes liked to paint their bodies: in their ears and noses, and round their necks, they wore rings fashioned from gold. Although they were skilled and artistically gifted craftsmen, especially in wood-carving, the Tainos had few weapons; they relied chiefly on flint-tipped spears. For water transport they used canoes made from tree-trunks, moved by oars, since they had no sails. The Tainos lived in villages of various sizes amid well-cultivated fields. The population of the island appears to have been divided into five provinces. Each of these had its own chieftain or *cacique*, with almost unlimited powers extending to matters of life and death. Below the *caciques* came the heads of smaller districts and villages, and they in turn were assisted by counsellors. Those islanders who did not belong to any of the ruling families tilled the fields and worked as craftsmen in the villages. There were also slaves.

The Tainos were a peaceable and hospitable people. Visitors whose intentions were clearly unwarlike were received as personal guests of the *caciques* and village headmen, and entertained by the community: the guest was invited to enjoy sexual intercourse with native women, and feasts were held in his honour. However, the islanders lived in fear of attacks by the Caribs from the neighbouring islands. These attacks generally took place at night and sometimes ended in the destruction of entire villages, the massacre of the male inhabitants, and orgies of cannibalism.

Most of the early encounters between the Spaniards and the Tainos were notable for their peaceful character. The islanders' behaviour was not, of course, uniform: at the beginning of contact some tribal groups were fearful and timid, others bold and inquisitive; and young people tended to be forthcoming, while older ones were reserved or unfriendly. For their part, the Europeans at first had no desire for conflict. Although Columbus clearly did not trouble himself about a coherent policy towards the natives, and later was often hesitant and inept in handling such matters, in the early stage of their encounters he advised his countrymen to treat the Indians considerately. Immediately after the landing on Hispaniola, armed soldiers were sent into the interior with instructions to secure the goodwill of the inhabitants by distributing glass beads, bells and coloured caps. A young woman who had been abducted and taken on board ship was given presents and sent home. News of this friendly behaviour spread, gaining the Indians' confidence. Only a few days after Columbus's arrival, the Tainos thronged to his ships, and the local chieftain sent a messenger to enquire when he could receive the seafarers.[4]

Unfortunately, it is possible to reconstruct only sketchily how the inhabitants of Hispaniola felt when they first saw the sails of the Spanish ships appearing on the horizon like heavenly bodies. There is no written record of this event, and the Tainos' oral tradition perished with them, half a century later, without being written down. Their reactions can be inferred only from the Spaniards' writings, and especially from Columbus's own journal. These suggest that the Tainos must have felt their visitors to be fundamentally different from themselves, and were profoundly disturbed by this discovery. What was crucial was the impossibility of comparing the Spaniards with any human beings with which they were acquainted, even with the Caribs. The latter's manner of life was familiar, even if some customs and skills had developed differently; but the strangers' beards, their white skin, the clothes covering their bodies, and the completely unintelligible sounds by which they conversed – for the Tainos, none of these things could be fitted into a meaningful relation with any historical experience. The same also applied to the instruments used by the newcomers. It was impossible to see the sailing-ship as a more highly developed canoe, and it was a long time before the Indians grasped the power by which it moved. Still more inexplicable, indeed positively uncanny, were the firearms and the ship's artillery, whose report alone, it seemed, could rip distant trees apart and, as the Indians found out soon enough, strike people dead. And what were they to make of the dignified Spanish notaries, who recorded the appropriation of their territory by painting strange black signs on a piece of parchment with a pointed quill?

Was it not the most obvious conclusion to regard these beings, so unfamiliar in their appearance, their behaviour and their powers, as supernatural? In the introductory chapter we noted that the civilized peoples of the Central and South American mainland, the Aztecs, Mayas and Incas, saw the advancing conquistadors as gods.[5] Similarly, the Spanish documents predating the occupation of Hispaniola repeatedly relate how the Arawaks called the voyagers gods and firmly rejected all attempts to correct this mistake. It is thus that Columbus himself describes his first encounter with a 'native king':

> Afterwards, in the evening, the king came to the ship; the admiral [Columbus] showed him due honour and caused him to be told that he came from the Sovereigns of Castile who were the greatest princes in the world. Neither the Indians whom the admiral carried with him, and who

were the interpreters, nor the king either, believed anything of this, but they were convinced that they came from heaven and that the realms of the Sovereigns of Castile were in heaven and not in this world.[6]

On Hispaniola, too, the arrival of bearded and fully clad strangers seems to have been prophesied, and, according to the historian Francisco López de Gómara, interpreted as an evil omen.[7] At all events, there is no doubt – even if the Spaniards maintained the contrary – that the Tainos were familiar with the conception of a supernatural being dwelling in heaven, and hence had at least some means of integrating the strangers' arrival into their own picture of the world.

Gods are to be welcomed with every sign of awe and with demonstrations of willingness to serve them. During Columbus's stay, accordingly, the Tainos vied with one another to show kindness to their visitors. They gave prompt answers to all enquiries, especially to the incessant questions about the whereabouts of gold; they hastened to supply their guests' every wish, whether for drinking water, fruit, precious metals or women; local rulers begged to receive the Spaniards or be received by them; and when Columbus's flagship, the *Santa Maria*, ran aground, the Indians showed deep distress and helped to unload the cargo. 'Finally [the journal tells us], the admiral says that it is impossible to believe that any one has seen a people with such kind hearts and so ready to give and so timorous, that they deprive themselves of everything in order to give the Christians all that they possess, and when the Christians arrive, they run at once to bring them everything.'[8] Such was their brotherly love that Columbus decided that he must have encountered a people predestined to accept the Christian message. Their obliging behaviour seemed completely unselfish, though it may have been influenced by the calculation that they had gained a powerful ally in their struggle against the Caribs.

On 26 December 1492, with the eager help of the *cacique* Guacanagari and his subjects, the Spaniards began building a fort, which they called *Villa de la Navidad* in commemoration of Christmas. Over forty men, many of them volunteers, stayed behind in this, the first settlement in the 'New World'. Columbus did not anticipate any danger from the islanders, for he judged the Tainos' military strength to be negligible and was convinced that a few armed men would be sufficient to control the entire island. His principal reason for building an observation tower and fortifications was to bring home to the Indians the technical capacities of Spanish carpentry. On 4 January 1493, at daybreak, Columbus weighed anchor and set out on his homeward voyage; on 15 March he arrived in the Spanish port of Palos.

Columbus had made great promises to the Catholic monarchs, Isabella of Castile and Ferdinand of Aragon, on whose orders he had set sail; and he had asked a great deal of them. In the 'Capitulations of Santa Fé', the treaties regulating the rights of sovereignty over whatever lands he might discover, he received very extensive benefits: he was raised to the rank of Admiral, Viceroy, and Governor-General, with the appropriate authority, and he was promised 10 per cent of the profit on all goods and products acquired in trade. The 'Capitulations' speak of the overseas territories – *islas y tierras firmas* – with such confidence and such visionary optimism that Columbus could not have afforded to return without accomplishing his mission. Having placed himself under such pressure to succeed, Columbus was no sooner back from his first voyage than he began energetically advertising his discoveries, though at that time, after such a brief examination, he was in no position to estimate their importance. In his famous letter to the Chancellor Luis de Santangel he writes:

> Española [Hispaniola] is a marvel. The sierras and mountains, the plains and arable lands and pastures, are so lovely and rich for planting and sowing, for breeding cattle of every kind, for building towns and villages. The harbours of the sea here are such as cannot be believed to exist unless they have been seen, and so with the rivers, many and great, and good waters, the majority of which contain gold.[9]

Columbus's notes on his first voyage contain several landscape descriptions that reveal him as a lover of nature and an accurate observer. Although these idylls are touched by a yearning for Paradise, they are not all that remote from the reality of the Caribbean archipelago. However, the Spaniards' desire for gold remains unpleasantly dominant: this theme and its variations appear undisguised throughout. 'It is true', writes the Admiral frankly in his journal, 'that if I arrive anywhere where there is gold and spices in quantity, I shall wait until I have collected as much as I am able. Accordingly I do nothing but go forward in the hope of finding these.'[10] Was that all he was doing? The reader cannot but suspect as much. Wherever Columbus and his followers made their appearance, their first thoughts were about precious metal. The simple gold ornaments sometimes worn by the Tainos gave rise to persistent questioning, conjectures and greedy bargaining. The Indians, obviously astonished to find gods displaying such unbridled cupidity, gave ready answers, saying that they had found gold accidentally in the interior or in a river, for it would never have occurred to them to mine systematically for gold. They soon learnt to carry on their dealings with the Europeans more artfully, by cutting their gold into chips and offering them individually in exchange for European goods. It seems, too, that many islanders, gradually tiring of the Spaniards' presence, exploited their obsession by directing them to distant sources of gold and thus encouraging them to travel onwards. At all events, the

Spaniards' vivid imaginations transformed the slightest, vaguest hint about gold into a certainty: gold-mines, rivers of gold, even whole islands of pure gold, seemed to be within easy reach. This immoderate greed for riches took precedence over all the other objectives of their voyage, such as the desire for geographical knowledge or the aim of making Christian converts. They sought salvation in gold alone. The blasphemous undertones of this sentence, far from being an exaggeration, may be found in Columbus's own writings. On 23 December 1492, off the coast of Hispaniola, he writes: 'Our Lord in His goodness guide me that I may find this gold.'[11] And in a letter about his fourth voyage, again referring to Hispaniola, he says: 'Gold is most excellent. Gold constitutes treasure, and he who possesses it may do what he will in the world, and may so attain as to bring souls to paradise.'[12]

Historians, particularly those chiefly concerned with Columbus's achievements as an explorer, have registered this greed with discomfort. It is strongly reminiscent of the collective psychosis that seized upon Californian gold-diggers in the mid-nineteenth century. In defence of Columbus and his companions it may be pointed out that subsequent conquistadors thought exactly the same, whether they appeared in Mexico, Panama or Peru. Even in the somewhat disillusioned *Historia general y natural de las Indias* by the chronicler Fernández de Oviedo, which was published in many volumes around 1540, the word 'gold' figures on almost every page. 'To many colonists', pronounces Georg Friederici, 'it never occurred to do anything but look for gold, and this frantic search for precious metals, jewels, and pearls prevented them from engaging in any productive economic activity.'[13]

There is no disputing that the Spaniards were primarily interested in the Arawak Indians as sources of information about where to find gold and of labour in extracting it. Columbus keeps emphasizing how ready the Indians were to supply information and to provide goods of every kind, even those that Europeans considered most valuable, in return for trifles. Similar criteria lie behind the stress on the Arawaks' peaceful and inoffensive character, which implied that any resistance by the Indians to the conquest and exploitation of their territory would be ineffectual. Columbus draws the logical conclusion in his diary: 'They are also fitted to be ruled and to be set to work, to cultivate the land and to do all else that may be necessary.'[14]

Secondly, the Spaniards were interested in the Indians, or rather in the Indian women, as sources of gratification. The early travellers unite in praising their unfamiliar nakedness and the beauty of their unhampered bodies. Not only did their nakedness confirm the Tainos' inoffensiveness, but it was the ultimate reason for the bewildering ambiguity in European opinion, which alternated between placing the Indians just above the beasts and regarding them virtually as inhabitants of Eden. In the travel narratives their absence of clothing is not condemned; it was seen, rather, as an entirely acceptable invitation to sexual intercourse. The brutality with which the Spaniards treated Indian women and children in order to gratify their lust is one of the most sombre episodes in the history of the encounter between these cultures.

Thirdly, the Indians ranked as objects of missionary activity. Columbus was a man of profound, medieval piety, who saw himself as the representative of the *Orbis Christianus*, just as the Crusaders had done.[15] He was familiar with the idea that the heathens overseas must be converted, to ensure their salvation and that of the proselytizer, and he often called himself the 'bringer of Christ', alluding to his Christian name. It is true that missionary concerns seem not to have been at the forefront of his mind when he was planning his first voyage. Salvador de Madariaga has rightly drawn attention to the extraordinary fact that there were no priests on the 1492 expedition.[16] However, Columbus frequently refers to his missionary ambition in his diaries and letters, and this project comes naturally to mind when he comments on the Indians' peaceable and inoffensive nature:

> I saw, as I recognise, that these people have no creed and they are not idolaters, but they are very gentle and do not know what it is to be wicked. [ . . . ] So your Highnesses should resolve to make them Christians, for I believe that, if you begin, in a little while you will achieve the conversion of a great number of peoples to our holy faith.[17]

In the instructions for Columbus's second voyage, the Crown clearly emphasized the Spaniards' obligation to convert the Indians; and the Papal Bulls which Isabella and Ferdinand had procured from Alexander VI in 1493 stated that the newly discovered territories should belong to Spain only on condition that missionary work was performed there. It is remarkable that in the image of the Indians formed by Columbus and his men, the conception of them as potential suppliers of gold never clashed with the conception of them as potential Christians. As will be shown, it would be left to the missionaries to make people aware of the repulsive double standard of morality implicit in such an evaluation of non-Europeans.

In sum, the Spanish seafarers' ideas about the inhabitants of Hispaniola concerned only their ability to satisfy the Europeans' material, sexual and religious expectations and requirements. There are no traces of any interest in the Indians for their own sake. Even external singularities, like the Indians' way of painting their bodies or arranging their hair, are neither described in detail nor interpreted. Far less do we find any observations about the Indians' social and political system, their economic life and religious cults, or their language. The extreme poverty of the ethnographical information cannot be explained or excused by the fact that communication with the Tainos was mainly conducted through expression and gesture. Nor can one blame the state of contemporary intellectual life, since the abundant European travel literature of the period shows a lively interest in anthropological peculiarities. No matter how one reads the sources, the scholarly balance sheet of these early contacts between Europeans and Indians in the Caribbean shows an alarming deficit. One must agree with the judgement of the French linguist Tzvetan Todorov, whose careful analysis of all the relevant documents leads him to the conclusion that Columbus had 'discovered America, but not the Americans.'[18]

When Columbus revisited *La Navidad* on 27 November 1493, during his second voyage, he found that the fortress had been completely destroyed and its garrison killed. The Tainos' behaviour was timorous and distrustful, and what little information could be got out of them revealed that the Spanish colonists had brought about their own downfall through their brutal treatment of the Indians, especially of the native women. The idyll of the first encounter had changed abruptly into the catastrophe of warlike collision – a process which can be observed in colonial history all over the globe. In the eyes of the Tainos, the Europeans did not behave like gods, but like exceptionally malicious demons; and as soon as these demons proved to be vulnerable and mortal, their supposed invincibility vanished. In attacking the garrison of *La Navidad*, the Tainos were following the logic of this discovery. Unlike conquistadors like Cortés and Pizarro, Columbus was unable to take decisions promptly and confidently, and so he found himself at a loss. This favoured the ascendancy of those people around him who wanted to bring Hispaniola under complete control as soon as possible and to lay hands on the gold of the interior, the quantity of which they grossly overestimated.

Thus began the period of extermination campaigns directed against the population of the island. First, small reconnoitering expeditions were undertaken from newly erected forts; then, in March 1495, a combat force including two hundred of the best soldiers, twenty horsemen and twenty bloodhounds was dispatched into the interior with instructions to reduce the Tainos to obedience. The Spaniards were thereafter to practise every imaginable form of aggression: deception and naked force were used to capture, blackmail and kill the native chieftains; entire settlements were conquered, pillaged and destroyed; commandos, practically out of control, roamed the island, looting, raping and murdering. The stirrings of Indian resistance provoked by such terrorism were suppressed with the utmost brutality, sparing neither women nor children. The Dominican monk Bartolomé de Las Casas later said that some 100,000 Tainos lost their lives in these campaigns. By 1496 active resistance was at an end. The 'pacification' of the island was complete.[19]

The direct extermination campaigns were followed by measures which were in the long run still more devastating because they were intended indirectly to destroy the basis of the Tainos' existence. These measures were linked with the settlement policy pursued by the Spanish Crown, which assumed ownership of all territories discovered overseas. This settlement policy began immediately after the *pacificación* of Hispaniola and assumed definite outlines when Nicolás de Ovando took office as governor in 1501. First, a series of fortified towns was founded at points of strategic and commercial importance: by 1509 there were already fifteen of these bases on Hispaniola. After this urbanization, modelled on the Iberian *reconquista* of the late Middle Ages, land was allotted to tenant farmers by the Governor or his appointed representative on behalf of the Crown. Plots of land outside the towns, sometimes far inland, were assigned to each Spanish citizen according to social status, family connections or military record. Legally, at least, the traditional possessions of the Indians were excluded from the allocation. However, since, at least in this early phase of overseas colonization, the Spanish colonists had usually come to America in order to enrich themselves by finding gold, not to till the soil, Ovando was obliged to use the natives as a labour force. An edict, issued in 1503 by Queen Isabella at the Governor's urging, introduced forced labour for the Arawaks, since, to quote the document, 'the Spaniards can find nobody else to work in their enterprises and to supply them with food, and to help them find the gold that is on the island.'[20]

Thus, the system of *repartimientos*, the allocation of Indian labour to Spanish immigrants, was introduced reluctantly and *faute de mieux*, in view of the colonists' refusal to do agricultural work. Yet this system must bear much of the blame for the extermination of the Tainos on Hispaniola.[21] Before Columbus arrived, the islanders had supported themselves with a modest subsistence economy based on cultivating a few plants by traditional methods and on the natural abundance which the island owed to its favourable climate and the waters surrounding it. They were now confronted with an agricultural system that not only included new elements like cattle, sugar-cane and tropical fruit, but was achievement-oriented and assigned a precise role to the wage-labourer, as the Indian was legally viewed. The change of outlook which the Indians were suddenly required to accomplish proved too much for them, both physically and mentally. This applied especially to the work involved in finding gold, for the Tainos were unaccustomed to digging for gold and washing the river sand, and could not see the point of doing so. Hence this work exacted the highest toll of victims.[22]

The Tainos employed in forced labour, men and women, were separated from their families for eight months in the year and often taken to remote places, which was itself a monstrous demand to make on members of a settled archaic culture with very slight mobility. They were ravaged by diseases, some of which, like smallpox, had been introduced by the Europeans. The high mortality rate among young and middle-aged men and women was accompanied by a sharp decline in the birth rate, which was all the more serious since Arawak women were less fertile than Spanish female immigrants. The break-up of the family when its members were sent to do forced labour led to an extraordinary increase in infant mortality, mainly because the Arawaks did not use animal milk and kept their infants at the breast for a long time, but also because the disintegration of the family destroyed the social space necessary for children's healthy physical and mental development. The social uprooting of so many people explains the periodical epidemics of suicide which are attested by trustworthy documents.[23]

The situation of the islanders was exacerbated by the death of Queen Isabella of Castile in 1504 and the replacement of the cautious governor Nicolás de Ovando with the arrogant Diego Colón, son of the discoverer. Isabella had agreed with the Vatican in seeing a close link between Spain's right to acquire possessions in the New World and its duty to convert the Indian heathen. On several occasions she had demanded that the potential converts should be treated humanely. Colón's assumption of the governorship gave an even freer rein than before to the unscrupulous conquistador types among the colonists. Moreover, the island's gold reserves were becoming exhausted: between 1503 and 1510 a steadily increasing quantity of gold, totalling 19 tons, had been sent to Spain, but after 1510 the quantity began to decline. The first people to be affected by this change were the Tainos, who were recruited in greater numbers and forced to work harder. Slavery was now also permitted in those cases where Indians were supposed, often wrongly, to be guilty of cannibalism or armed resistance. The growing importation of more robust slaves from West Africa did nothing to relieve the Indians' burdens.

The mainland Indians could escape the conquistadors' aggression, partly at least, by fleeing into the jungle or into rough mountain areas, but the Tainos had no such resource. As early as 1520 impartial observers recognized that the extinction of the islanders was only a matter of time. Hence, a Spanish envoy wrote home in 1518 that the Indians were in the state of a dying man, 'given up by the physicians, with the candle placed in his hand.'[24]

For the historian trying to assess the consequences of the collision between Europeans and Indians on Hispaniola, it is important to know the population of the island before Columbus's arrival. Even at the end of the fifteenth century, contemporary commentators offered widely differing estimates. Referring to a remark by Columbus, Las Casas spoke of 1,100,000 inhabitants; elsewhere he suggested that they might have numbered three million. Since the chronicler Oviedo, an opponent of Las Casas who represented the Spanish treatment of the Indians in the best possible light, likewise estimated the island's population at one million, and since almost all reports speak of the island's great population density, a figure of over a million in 1492 has been generally accepted.[25] However, by demonstrating the fertility of the low-lying areas of the island and the simple diet of the islanders, the American historian C. O. Sauer has suggested that Hispaniola could have supported well over three million inhabitants.[26]

After the island had been completely subjugated in 1502–4 and the Arawaks subjected to forced labour on instructions from Spain, administrators were asked to supply demographic information about the native population. Even Columbus, during his fourth and last voyage, is said by Las Casas to have uttered the doubtless exaggerated statement that six out of every seven Tainos had died since the discovery of the island.[27] In 1508 the royal treasurer was sent to Hispaniola and declared that after a careful count 60,000 surviving Indians had been found. Finally, Oviedo reported in 1548 that of the original inhabitants only 500 now survived, and soon afterwards the extermination of the Arawak Indians was complete. At least a million, perhaps several million people of another race with their own culture, had been annihilated within half a century: in the perspective of world history this must be described as the first genocide perpetrated by Europeans, and one which we are well informed about thanks to relatively good documentation.

Inexcusable as this genocide is, it is nevertheless important to point out that the Spaniards' dispossession, exploitation, oppression and final liquidation of the Indians on Hispaniola met with forceful opposition and protests from humane contemporaries. Protests occurred on two levels: among the eye-witnesses who knew about conditions overseas at first hand, and among Spain's leading theologians and lawyers. It is worth pursuing these early stirrings of anti-colonialism and examining the arguments from theology and international law which formed the intellectual context of colonization at that time.

The first voice to be raised in public in support of humane treatment for the population of Hispaniola was that of the Dominican monk Antonio de Montesinos. In a sermon delivered in 1511 before the Governor, highly placed officials and influential settlers, he made an impassioned appeal to the Christian consciences of all those responsible for Spain's policy towards the Indians:

In order to make your sins against the Indians known to you I have come up on this pulpit, I who am a voice of Christ crying in the wilderness of this island, and therefore it behooves you to listen. [ . . . ] This voice says that you are in mortal sin, that you live and die in it, for the cruelty and tyranny you use in dealing with these innocent people. Tell me, by what right or justice do you keep these Indians in such a cruel and horrible servitude? On what authority have you waged a detestable war against these people, who dwelt quietly and peacefully on their own land? [ . . . ] Why do you keep them so oppressed and weary, not giving them enough to eat nor taking care of them in their illness? For in the excessive work you demand of them they fall ill and die, or rather you kill them with your desire to extract and acquire gold every day.[28]

Montesinos's speech produced startled incredulity followed by immense excitement. Both the passionate tones of his indictment and the violence of the public reaction suggest that Montesinos had raised a topic that had long been ripe for discussion but repeatedly suppressed. The Dominicans, who showed remarkable solidarity with Montesinos, sent him to Spain to give a report to King Ferdinand. Montesinos's account, combined with news of the dwindling of the native population, made a sufficient impression on Ferdinand to make him summon a number of leading theologians and legal scholars to discussions in Burgos in 1512. In December of the same year the *Leyes de Burgos* were passed, the first attempt at general legislation on behalf of the Indians.

The Laws of Burgos did not encroach on the Crown's right to acquire possessions overseas, nor on the system of forced *repartimientos*. They did, however, provide a series of measures directed against abuses in the treatment of the Indians. It was laid down that the Indians must be well fed and clothed and suitably paid; they must also be instructed in Christian doctrine and converted to the true faith. These rules were intended to apply not only to the Arawaks of Hispaniola but to the entire area of the West Indies. However, this legislation raised more questions than it could answer. It did not solve the problem of the legality of Spanish conquests overseas, as later became apparent. The belief in Spain's mission to convert the heathen was based on premisses that had received too little analysis. There remained the question whether the Indians were willing and able to accept Christianity; and if they offered resistance, what gave European colonists the right to convert them by force? If missionary work could only be accomplished through violence, was it still that apostolic mission which the Papal Bulls of 1593 had declared to be the precondition for acquiring overseas territories? Was there not, rather, a danger that the obduracy of the savages might be cited as a retrospective justification for the violent seizure of their land? Between 1512 and 1542 this cluster of questions was to be

passionately debated and pursued into its furthest ramifications.[29] The
leading spokesman in this discussion was Bartolomé de Las Casas.[30] The
'Apostle to the Indians' had emigrated to Hispaniola in 1502, had later
settled on Cuba, and had himself employed Indians to search for gold
and work on his estate. It was not until 1515 that he began to support the
Indians' cause, but he did so with an impassioned persistence that he
retained during the following fifty years of his long life. In 1515 he
struggled to persuade the Spanish court that the Laws of Burgos should
be more strictly observed. As a result of his efforts a commission of
inspection, consisting of three Jeronimite monks, was sent to Hispaniola,
while he himself was charged with supreme responsibility for Indian
affairs. The commission of inspection and inquiry took evidence from
Spanish colonists on the island – not from the Tainos – which led to the
conclusion that the Indians, unable to live in freedom, were vegetating in
a barbaric fashion, and that the missionaries' efforts were wasted on
them. The commission's negative and prejudiced report did not deter Las
Casas from continuing to advocate the abolition of the *repartimiento*
system; in its place he recommended the founding of mixed settlements
including both Spaniards and Indians, in the hope of preparing the
Indians for the inevitable transition to agriculture, helping them to
assimilate, and reducing racial prejudice. In his campaign Las Casas
received support from the Crown. However, his first such project,
established on the coast of Venezuela, was a failure. The Spanish settlers,
who had been reluctant to take part in such an enterprise, did not
understand how to run it. Besides, the mainland was already infested by
slave-hunters, so that the basis of mutual trust on which Las Casas had
hoped to found co-operation between cultures had been destroyed.

A later settlement project, promoted between 1537 and 1550 among
the warlike inhabitants of the Guatemalan jungle, likewise proved a
failure in the long run. Here Las Casas had laid down the condition that
only Dominican monks should have access to the settlement. Peaceful
conversion was its principal aim, and at first the monks, who had been
remarkably quick to familiarize themselves with the local language,
managed to arouse not only the Indians' curiosity but also their
sympathy. The final collapse of this second experiment in colonization
occurred for reasons similar to those which had earlier frustrated
Portuguese missionary work in West Africa. In both places the
missionaries failed to realize that their arrival put the complex ethnic
structure of archaic peoples under considerable strain, altered the
balance of power, and thus released latent aggression.

Besides his attempts at colonization, which anticipate the seventeenth-
century Jesuit settlements in South America, Las Casas devoted intense
effort to a theoretical understanding of the problem of colonialism. After

entering the Dominican monastery on Hispaniola he spent thirty-five years, from 1527 until shortly before his death, labouring on his main work, the *Historia de las Indias*. This rich and copious work is a major source for the history of Spanish colonization: its author's indefatigable support for the native population permits insights denied to other contemporary chroniclers, whose purpose was mainly apologetic.[31]

This book, however, did not become nearly as famous as the *Short Account of the Destruction of the Indians* which appeared in 1552, after its author had finally returned to Spain. The *Account* is a fiery pamphlet directed against the conquistadors' dealings with the Indians, a 'hair-raising catalogue of atrocities',[32] which circulated widely outside Spain and, especially in the eighteenth century, was translated into most European languages. 'I think', concluded Voltaire, 'that Las Casas' account exaggerates at several points; but even assuming that he says ten times too much, what is left suffices to fill one with horror.'[33] Modern historians, too, have repeatedly enquired into the veracity of the treatise, and not only the author's credibility but even his sanity has been questioned. The general view nowadays is that Las Casas's criticism was justified, even if the Dominican is still considered sensationalist in highlighting certain abuses.[34]

The *Account* is arranged chronologically and geographically, following the sequence of Spanish discoveries and the territories discovered: Hispaniola, Cuba, Mexico, Venezuela, Florida, Colombia. It has little to say about landscape, history, colonial administration; the *Historia de las Indias*, after all, supplies all the information one might want about such matters. Las Casas confines himself to the Spaniards' policy towards the natives, if indeed it can be called a 'policy' at all. He places an obvious emphasis on the conquistadors' atrocities, especially those committed without any discernible motive but seemingly from a mere excess of sadistic energy. We read of children being killed and mutilated, of old men chased by bloodhounds, of innocent people roasted over slow fires, of women being raped and murdered. In Las Casas's account all this appears completely wanton; for Indians as the author sees them, in their child-like innocence and docility, can give no occasion for such brutal punishments. The central passage in Las Casas's account deals with Hispaniola and runs as follows:

> These gentle lambs, endowed by their Maker and Creator with the qualities mentioned above, no sooner became known to the Spaniards than the latter fell upon them like ravenous wolves, tigers and lions. For forty years they have done nothing to them, and even today they do nothing to them, save maim, strangle, afflict, torment, torture, and destroy them through a thousand new and strange agonies, such as were never before seen, heard or read of and of which I shall cite some examples below. Thus they have

brought it about that of the over three million people, whom I formerly saw with my own eyes on the island of Hispaniola, only two hundred natives still survive.[35]

This text was of little help in coming to grips intellectually with the problem of colonialism. More important for this purpose was a treatise published by Las Casas in 1537 under the title *The Sole Method of Converting all Nations to the True Faith*.[36] Here he argues the necessity of peaceful missionary work among the Indians. All people on earth, declares Las Casas in his introduction, are God's creatures, and as such equipped and summoned by God to accept faith as a free gift. Hence, it is wrong to deprive the Indians of their freedom or their possessions, even if they have not yet adopted the Christian faith. Missionaries, the author goes on, must employ more gentleness and patience and rely much more on persuasion and on setting an example than on force and intimidation. In his arguments Las Casas appeals to a bull issued by Pope Paul III in that same year, which stressed that non-European peoples were capable of conversion, but warned against trying to convert them by force under the pretext of a 'just war'.

In rejecting forcible conversion, Las Casas found himself in opposition to the Court lawyer Juan Gines de Sepúlveda, a cultivated and much-respected man, who had adopted Aristotle's notion that barbarous peoples should be regarded as natural slaves.[37] In his treatise *The Just Reasons for War against the Indians*, Sepúlveda appealed to the charter of 1493 granted by Pope Alexander VI, in which Columbus's discovery was sanctioned on condition that efforts were made to convert the new-found peoples.[38] Sepúlveda argued that the Church could only fulfil the Christian duty to spread the gospel if the unbelievers had first been subjected to political authority. 'As may clearly be seen from the bull', writes the lawyer, 'it was Pope Alexander's will that the barbarians should first be made subject to the Crown of Castile and that the gospel should be preached to them only afterwards.'[39] Unlike Las Casas, who knew conditions overseas at first hand, Charles V's lawyer did not see that such an interpretation risked providing a legal basis for the wanton savagery of the Spanish colonists. Hence, Las Casas replied sharply that such a 'godless and Mahometan' method of conversion must be rejected out of hand, because it was wholly contrary to Christianity.[40]

This debate over the 'just war' was extended by the reflections on the Spanish claim to property overseas put forward by Francisco de Vitoria, a lawyer at the University of Salamanca.[41] The Spaniards' right to conquer and settle new territories rested, as stated earlier, on three main supports: the right of the discoverer or finder; papal approval subject to missionary work; and an agreement of 1494, the Treaty of Tordesillas, in which Portugal and Spain had divided up the world between them. Vitoria queried the validity of these legal titles by referring to Aquinas's ideas on natural law and maintaining that the formation of political bodies was as natural as the right to personal property, both being part of the organic harmony of creation. The relations between states, like those between individuals, were accordingly based on reciprocity acknowledged by all authorities concerned. Dealings between sovereign states and independent individuals might extend to trade, peaceful political contacts, and the possibility of conversion by missionaries; but for any spiritual or secular power to assume world dominion was contrary to nature and impermissible. Vitoria did concede that in certain special cases Spain had the right to conquer a territory: for example, if a newly discovered territory proved to be uninhabited, or if a non-European nation itself violated natural law, as was the case, in Vitoria's opinion, when cannibalism could be proved to have taken place. Vitoria denied any possibility of a 'just war' against the Indians, though he left room for interpretations that fundamentally contradicted his thinking by saying that if a war served the interests of the non-Europeans themselves – for instance, if it meant protecting the Arawaks by fighting the Caribs – it could be tolerated in a moderate and suitable form. Vitoria had very little contact with Las Casas, and did his best to avoid disputes about the actual fate of the West Indies. His reflections, however, helped to guide later debates on colonialism, when the Dutch, French and English began to claim territories overseas.

In 1542 Las Casas and his associates managed to induce Charles V to issue the *Leyes Nuevas* to safeguard the Indians. These laws forbade the extension of the *repartimiento* system and directed the local courts overseas, the *audiencias*, to ensure that the Indians doing forced labour were humanely treated. However, when the 'New Laws' became known across the Atlantic, they aroused such resistance among officials, landowners, and even clerics that three years later Charles V was obliged to repeal the important provision of the legal package forbidding the creation of new *repartimientos*.[42]

By now the fate of the Tainos on Hispaniola was already sealed. The laws came too late; and even if they had come thirty years earlier, the colonists would scarcely have obeyed them, nor could Spain have monitored their operation. It is beyond question that Spain as a colonial power completely ignored its human responsibility towards the Indians of Hispaniola, both passively and actively. The Indians were granted no freedom, such as a reservation might have provided, to preserve their own way of life; nor were they integrated into the colonists' cultural and social life in any ethically defensible manner. The most trenchant formulation of this sad fact is probably that by the eighteenth-century

German writer Georg Christoph Lichtenberg: 'The American who first discovered Columbus made a bad discovery.'[43]

Are we to conclude, then, that the debate about legal rights and the treatment of the Indians, which the discovery of Hispaniola set in motion, merely testifies to the helplessness of all intellectual and ethical endeavours when faced with historical action? Such a view would focus on only one aspect of the debate, that is, its power to bring about concrete change. In other ways, however, the Spanish discussion of colonialism has its special importance and value. There is no other colonial power, neither Portugal nor at a later stage Holland, England or France, which accompanied its early overseas expansion with such efforts to subject the fact of cultural contact to theoretical analysis and bring it under legal control. Yet it was difficult to conduct this analysis on the basis of late-medieval legal concepts and a Christocentric world view, and its results failed to achieve the general moral authority on which effective political action must be based.

# Missionary Work as a Cultural Relationship
## The French in Canada

Strictly speaking, the history of relations between Europe and Canada begins with the Viking voyages around AD 1000. These are recorded in the Icelandic sagas, which were written down in the thirteenth and fourteenth centuries and have been found, after critical comparison with other sources, to contain a large element of historical truth. They tell us how the unruly Erik the Red fled to Greenland to avoid punishment for his criminal deeds, and how his son Leif visited Baffin Island and the Labrador coast and settled in the extreme north of Newfoundland. The archaeological excavations conducted by Anne and Helge Ingstad between 1961 and 1968 have found indisputable evidence at L'Anse aux Meadows of settlements dating from the Viking period which cannot have been made by Indians or Eskimos. They would seem to have been abandoned for some reason during the fourteenth century.[1]

After these first contacts, it was another five centuries before Giovanni Gabotto, an Italian voyager in the service of England, reached the Canadian coast in his search for a convenient passage to the riches of the Far East. In the summer of 1497 John Cabot, as he is called in English, reached a point only a few miles from Leif Eriksson's landing-place, but was prevented by drift ice from advancing any further. Cabot made a second voyage, from which, so far as we know, he never returned.[2] In the succeeding century the coasts and islands of Canada were occasionally visited by fishermen and by Spanish and Portuguese explorers, and stretches of them were mapped in a rough and ready fashion. The next major explorations after Cabot's, however, were the Atlantic voyages made by Jacques Cartier from 1534 onwards.

Little is known about Cartier's life, except that he came from St Malo and was an experienced sailor, familiar with the deep-sea fisheries off the Newfoundland coast.[3] His expedition was financed by King François I of

France, and his instructions were to look for a north-west passage to China and 'discover certain islands and countries where it is said that great quantities of gold and other precious things are to be found'.[4] These extravagant hopes were dashed, however, by the sight of the barren southern coast of Labrador: Cartier wrote in his account of the voyage that it reminded him of 'the land God gave to Cain'.[5] On 24 June 1534 the French landed on the North American mainland in the Bay of Gaspé, south-east of the mouth of the St Lawrence River, where they erected a cross and took possession of the land for the French Crown, vowing to spread Christianity there. Some Indians had gathered and watched the ceremony with interest from a little distance. To prove that he had found a previously unknown continent, New France, Cartier took two Indians, sons of the chief, with him on his return voyage.

Cartier's second voyage led to more significant results. It brought the French to the Huron settlement of Stadaconé, later Quebec, and further upstream to Hochelaga, later Mont Royal, now Montreal. In Hochelaga, a fortified centre of the Hurons, the seafarers received an enthusiastic welcome from over a thousand Indians. Presents were exchanged, and the Indians strove to touch the newcomers and asked them to lay their hands on children and the sick. Impressed by his friendly reception and the autumnal glory of the 'Indian summer', Cartier decided to spend the winter in Canada, and set up camp near what is now Quebec. However, he had underestimated the severity of the Canadian winter. His crew was devastated by cold, starvation and scurvy. They were ordered to hammer on the poles surrounding their encampment for hours at a time in order to delude the increasingly hostile Indians about their numbers. Tradition has it that they were only saved from dying of scurvy by a mysterious plant which the Indians recommended as a remedy.[6]

Although Cartier's third Canadian expedition (1541) was, all things considered, a failure, it remains important because its origins are thoroughly documented. François I had become keenly interested not only in trade with Canada but also in projects of colonization. He was well aware that French penetration into the regions assigned to Spain with Papal approval under the Treaty of Tordesillas (1494) would eventually bring him into conflict with both the Emperor Charles V and Pope Paul III. It is now known that Spain followed Cartier's voyages with suspicion and maintained informants in the Atlantic and Channel ports of France to keep an eye on shipping movements and unusual preparations for voyages. François I could not risk a destructive privateering war in the Atlantic. On the one hand, he declared that he did not regard the Treaty of Tordesillas as binding on France, and that he would like to be shown such a division of the world laid down in Adam's will; on the other, he adopted a flexible policy, disclaimed any hostile intentions towards the position of Spain and Portugal in the New World, and promised to avoid the territories and harbours held by these powers. Probably in order to appease the Pope and clergy, care was taken to emphasize the missionary purpose of Cartier's third voyage. Thus, a memorandum composed by the captain begins with the sentiment that the only profit expected from the voyage is the conquest of innumerable souls at God's behest.[7] C.-A. Julien has convincingly shown that this pious formula was a mere pretext: the main purpose of the journey was clearly the economic exploitation of the newly discovered territories, whether through mining, agriculture or trade in spices and furs.[8] Later, of course, the Jesuit missionaries were to point to this early declaration in order to justify their own activity and seek support for it.

Cartier's expeditions produced no immediate results. Indeed, they passed into a proverb signifying the collapse of extravagant hopes: the French even today say 'as false as a Canadian diamond' when they are suspicious. Not until sixty years later did France pay any further attention to its discoveries on the St Lawrence River. Between 1603 and 1615 Samuel de Champlain visited its estuary, explored the coasts of Nova Scotia and Acadia, and sailed past what is now the state of Maine as far as Cape Cod. In 1608 he founded Quebec. Further expeditions took him beyond Montreal to Lakes Huron and Ontario.[9]

Very little is known about Champlain's life before he set out on his voyage, but, thanks to his own records, his later achievements are far better documented than Cartier's. He came from the area south of La Rochelle, may have been baptized a Protestant but later converted to Catholicism, and belonged to the minor rural nobility. He went to sea at an early age and took an interest in problems of navigation and cartography; he also travelled, possibly in the service of Spain, to the West Indies, where he is said to have spent two years. Having been present in a subordinate capacity on the Canadian voyages of 1603 and 1604, which confirmed and slightly supplemented the findings of Cartier's expeditions, he achieved distinction by composing an account of the voyages. His third voyage in 1608, the decisive step towards French colonization in this part of North America, was undertaken as commander of three ships which sailed from Honfleur. The expedition was organized by the merchant Pierre de Mont, who in turn had received the necessary authority from King Henri IV.

From 1608 Quebec became the centre of French colonization and the starting-point for further exploration. At first the settlement consisted solely of three two-storey houses standing close together and protected by a rampart and a ditch; each house had a small front garden in the French style. It was occupied by only twenty-eight men, the majority of whom died of scurvy in the first winter. Along with a few hundred

Spaniards in Florida and a hundred or so Englishmen in Virginia, they were the only Europeans on the North American continent at that time. However, Samuel de Champlain was not the man to be satisfied with erecting a couple of fortresses. He worked ceaselessly until he was appointed governor of 'New France' in 1627. In Quebec he devoted considerable effort to establishing the fur trade; he undertook daring expeditions into the interior; and in France, especially after the death of Henri IV in 1610, he drummed up financial support and recruited enterprising settlers.[10] As early as 1609 he let himself be drawn into conflicts among the Indians by agreeing to support the Hurons and Algonkins in their struggle with the Iroquois. The use of firearms made it child's play to defeat the Mohawks, one of the five tribes composing the Iroquois League. By doing so, however, Champlain ensured the enmity of the Six Nations, the most powerful body of Indians anywhere on the east coast. This fatal misjudgement of the ethnic and demographic situation was one reason why France came off worse in its conflict with Britain in the eighteenth century.

Champlain expressed remarkably nuanced views about the Indians whose friendship and commercial support he sought. Like the Jesuit missionaries later, he generally reserved his censure for their unbelief and certain vices associated therewith. In his account of his voyages, a document of anthropological importance, he writes:

> All these tribes suffer so much from hunger that sometimes they are obliged to live on certain shell-fish, and to eat their dogs and the skins with which they clothe themselves against the cold. I consider that, if anyone were to show them how to live, and how to till the soil, and other things, they would learn very well; for there are many of them who have good judgement, and reply pointedly to the questions put to them. [ . . . ] I asked them what sort of ceremonies they used in praying to their God. They told me that they had no other than this, that each one prayed to God in his heart, just as it suited him. That is why there is no law amongst them, and that they do not know what it is to pray to and worship God, living as they do like brute beasts. I believe they would soon be brought to be good Christians, if one were to live in their country, as the majority of them desire.[11]

This view of the Indians broadly corresponded to that held by the missionaries, who were to play such an important part in the encounter between cultures in Canada. Like Champlain, they assumed that the Indians were endowed with reason and able to learn, and that their personal and moral shortcomings would disappear under the missionaries' influence; and also that the Indians would eagerly accept the Gospel and the education offered to them. In this last assumption, as we shall see, Champlain and the missionaries were completely wrong.

After exceedingly difficult beginnings, an important step forward came with the founding of the *Compagnie de la Nouvelle France* by Louis XIII's minister, Richelieu, in 1627. At this time there were altogether only 107 Frenchmen living on the St Lawrence, while Virginia, a colony which had cost similar efforts to establish, already numbered about a thousand inhabitants. The colony's food supply in winter was still very meagre, its administration was haphazard, and there was no ecclesiastical organization. Clear progress had been made only in building up commercial relations with the Indians of the interior in order to export furs: an estimated 15,000 beaver pelts were supplied annually. The new trading company, modelled on the East India Company (founded in 1600) and the Dutch *Oost-Indische Compagnie* (founded in 1602), was based in Paris and provided with capital by 100 partners, mainly government officials and merchants, each of whom contributed 3,000 *livres*.[12] The company was guaranteed a monopoly of the fur trade in New France for fifteen years, while it undertook to send out 4,000 settlers during that period. The implementation of this plan was delayed by conflict with the English, who conquered Quebec in 1629. The little group of colonists held out, and their territory, very much the worse for wear, was restored to France in 1632. Plans for building up the colony were once more taken in hand. The *Compagnie de la Nouvelle France* managed to encourage some emigration, though on nothing like the scale that had been hoped for. By 1662 about a thousand colonists had arrived in Canada. Efforts were also made to extend the network of fur trading by sending *coureurs de bois* into the interior. One of these vagrants, Jean Nicollet, reached Lake Michigan in the company of Huron Indians. Various small trading-posts were set up near Quebec: Trois Rivières, Sillery, Ville Marie and finally Montreal, at the very spot where Jacques Cartier had come upon the Indian settlement of Hochelaga. Then stagnation returned.

By 1645 the trading company was so deeply in debt that it decided to transfer the monopoly of the fur trade to a group of colonists, the *Communauté des Habitants*, a measure which encouraged growth, though on a modest scale. At the same time, however, social tensions increased within the settler community, especially between the rich families who had concentrated on the fur trade and the poorer ones who lived by farming. The existence of both groups was increasingly menaced by the Iroquois. Their attacks, which became more and more frequent from 1640 onwards, interfered with trading links and devastated the fields. The other Indians no longer dared to bring beaver pelts to Quebec in exchange for firearms, brandy and other goods, while the colonists were afraid to leave their houses in Trois Rivières and Montreal. The hope of reaching a peaceful agreement by playing off the various tribes against one another came to nothing. In July 1649 news reached Quebec that the Hurons, the most peaceable allies of the French merchants and missionaries, had been completely defeated by the Iroquois. In this emergency Quebec attempted to negotiate with the English in Massachusetts, independently of Anglo-French relations in Europe, in order to form a defensive alliance against the Iroquois; but this plan also came to nothing. In Quebec, wrote a colonist in 1653, 'there is nothing but poverty'; Trois Rivières had to spend its scanty earnings from the fur trade on its own defence; and the depots in Montreal contained not a single beaver pelt.[13]

Once again, however, a precarious peace was concluded and followed by short-lived commercial growth. Between 1654 and 1657 it looked as though the crisis had been overcome, but by 1663 it was finally clear that New France, the colony which Champlain had founded with such hopes, could not survive unaided. By this time the French possessions contained only 3,000 colonists, while the English settlements in North America had forged ahead, numbering some 73,000 inhabitants between them by 1660.[14] Between 1654 and 1661 the Canadian immigration figures sank to between thirty and forty people per year. Several bases, on the coast and further upstream, had to be abandoned, while the route linking Quebec, Trois Rivières and Montreal was at times impassable. In this desperate situation the colonists decided to return the administration of their settlements to the Crown. Under Colbert, Louis XIV's minister of finance, Canada became a French province. The *Communauté des Habitants* and the *Compagnie de la Nouvelle France* lost their privileges, and the colony's economic development was directed from Paris in accordance with the doctrines of mercantilism and underpinned by sending out colonial troops who soon checked the Iroquois threat. A new and happier chapter of Canadian history began.

During the difficult early years of the colony's existence, there was only one form of European influence which was marked by continuity and tireless commitment: the Jesuit mission. Canada's first missionary endeavours go back to 1611, when two Jesuit priests, Pierre Biard and Ennémond Massé, arrived on the peninsula of Acadia, just outside the mouth of the St Lawrence. In the next few years the Indians of this coastal region received the attentions of a small number of Franciscans belonging to the strict order of Recollects, but their work was soon abandoned because support from France was lacking. Between 1632 and 1657 the Jesuits acquired a clear monopoly in the colony's religious life. They concentrated their efforts on the Huron nation, and by 1640 they had erected five churches and performed over a thousand baptisms in the Hurons' area of settlement. The Jesuits continued their work under conditions of extreme hardship until 1649, when the Hurons were slaughtered and dispersed by Iroquois assaults. Since the missionaries were required to send in regular reports on their work, a rich body of documentation has survived from this period, enabling us to form a detailed picture of their motives and their achievement.[15]

First, however, a few words about the Hurons. About 1615, when the first Frenchmen made contact with them, the Huron heartland covered a relatively small area in the south-east of the country, between Georgian Bay, on the lake that bears their name, and Lake Simcoe.[16] It is thought that the Huron population, ethnically and linguistically related to the Iroquois, numbered over 20,000, and that its density was considerably greater in this area of settlement than along the coast. The Hurons lived in a tribal federation composed of several different ethnic groups, the most important being the tribe of the 'Bears', to which half the total population belonged. Their dwellings were long, hall-like bark huts, which could each accommodate over twenty families with an average of five members. Communal life in such confined space was remarkably free from conflict, and is commended in all the missionaries' reports. 'They are very much attached to each other', writes the Jesuit Father Le Jeune, 'and agree admirably. You do not see any disputes, quarrels, enmities, or reproaches among them.'[17] The atmosphere inside these Indian dwellings has been vividly described by the classic American historian Francis Parkman:

> He who entered on a winter night beheld a strange spectacle: the vista of fires lighting the smoky concave; the bronzed groups encircling each, – cooking, eating, gambling, or amusing themselves with idle badinage; shrivelled squaws, hideous with threescore years of hardship; grisly old warriors, scarred with Iroquois war-clubs; young aspirants, whose honors were yet to be won; damsels gay with ochre and wampum; restless children pellmell with restless dogs. Now a tongue of resinous flame painted each wild feature in vivid light; now the fitful gleam expired, and the group vanished from sight, as their nation has vanished from history.[18]

The Hurons' name comes from the French *hure* (bristly or ugly head), because the colonists thought they looked like wild boars.[19] They lived in some twenty-five villages and hamlets, but the number and location of these settlements kept changing, because the Hurons tended to move on whenever the firewood was used up and the fields, which they did not manure, were exhausted. Some villages were protected against surprise attacks by ditches, ramparts and palisades and served also as refuges for the inhabitants of undefended settlements. Private possession of land was unknown, but each family was assigned as much land as it needed for a limited period. Maize, beans, pumpkins, sunflowers, hemp and tobacco were cultivated. The rivers and lakes in Huron territory were full of fish, and the Hurons' fishing techniques were highly developed. On the other hand, game was sometimes in painfully short supply, even though in autumn large numbers of deer were often driven into pens and killed. Women were normally responsible for all the work in the fields and in the home, while in summer and autumn the men travelled in all directions in order to trade with neighbouring Indian tribes and with colonists, to await the draughts of fish in the Great Lakes, to hunt, and to fight wars. In winter they again gathered in their villages.

Since their lives were normally so impoverished, the Hurons attached great importance to their festivities. The Jesuit missionary Father Brébeuf, who lived among them around 1630, distinguishes four kinds of feast: one devoted to singing and eating, another to celebrate recovery from serious illnesses, a feast of thanksgiving, and a farewell feast. These feasts, whose excesses caused the missionaries great disquiet, were held in the settlement's assembly house and lasted up to two weeks. The medicine-men took a major part in them by making weather, diagnosing illnesses or interpreting dreams. The missionaries regarded these medicine-men as their principal adversaries, especially as their know-ledge and skills often gave them immense influence among their fellow tribesmen. Thus, Father Brébeuf writes: 'No one dares to contradict them. They are continually at feasts, which take place at their command. There is, therefore, some foundation for the belief that the Devil occasionally gives them assistance, and reveals himself to them for some temporal profit, and for their eternal damnation.'[20]

The Hurons certainly acknowledged the existence of a higher being and believed in the immortality of the soul, as the missionaries noted with relief. However, Christian conceptions of the afterlife were as alien to them as was the moral notion of the godly life. As Champlain was the first to report, their prayers were intended to conjure up the indwelling powers of the surrounding natural world and to gain these powers' goodwill for their undertakings. The fundamental differences between the two sets of religious ideas explain many of the difficulties and misunderstandings which the Jesuits found themselves facing in their missionary work.

As mentioned earlier, the Hurons' main enemy was the Iroquois nation south of the St Lawrence. Anyone who did not submit to the Iroquois could expect their unremitting hostility. Warfare between the Hurons and the Iroquois was carried on by surprise attacks, massacres and vandalism. Both sides were armed with clubs, bows and arrows; and after contact with the Europeans they made increasing use of tomahawks and rifles. Neither nation had universal military service, a clearly defined military organization, or long-term strategic planning: questions of war and peace were decided by the chiefs in consultation with their immediate followers. In the art of war and in their military equipment the Iroquois seem to have been markedly superior to the Hurons and to other neighbouring tribes.[21]

Let us return, however, to the Jesuit missionaries in Canada. What were their motives for wanting to Christianize the Hurons, an impressively self-sufficient people who had developed no urge to attain salvation? A brief historical retrospect must suffice.

In the introduction and in the chapter on the Portuguese 'system of limited contacts' (Chapters 1 and 2 respectively), it was pointed out how closely the fifteenth and sixteenth centuries associated the concept of colonization with the obligation to convert the heathen. For theorists of colonialism, it was this alone that justified the conquest of foreign territory and the claim to supremacy over other peoples.[22] This principle also governed the activities of the Jesuit missionaries. The Jesuit order, of course, was created by Ignatius Loyola, a nobleman from Navarre who turned to the study of theology after being injured in war and who, along with six associates, founded the order in Paris in 1534. These young men vowed to serve God in absolute poverty, to devote their entire lives to the active care of souls, and to maintain themselves in readiness to carry out the instructions of the Holy Father with unquestioning obedience. Their vow, confirmed by Pope Paul III, envisaged that they would make a pilgrimage to Jerusalem and do missionary work in the Holy Land – a plan which the founders of the order were unable to carry out. The Jesuits' belief in their mission was rooted in the *Spiritual Exercises* devised by Ignatius Loyola, to which every member of the order had to submit twice in his life.[23] Although the idea of converting non-Europeans is not central to these *Exercises*, they nevertheless provide the framework into which the Jesuits' missionary work had to fit and which gave it meaning. Thus, the characteristic features of the seventeenth-century mission to Canada were already present in the demands made by the *Exercises*, notably the missionaries' complete indifference to personal wealth, social status and outward prestige; their obligation to imitate Christ and their uncompromising devotion to the service of God; the militant interpretation of the apostolic spirit, which had to prove itself in perpetual combat with the menacing forces of evil; and finally the flexibility of their methods in pursuit of an unchanging aim.[24] The spirit of the *Exercises*, enhanced by the rigours of practical missionary work, was perhaps most forcefully expressed in the words of the Jesuit Father Le Jeune, written in 1635:

> Three mighty thoughts console a good heart which is in the infinite forests of New France, or among the Hurons. The first is, 'I am in a place where God has sent me, where he has led me as if by the hand, where he is with me, and where I seek him alone.' The second is, in the words of David, 'according to the measure of the pain I endure for God, his Divine consolations rejoice my soul.' The third, that we never find Crosses, nails, nor thorns, in the midst of which, if we look closely, we do not find J. C. [Jesus Christ].[25]

The labours of the missionaries among the Hurons were also supported by the increasing renown of their order throughout the world. In Europe the Jesuits had rapidly become the animating force of the Counter-Reformation. Thanks to their adroit manoeuvres, the Reformation, particularly in educational matters, had been kept firmly within bounds, and the Council of Trent, which concluded its deliberations in 1563, had restored the authority of the Pope and the Catholic Church. Outside Europe the Jesuits had succeeded in preventing the Huguenots from infiltrating the areas dominated by Catholic powers, such as Florida, Brazil and Canada itself. One of the co-founders of their order, the pioneer missionary Francis Xavier, had become an exemplary figure on whom the Jesuit missionaries overseas modelled their behaviour.

Francis Xavier had left Europe in 1541 and gone to India as papal nuncio on the instructions of Pope Paul III and at the request of the King of Portugal.[26] After devoting himself intensively to pastoral work in Goa, he continued his journey to the south-eastern tip of the sub-continent, where he conducted missionary work with great success among the local inhabitants, the Paravas; and thereupon he sailed to Malacca and the Spice Islands. After successful activity in Japan, Francis Xavier set out for China, but died in 1552 on a small island outside the bay of Canton. His abortive mission to China was carried on by the Italian Jesuit Matteo Ricci, who reached China three decades later, and the members of the order in Europe received regular reports informing them about the progress of missionary work in the Middle Kingdom.

The reports that arrived from South America towards the end of the century sounded no less encouraging. The first Jesuits, coming from Brazil, had arrived in Paraguay about 1590, where after 1606 they founded the earliest 'reductions', communities in which the nomadic Guaraní Indians were helped by the missionaries to adopt a settled way of life and were taught agriculture, crafts and the Christian religion.[27] The Jesuits working in Canada knew Francis Xavier's life story and were aware of the successes of their fellows in China and South America. Now and again their reports reveal the desire not to lag behind such achievements.

If the believing Christian in the early period of discoveries had no doubt of the obligation to convert the heathen, he might nevertheless ask how great were the missionaries' prospects of success in a given case. This question was linked with another, concerning the nature and character of the people whose conversion was being sought. What did the Jesuit missionaries think of the Hurons in this respect?

It must be stated at the outset that the Indians' membership of the human species, 'the race of Adam' as the phrase went, was never denied. One of Champlain's companions, Marc Lescarbot, took pains to

demonstrate in his *Histoire de la Nouvelle France* that the second father
of mankind, Noah, must have known America, and that after the Flood
he had even seen to it personally that the continent should be populated
by his descendants.[28] Such reasoning was by no means exceptional; it
indicates what efforts were made to integrate into the scheme of
Christian history the exciting discovery of a 'New World' that was
nowhere mentioned explicitly in the Bible. The Jesuit priest Joseph-
François Lafitau, author of the first comprehensive ethnographic study of
the native population of North America, was more cautious in his
conjectures about the Indians' origins. In his work *Moeurs des sauvages
américains* (1722), Lafitau surmised, long before light was cast on the
matter by the voyages of James Cook in the North Pacific, that the
Indians might have migrated from eastern Mongolia across a land bridge
– a thesis which brought him very close to the findings of modern
research.[29] Admittedly Lafitau also strayed into speculations when he
supposed that the Indians were descended from barbarians who had left
Greece before the Indo-European invasion; and in general, supported by
other contemporary authors, he divided the chronology of these events
into phases that were much too short.[30]

In the missionaries' opinion, such early migrations explained why the
Indians, though undoubtedly human, had not been able to share the
Christian revelation. It might be that their connection with the West had
been severed before the birth of Christ, or that, unable to maintain this
connection, they had gradually forgotten their Christian heritage. Hardly
anyone doubted, however, that the Indian was a creature endowed with
reason and accessible both to theological arguments and to religious
feeling. Many thought, indeed, that by being detached from the general
course of human history the Indian had remained free from corruption,
closer to the childhood of humanity, and hence peculiarly apt for
conversion. Not that this latter argument lacked opponents: Father
Brébeuf, for example, regretted that the Hurons had not reached the level
of civilization of the Chinese or Japanese, since this would have made the
missionaries' work considerably easier.[31] Nevertheless, the Indians
seemed worthy of intensive missionary efforts. 'But, after all', says Father
Jérome Lalemant in his report, 'they are rational creatures, capable of
Paradise and of Hell, redeemed by the blood of JESUS CHRIST, and of
whom it is written, *Et alias oves habeo quæ non sunt ex hoc ovili, et illas
oportet me adducere.*'[32] And Le Jeune speaks yet more clearly:

> As to the mind of the Savage, it is of good quality. I believe that souls are all
> made from the same stock, and that they do not materially differ; hence,
> these barbarians having well formed bodies, and organs well regulated and
> well arranged, their minds ought to work with ease. Education and
> instruction alone are lacking. Their soul is a soil which is naturally good,

but loaded down with all the evils that a land abandoned since the birth of the world can produce. I naturally compare our Savages with certain villagers, because both are usually without education, though our Peasants are superior in this regard; and yet I have not seen anyone thus far, of those who have come to this country, who does not confess and frankly admit that the Savages are more intelligent than our ordinary peasants.[33]

Besides humanity and rationality, the missionaries ascribed to the Indians in general, and the Hurons in particular, further characteristics which implied readiness for conversion. Thus, they praised their charges for the simplicity of their way of life, their independence of material goods, their calm dignity, their scrupulous observance of treaties, and their love of their families. In all these virtues, and in the degree of happiness derived from them, the Hurons struck the missionaries as far superior to most Europeans. According to Father Le Jeune there were two passions which devastated the European colonists but made no impact on the Hurons – ambition and avarice. They had no police, taxes, titles or commands, but obeyed their chiefs out of sheer goodwill.[34] The obvious implication of such an assessment, both in Canada and earlier in Paraguay, was that the Indians had to be protected from the corrupting influence of the colonists. In Canada the main source of concern was contact with fur traders, who introduced alcohol and confused the Hurons by their unbridled sexuality (though the Hurons themselves were far from abstemious in this respect); and for several decades the Jesuits did indeed manage to shield Huronia from such harmful contacts.[35]

The above-mentioned virtues of the Hurons had to be set against a catalogue of vices which amazed and disgusted the missionaries. The Jesuits' principal complaints were about polygamy, pre-marital intercourse, provocative nudity and obscene conversations, all of which were regarded as sexual excess; but the Hurons were also criticized for swinish gluttony, thievishness, maltreatment of prisoners taken in war, and cannibalism. The missionaries thought that the Hurons' shortcomings and lack of self-control could be ascribed to their rudimentary and grotesquely misguided religious conceptions, and hoped that, once their deplorable idolatry had been extirpated, all the rest would follow. It is noteworthy that idolatry and its associated vices were scarcely ever accounted for by claiming that the Indians were naturally corrupt. On the contrary, it was taken for granted that the Indians were basically good and desirous of the good; but it was argued that their very innocence exposed them to attacks from the Evil One, who had been unceasingly active everywhere since the Fall. For the rest, it may be said that many Jesuits were perfectly aware of the relativity of their judgements. Father Le Jeune writes:

Oh, how weak are the judgements of men! Some place beauty where others see nothing but ugliness. The most beautiful teeth in France are the whitest; in the Maldive Islands whiteness of teeth is considered a deformity, they paint them red to be beautiful; and in Cochin China, if my memory serves me, they paint them black. Which is right?[36]

As far as missionary work was concerned, the Jesuits were convinced that they should proceed peacefully, with no pressure or compulsion placed on the native population. The glad tidings of Christianity, wrote Le Jeune, should rise over Canada like a sun. He even dreamed (perhaps with propaganda in mind) of a future Golden Age which would have no need to adorn itself with the wealth of Peru but would be marked by innocent relations between Europeans and Indians.[37] No doubt the missionaries would have been glad if the colonists had been able to ease their labours by offering military resistance to the constant attacks from the Iroquois; and perhaps they also occasionally envied the Portuguese, whose brilliant display of power in Asia seemed to give more support to their missions.[38] However, the Jesuit missionaries never for a moment contemplated forcible conversion or a 'just war' against Indians who refused to be converted.[39]

The Jesuits wanted to win the Hurons over to Christianity by gentle means. They were determined to approach them sympathetically, to persevere in instruction without forcing doctrine upon them, and to set an example worthy of imitation. There would seem to be no grounds for questioning the sincerity and unselfishness of this enterprise; the rich source material of the *Jesuit Relations* provides impressively consistent evidence of these qualities. Moreover, the Jesuits were fully aware of the extreme difficulty of their task. During their first attempts at conversion, before 1615, the missionaries had thought it best to emulate the *coureurs de bois* and accompany the Indians on their hunting expeditions through the wilderness, enduring the utmost hardships. Later they concentrated on the Hurons' settlements and tried to urge them to adopt a settled way of life, which would make missionary activity easier. However, the Jesuits were still governed by the precept that they should accommodate themselves to the Indians' way of life. It is known that the *coureurs de bois* sometimes carried this accommodation so far that they not only shared the Indians' houses and food but also imitated their social and moral behaviour, much to the regret of the missionaries, who deplored this *vivre à l'indigène*.[40] However, the Jesuits too, to a large extent, ate and lived as the Hurons did, paddled canoes skilfully, used the sauna, employed local herbs as remedies when ill, and went on hunting and fishing expeditions. In any case, the rejection of material comforts enjoined by the rules of their order brought them close, in a sense, to the Indians' way of life. The *Instruction pour les Pères de Nostre Compagnie qui seront enuoiez aux Hurons*, published at Paris in 1638, explicitly recommended the missionaries to share the Indians' way of life, whatever privations it involved, as the best way of gaining their confidence.[41]

Many sources agree, however, that the simple and austere life in the seclusion of the Canadian forests was seen by the missionaries primarily as a means towards religious contemplation and purification, and was deliberately sought for that reason. Father Brébeuf remarks in his account that anyone who enters Huron territory full of reverence and love for God need not fear for his soul. He continues: 'Is it not a great deal to have, in one's food, clothing, and sleep, no other attraction than bare necessity? Is it not a glorious opportunity to unite oneself with God, when there is no creature whatsoever that gives you reason to spend your affection upon it?'[42] In the eighteenth century the Jesuit Charlevoix, composing his history and description of New France, was to evince some melancholy as he recalled the self-sacrifice of his fellow-Jesuits in Huronia, who had entirely cut themselves off from the world in order to attain that spiritual peace and innocence of which Christ had spoken to his disciples.[43]

Besides sharing the Indians' way of life, it was no less important that the missionaries should learn their language. Even the earliest Jesuit missionaries, Fathers Biard and Massé, who worked among the Micmac Indians in Acadia around 1610, realized that there was no serious prospect of converting the Indians unless one mastered their tongue. Biard and Massé were of course not the first to advocate learning native languages: the Jesuits in China and South America had long since realized the importance of this step in approaching an alien people. Yet one is struck by the high value that was placed in Canada on the ability to communicate with the Hurons in their own language: the missionaries who did so stood out from the other colonists and from their fellows who had stayed in Quebec, and demonstrated the inner commitment which drove them to work on the remotest frontier of cultural contact. Father Brébeuf, who was thought specially talented as a linguist, writes: 'The Huron language will be your Thomas [Aquinas] and your Aristotle; and clever man as you are, and speaking glibly among learned and capable persons, you must make up your mind to be for a long time mute among the Barbarians. You will have accomplished much, if, at the end of a considerable time, you begin to stammer a little.'[44]

Learning the language and using it to proclaim the Christian message created problems even for the most committed missionaries.[45] It went without saying that the missionary had to spend long periods in the Indians' company and engage a teacher whose services had to be rewarded. Both these things, however, were possible only where the natives led a settled life. The Indian languages were, of course, not recorded in writing: there were no grammars, their phonetics followed unfamiliar laws, and the vocabulary lacked precisely those abstract terms, like 'guilt', 'penitence', 'grace', 'temptation', 'faith', which played a major role in religious instruction. People made do as best they could with transcriptions, dictionaries and glossaries. Father Brébeuf spent the winter of 1625 among the Montagnais Indians and composed a grammar of their language; a year later he did the same among the Hurons. The next step was an attempt to translate the catechism into the native language. In one of the earliest works of this kind, the *Doctrine chrétienne* published at Rouen in 1630, the French version was accompanied by a clearly presented translation into the Montagnais language. In 1632 the Recollect monk Gabriel Sagard published a 132-page dictionary of the most important language in the Great Lakes area, Huron. It was the first such work produced in North America, and it is still the best study of the Huron language.[46]

Even with such guidance, however, there were still obstacles to conveying the substance of the Christian faith. Every language, and particularly the language of a primitive people, is intertwined with the entire culture to which it belongs; it is at once an element in the culture and a dynamic factor in cultural change.[47] If a concept from Western thought was to be introduced into an Indian language without altering its meaning and causing misunderstanding, the language in question had to be broadly similar to Western languages in its grammatical structure, and had to embody at least a comparable state of social, economic and cultural awareness. It was not enough to extract an Indian word from the half-understood utterance in which it had occurred, and to declare it synonymous with a French word: the real task was to trace the complex ties between the Indian word and its entire cultural background. The missionaries would have had to adjust their conceptual language to this cultural framework, even at the considerable risk of distorting the very essence of their message – a problem which brought about the ultimate failure of the Jesuit mission in China.[48] Finally, they faced the deep-seated problem that the religious language of primitive peoples, unlike that of Christianity, does not reflect a tragic sense of life; instead, it is directly related to ritual action and represents a pragmatic attempt to cope with external dangers, as when a god is invoked before a military campaign or in economic distress.

Another way to facilitate communication for missionary purposes would of course have been to teach the Indians French. The Jesuits soon found that the Indian children, in particular, proved bright and teachable, as long as their enthusiasm was maintained by little presents and the lessons were made attractive. The latter was done by exploiting their natural love of singing and making them memorize verses from the

Bible by chanting them. As early as 1635 the Jesuits in Quebec had opened a modest *Collège*, the first of its kind north of Mexico, and older by two years than Harvard College. Soon afterwards they began to teach young Indians who had been voluntarily surrendered by their families for this purpose. Great expectations were attached to the founding of the seminary 'Notre Dame des Anges' in 1651. It was intended as a school for Indian missionaries who would subsequently return to their own people – a method already tried out by the Portuguese, who had begun missionary work in the Congo in the late fifteenth century.[49] Although they were looked after with touching affection, however, the young Indians seem to have found Quebec uncongenial. Many of them died or fled, and as Indian families became less inclined to let their children leave for the town, the schoolrooms were soon standing empty. The missionaries did not forget to establish a school for Indian girls, which was run by Ursuline nuns from France and had over forty-eight pupils in 1640; but this experiment too was doomed to failure.

Finally, the Indians' instruction in Christianity was to be completed by prolonged residence in France. There was already a tradition of transporting inhabitants of the New World to Europe: Columbus, Cartier and many other explorers had repeatedly brought home 'savages' as living proof of their achievements. It is in this context that we should mention the famous remarks by Montaigne, who saw a group of Brazilian Indians displayed publicly in Rouen in 1562, and wrote of them in his *Essais*:

> They are even savage, as we call those fruits wilde which nature of herselfe and of her ordinarie progresse hath produced: whereas indeed, they are those which our selves have altered by our artificiall devices, and diverted from their common order, we should rather terme savage. In those are the true and most profitable vertues, and naturall properties most lively and vigorous, which in these we have bastardized, applying them to the pleasure of pour corrupted taste.[50]

The problem that Montaigne had pointed out was also apparent to the Jesuits. They felt it necessary to ensure that residence in France would not paralyse the Indians' fresh, unspoilt receptiveness but rather encourage it, and they imagined future Indian missionaries who would preserve and propagate the Christian message in a purer form than Europeans, indelibly marked by the temptations of an advanced civilization, could hope to do. However, it soon turned out that the Indians, in striking contrast with the black Africans, found the European climate uncongenial and soon died, mostly of consumption.

Another interesting experiment in the linguistic and religious education of Indians, mainly adults this time, was the establishment of an Indian village community at Sillery, just outside Quebec. Like the educational institutions described earlier, this was financed by generous donations from aristocratic sympathizers in France. The first years after the foundation of this settlement in 1637 seemed to promise success. In the reservation some thirty families, chiefly Montagnais Indians, were encouraged to lead a settled life, and in 1645 they included 145 baptized Christians. Land was made arable and allocated to the converts; they operated a windmill, a bakery, even a brewery, and built a school, a hospital and a church. The language of daily use was French, and religious life developed so quickly that the Jesuits occasionally had to intervene to check the immoderate fervour of their converts.[51] However, as the settlements of the French colonists approached closer to the reservation, so it became harder to shield the Indians from damaging influences. Alcoholism spread alarmingly, and when a fire broke out in 1657, the Indian inhabitants began to scatter in the forests.

How did matters develop at the remotest frontier of cultural contact, 300 miles inland from Quebec, in the Huron heartland itself? Before 1632 this region contained only a few Recollect and Jesuit missionaries at Lake Simcoe, and during the English occupation (1629–32) their activity came almost to a standstill. The restoration of Canada to the French, however, gave a powerful impetus to the conversion of Huronia. Two preconditions that seem particularly to have favoured the Indian mission were the settled life of the 30,000 or so Hurons living in this area, and the fact that the fur trade was already in full swing and had generated new needs which the natives wanted to have satisfied. As early as 1638 ten Jesuit missionaries were at work between Lake Simcoe and Georgian Bay, and by 1649 this number had risen to eighteen missionaries, over twenty deacons, and eleven further assistants. Around the year 1640 a central mission station, consisting of a church, dwelling-houses and storerooms surrounded by fortifications, was built in Sainte Marie, the present-day Midland.[52]

The Jesuits' selfless dedication is beyond doubt, and yet by 1650, scarcely two decades after its resumption, it had to be admitted that the missionary experiment in Huronia had failed completely. Some of the reasons were directly connected with missionary activity, others were unrelated to it. Among the former was the fact that, as an authority on these matters bluntly puts it, 'the Hurons were obviously not at all interested in what the Jesuits had to teach.'[53] In other words, even though the missionaries adopted an alien language and way of life, they failed to convey the substance of the Christian faith to a mentality that differed in crucial respects from the European one. Indeed, most of the missionaries soon acknowledged that the conversions they achieved were neither numerous nor entirely trustworthy. Father Le Jeune wrote in 1635:

It is quite true that, if these people were as desirous of learning as are all civilized nations, some of us have a good enough knowledge of their language to teach them. But as they make living, and not knowledge, their profession, their greatest anxiety is about eating and drinking, and not about learning. When you speak to them of our truths, they listen to you patiently; but instead of asking you about the matter, they at once turn their thoughts to ways of finding something upon which to live, showing their stomachs always empty and always famished. Yet if we could make speeches as they do, and if we were present in their assemblies, I believe we could accomplish much there.[54]

In 1640 Father Jérome Lalemant reported to France:

The Gospel has been announced to more than ten thousand savages, not only in general, but to each family, and almost to every person individually; more than a thousand have been baptized, in the extraordinary epidemics which have come upon them, and of these many little children, at least, have taken flight to Heaven; and to crown this good fortune, we have endured many persecutions.[55]

To an attentive reader, these accounts of the missionaries' successes sound very half-hearted. It is clear, too, that most of the people converted were dangerously ill, indeed *in extremis*, in which state many Hurons took care also to call on the services of their medicine-man. Converts who made unexpected recoveries often abandoned the true faith. Since genuine changes of heart were so rare, many missionaries were content to record with pleasure the outward professions of faith made especially by young Indians, without sufficiently acknowledging their fondness for parody and masquerade. Thus, the Jesuits' narratives proudly describe how willingly the Indian children go to church, sing in the choir, listen to the sound of the church bells, and take part in prayers. Often the authors of these narratives went so far as to contrast the Hurons' zeal and devotion polemically with the religious indifference of the European colonists. Again and again, however, the missionaries were brought down to earth by discovering that this display of enthusiasm resulted only from curiosity and calculation, and that it evaporated as soon as the novelty had worn off and the promised rewards had failed to materialize. From 1640 onwards, when famine broke out among the Hurons and the Iroquois' attacks became more frequent, occasional mass conversions took place; but how genuine these were is a question better left unanswered.

There is no avoiding the impression that in the course of time the missionaries came to attach less importance to conversion, and regarded their work more as a personal trial of strength through tribulation and struggle with the Evil One. It is obvious that many Jesuits looked forward with composure, sometimes even with a kind of ecstatic yearning, to an early death from starvation or hardship, or at the hands of the Indians, and that the failure of their divinely appointed mission was to be glorified by the sacrifice of their own lives. Many of the accounts that appeared in the mid-seventeenth century described martyrdom with an extravagant profusion of morbid fantasies that display fascination, rather than disgust, with torture and cannibalism, and for many missionaries the stake where their Iroquois enemies would martyr them symbolized the cross on which Christ had suffered. Sometimes Jesuits who had narrowly avoided perishing – Father Isaac Jogues, for example – would again go among hostile tribes in order to be sure of meeting death; others, such as Father Jean-Pierre Aulneau, seem to have prepared themselves for martyrdom in systematic meditations, and finally to have accepted it with joy.[56]

Missionary work was made yet harder by a number of epidemics, probably smallpox introduced by the Europeans, which afflicted the Hurons even before 1640 and are thought to have reduced their population by half.[57] The Jesuits' arrival coincided so clearly with the outbreak of the plague that the terrified Hurons could not fail to connect the two. It goes without saying that this suspicion was, if anything, increased by the sympathy which the missionaries showed to dying Indians and by the ritual of baptism. In a letter to Quebec, Father Brébeuf reported that the missionaries' lives were in imminent danger and that a show of resolution had been needed to dispel the Hurons' anger.[58] Today we know that the council assemblies of three Huron tribes considered either killing the missionaries or else hiring murderers from a neighbouring tribe so that their deaths would not jeopardize the fur trade with the French.[59] On this occasion the Jesuits apparently owed their survival more to the commercial interests of the Hurons than to their own protestations of innocence. It is certain that the Indians were deeply divided in their views about the missionaries, especially after the outbreak of plague had cast an ominous light on the latter's presence. In this context the activities of the Indian medicine-men had a particularly harmful effect on the missions. It had not taken the Jesuits long to regard the medicine-men as their most dangerous adversaries, sorcerers and emissaries of the devil. Le Jeune writes:

> These persons, in my opinion, are true Sorcerers, who have access to the Devil. Some only judge of the evil, and that in diverse ways, namely, by Pyromancy, by Hydromancy, Necromancy, by feasts, dances, and songs; the others endeavor to cure the disease by blowing, by potions, and by other ridiculous tricks, which have neither any virtue nor natural efficacy. But neither class do anything without generous presents and good pay.[60]

It is no wonder that the medicine-men for their part were unsympathetic to the missionaries, whom they saw as trespassing on their own professional territory. Since these medicine-men often played a major part in the life of the tribe and were consulted about political decisions, they confronted the Jesuits with an unremitting hostility which could be appeased only temporarily by bribing them with presents.

The missionaries also had difficulty coping with the sharp minds of the Hurons, who often challenged them to engage in discussion and embarrassed them by critical remarks. Here is a sample of the Indians' reasoning: if it was true that Eve's apple had plunged the whole of humanity into misfortune, was it not glaringly unjust that Christ's death on the cross could redeem only half of humanity, namely the Christians? Dying natives were also heard to say that they set no great store by getting to heaven, which was swarming with Frenchmen who would only let one starve; nor could they see why the Christians found the next world so attractive, if, as the missionaries asserted, there was no hunting, no polygamy, no feasting, and no warfare in heaven.[61] These questions and objections, and others like them, obliged the Jesuits to rethink their own views critically and to agree among themselves on a common conception of their faith; for the Indians had superb memories and took great delight in catching the missionaries out in self-contradictions. In their narratives the Jesuits give many of their Indian acquaintances ample credit for intelligence and acuteness, and it is certainly no accident that Enlightenment authors gave the Hurons a prominent place in stories exposing European culture to criticism.[62]

The principal reason for the failure of the missionary experiment in Huronia did not lie, however, in the activity of the Jesuits and the contumacy of their Indian charges, but is to be sought in the intensification of hostilities between the Iroquois and the Hurons. In discussing the general decline of the French colony in the second half of the seventeenth century, we have already mentioned that Iroquois attacks became more frequent after 1640. On his way to Huronia in 1642, Father Jogues, along with over twenty converted and baptized Hurons, was taken prisoner by the Iroquois, and subsequently there were repeated attacks and massacres with Christians as their victims. In March 1649 two pillars of the Jesuit mission, Fathers Brébeuf and Lalemant, were martyred at the stake by the Iroquois. Huron counter-attacks eased the situation only temporarily: the Jesuits' appeals for the encouragement of immigration were ignored in France, and Quebec in its enfeebled state could not provide the military support they requested. In the summer of 1649 those Hurons who had survived the Iroquois attacks left their territories to seek refuge with neighbouring tribes further north, ceasing to exist as a tribe in their own right. At the same time the Jesuits evacuated Sainte Marie, their last and most important base in Huronia.

Father Paul Raguenau had the melancholy duty of reporting the end to his superiors:

> But on each of us lay the necessity of bidding farewell to that old home of sainte Marie, – to its structures, which, though plain, seemed, to the eyes of our poor Savages, master-works of art; and to its cultivated lands, which were promising an abundant harvest. That spot must be forsaken, which I may call our second Fatherland, our home of innocent delights, since it had been the cradle of this Christian church; since it was the temple of God, and the home of the servants of Jesus Christ. Moreover, for fear that our enemies, only too wicked, should profane the sacred place, and derive from it an advantage, we ourselves set fire to it.[63]

The Jesuit missionaries were, of course, only too ready to see the conflict between Iroquois and Hurons as the work of the devil and a product of Indian intrigues: their reports provide scanty help towards a deeper analysis of these events.[64] The clergy were not and perhaps could not have been aware that the outbreak of these hostilities was closely linked with the state of the fur trade in the American–Canadian frontier area. Today we know that about the year 1640 there had been a sharp decline in the number of beaver pelts offered for sale, both on the upper Hudson River, where the Iroquois hunted them on behalf of the Dutch and English, and on the upper St Lawrence and east of the Great Lakes. Modern research suggests that in advancing into the territory of their Huron kindred, the Iroquois were not primarily in search of new hunting grounds, but wanted rather to force the Hurons to break off their trade with the French and serve thenceforth as intermediaries for the tribes living further north.[65] This would have allowed the Iroquois to send their European trading partners in New York an undiminished supply of beaver pelts, though taken from remoter areas. We know also that among the Hurons at this time a party favouring such a peaceful union with the Iroquois began to form: it consisted of the traditionalist forces that rejected the cultural changes introduced by the Jesuits' arrival. These groups may also have recognized that the Iroquois were generously equipped with arms and munitions by their Dutch and English trading partners, while the Hurons themselves were armed only sparingly and reluctantly by the French.[66]

On the other hand, there is no doubt that once the wave of epidemics had passed, the missionaries rapidly succeeded in securing a natural authority. However dubious their conversions may in general have been, the missionaries' authority was based on their steadfast courage, their skill as craftsmen, and their integrity. This was why a majority of the influential Hurons were inclined to expect greater benefits in future from the relationship with their French partners and probably also became increasingly ready to learn from the Jesuits where this seemed advantageous. Nobody can now say what would have become of the Huron tribes if they had expelled or killed the missionaries and joined the Iroquois. It is, however, beyond question that their fragile but touching loyalty to their spiritual teachers ensured the Hurons' downfall.

Anyone who knows the ample source material on the Jesuits' missionary experiment in Huronia cannot but respect this European achievement, no matter how unsuccessful it may have been. One may disapprove of missionary activity on principle, but it is indisputable that as far as the methods and aims of the Europeans involved were concerned, this experiment was marked by genuine understanding, a high sense of responsibility, and an extraordinary material disinterestedness. These qualities could have provided a humane basis for a relationship, even a prolonged one, between two cultures. However, such a relationship was opposed by far more powerful forces of colonial development, in this case the interest in the fur trade shared by rival nations and alliances. Soon afterwards, the English Quakers, who were fully comparable with the Jesuits in their ethical standards, were to find to their chagrin that their 'holy experiment' in seventeenth-century Pennsylvania came to nothing, this time because of the settlers' greed for land.

# Cultural Relationship as 'Holy Experiment'

## *The English in Pennsylvania*

The open aggressiveness of Spanish colonial expansion in the sixteenth century reflected the ruthless struggle that Habsburg Spain was waging simultaneously against the hegemonic ambitions of France and against the Ottoman advance in the Mediterranean. The conquistador spirit combined the mentality of a robber knight and the emotional afflatus of the Crusades to produce a mood of fierce determination. The native American Indian population, unsuspecting, docile or internally divided, could put up no resistance. Moral considerations were swept aside by the uninhibited lust for easy wealth which the first generation of colonists displayed. Nor was there much to hinder the Europeans' onward progress. Tropical diseases claimed fewer victims than in Africa, and most of the geographical obstacles had already been overcome by the highway system of the advanced Indian civilizations. The conquistadors saw themselves as representatives of the Crown, enhancing its renown by their victorious deeds, and this alliance was fostered by the fact that emigrants were chosen from the most ambitious and energetic of the minor nobility, artisans and peasants. Spanish travel narratives combine elements of the heroic epic and the medieval chronicle: their main themes include glorious feats of arms, miraculous events and the courtly magnificence of Indian potentates, and every incident finds an unassailable meaning in the framework of Christian history.

By contrast, English expansion across the Atlantic in the seventeenth century has an entirely different character, even if the motives and results are similar. The first striking difference is that the settlement of North America, initially at least, was a hesitant, faltering process. Admittedly, as early as 1497 the Italian Giovanni Gabotto (John Cabot), in the service of England, had reached Newfoundland, but although there were already vague plans for settlement, this voyage remained a dead end for the time being.[1] More than sixty years were to pass before Humphrey Gilbert and Martin Frobisher proposed further voyages of exploration to North America, with the particular aim of discovering a north-west passage, a direct sea route to China. Between 1577 and 1580 Francis Drake circumnavigated the globe, plundering and burning the ports along the west coast of South America as he went, and thus proving to the world how vulnerable was the Spanish position in the Western hemisphere. Queen Elizabeth's support for these maritime enterprises was kept secret at first in order to spare Spanish sensibilities, but became more and more overt as time went by. The Queen was also involved in financing an expedition which Walter Ralegh sent to Virginia in 1585. This was the first concerted attempt at settlement, but it soon had to be abandoned. Further enterprises, again inspired by Ralegh, failed likewise, and the Crown temporarily withdrew its support owing to the challenge of the Spanish Armada in 1588. It was not until after Elizabeth's death, and after her successor, James I, had made peace with Spain, that a new and fruitful initiative was taken. In April 1607 three small ships with some 140 people on board arrived in Chesapeake Bay, landed in the region called 'Virginia' in honour of the Virgin Queen, and founded the settlement of Jamestown, named after James I. Its early years were extremely hard, but additional settlers followed, and tobacco plantations were set up and yielded a profit. By 1620 there may have been some 850 settlers in Virginia.[2]

Not only did the English settlement of North America lack the pioneering *élan* of the conquistadors, but it also lacked a homogeneous character. By 1640 North America had some 25,000 colonial inhabitants. More than half of them were settled in the northern colonies, the 'New England' states of New Hampshire, Massachusetts, Rhode Island and Connecticut. Some 2,000 colonists lived in New York, which had been founded by the Dutch and was the oldest of what were called the 'middle colonies'. Finally, the southern states, which in 1640 consisted only of Maryland and Virginia, numbered about 11,000 souls.[3]

A distinction is to be drawn between colonies founded by privileged commercial companies and those created by the allocation of land to a particular individual. Virginia, for example, was founded by an association of small shareholders, the Virginia Company. This commercial body received a charter from the King setting out the principles, based on English law, on which the colony was to be established. At the outset the colonists still had no private property, and such profits as they laboriously reaped ended up in the pockets of the shareholders back home. Not until seven years after the founding of the colony was the private ownership of land permitted. The year 1619 saw the first meeting of the General Assembly, the colony's first legislative body, composed of twenty-two respected and well-to-do citizens. As in the other colonies, the interests of the Crown were represented by the governor, who was a nobleman appointed by the King.

Unlike Virginia, Maryland was the property of an individual. In 1623 Charles I transferred to Lord Baltimore, a Catholic convert, a territory north-east of the Potomac River. Baltimore's son Cecil was given a completely free hand in drawing up a charter, in which he declared the colony to be the property of his family in perpetuity and reserved to himself the power of decision in administrative and judicial matters and in the distribution of land. His younger son was sent to America as governor. As in later privately founded colonies, the members of the founder's family exercised very extensive influence. Maryland also had an Assembly, composed of landowners of blameless reputation, who were soon entitled to propose laws and who steadily increased their influence. It was a peculiarity of Maryland that it was founded by a religious minority, the English Catholics. It was soon realized, however, that the colony could only survive if it tolerated immigrants belonging to other religious groups, and so articles providing for religious toleration were added to the Constitution.

Although the English possessions in North America were kept on a loose rein, control could be tightened at any time. Thus, after disturbances among the settlers, both Virginia and Maryland were brought under direct administration from England, though without abolishing the Assemblies. Although these possessions were ruled in a remarkably democratic fashion by contemporary European standards, the settlers' sovereignty was not unlimited. No share in government was taken, for example, by the indentured servants, who had to pay for the expenses of their voyage by a specified amount of labour. In New England such servants were relatively rare, but around 1640 they probably accounted for approximately one-third of the population of Virginia and Maryland.[4] There were also, especially in the Southern States, imported black slaves who had no legal rights whatever: Virginia had 150 of them in 1640, but a century later they already numbered 60,000.[5] Nowhere was the Indian population integrated into the settler community.

The North American possessions, however, did not differ from one another only in being founded by joint-stock companies or by private individuals. There were also differences, sometimes very marked, in the origins and mentalities of the immigrants. Most of the settlers who colonized New England during the seventeenth century were Puritans, originating from the country or from small towns. Their economic circumstances ranged from poverty to at best moderate prosperity. Under the Stuarts they had suffered various restrictions imposed by the

Established Church, and they hoped that their piety, virtue and industry would enable them to form new and godly communities across the Atlantic. The first Puritan colony was founded in 1620 in Cape Cod Bay by the Pilgrim Fathers, who had arrived on the *Mayflower*. A particularly rigorous group founded Salem, north-east of Boston, later to become notorious for its witch-trials. Strict Puritanism also produced separatist movements, such as the founding of Rhode Island by Roger Williams, who brought about an almost complete separation of Church from state. Although the Puritans, like other colonists, occasionally contemplated missionary work among the Indians, their religious spirit remained introverted, largely confined to private and family life. Towns were soon founded in New England, and grew rapidly, with commerce and crafts flourishing. Infant mortality seems to have been lower than in England, so that immigration from Europe soon ceased to be necessary to supplement the population.

In other cases, however, it was material hardship rather than religious loyalties which encouraged emigration. This applied particularly to the settlers in the Southern States, where, as mentioned earlier, indentured servants were particularly numerous. These were often English peasant farmers who could no longer support themselves from their land: their poverty seems to have been due less to the enclosure of common land by large landowners than to the spread of sheep-farming. The general rise in prices since the sixteenth century and the increase in unemployment produced an urban proletariat, especially in London, where crime grew enormously. As early as 1615 a Royal Commission proposed sending convicted criminals overseas, but large-scale transportation did not begin until after 1660. During the Civil War (1642–8) and the subsequent campaigns in Ireland and Scotland, prisoners of war were often sent overseas.

The opportunities for social mobility among poor settlers were considerably fewer than was claimed in propaganda tracts and in early American historiography. Even in colonies where at certain times a piece of land was allotted to every immigrant, by no means all people managed to make use of their land; many sold it instead. It is estimated that in the seventeenth century only one-tenth of indentured servants became successful farmers; a similar proportion made a secure income from crafts and trades; and the remainder, if they survived at all, sank to the level of 'poor whites', day-labourers and occasional workers whose lives were often more miserable and shiftless than those of the black slaves.[6] Moreover, disparities in income were considerably greater in the South than in the North, and the small group of wealthy plantation owners who established themselves in Virginia, Maryland and later in North and South Carolina, favoured an exclusive life-style very different from the conscious austerity of the Puritans in New England.

The differences among the various groups of North American settlers often resulted from differences in geography and natural resources. In the North, which had harbours in convenient locations, foreign trade soon acquired great importance. The immense forests provided wood for shipbuilding, the sea produced fish, especially cod, in vast quantities, and whaling supplied the sperm-oil which was much in demand for lighting. Thanks to the co-operation of the Indians, the interior supplied various animal furs, especially beaver, which was in huge demand in Europe: in the mid-seventeenth century a single successful fur-trader from Massachusetts sent almost 9,000 pelts across the Atlantic in five years.[7] Had it not been for their trade and customs agreements with England, the settlers in New England could have been self-sufficient even before 1700, not only because they had the necessary resources, but also thanks to their technical skills. The Puritans' efforts to create an educational system provided a model for other parts of America and even for Europe. Schools, along with churches, were among the earliest public buildings in New England: a Latin school was set up in Boston in 1635, and Harvard College was founded a year later. Although England tried to prevent the growth of printing and newspapers in the colonies by keeping a careful watch on the export of printing presses, the first American book, the *Bay Psalm Book*, was printed in Boston as early as 1640. It was not long before towns like Boston and New York, joined somewhat later by Philadelphia, contained a class of educated citizens, born and brought up in America, who were fully equal to the English in education, self-confidence and cultivated manners.

The Southern States also had fisheries, fur-trading and a little shipbuilding in the seventeenth century, but far and away their most important product was tobacco. This was the first exotic product to be imported simply as a source of enjoyment, and in Europe its popularity spread rapidly after 1550, when small quantities first arrived from Central America and Canada. Colonies like Virginia and Maryland literally owed their survival to tobacco. For the early settlers it was crucial that tobacco can thrive in a great variety of different soils and climatic zones. In 1619 one of the first tobacco planters in Virginia, John Rolfe, calculated that by cultivating a thousand tobacco plants and four acres of maize, landowners could support themselves, pay a servant, and buy such European imported goods as they might still need.[8] The cultivation of tobacco, like that of cotton and sugar cane later, helped to determine the social structure of the Southern States. Clearing the ground, sowing and tending the seeds, harvesting and drying the crop, all required a large number of unskilled labourers. At first these were mostly indentured servants; later slaves predominated. The great landowners were not much interested in encouraging education. They lived like the English landed nobility, sent their sons to college in England, subscribed to English journals. The first printing press began operating only in 1730, and the first university, William and Mary College, founded in 1700, never attained the renown of Harvard or Yale.

It is instructive to compare the travel writing of the English in seventeenth-century North America with that of the Spaniards in the preceding century.[9] The English colonists did not see themselves to any significant extent as chroniclers of world-shaking events. Their reports contain few traces of expansionist zeal or of a conviction of leading the struggle against barbarism for the honour of the Crown and Christianity. Nor are their experiences described dramatically. This is partly because they had fewer such experiences, and it is difficult to make a stirring, rhetorical narrative out of hunger and hard work; but it is also because the English settlers were realistic, down-to-earth, practical people who concentrated on the task before them. The English were wary of far-fetched expectations and dreams, and those few who still talked of easy passages to the wonders of China and wealth beyond the dreams of avarice were soon reduced to silence. Reports from New England, Virginia and Maryland seldom touch on the topics which so much preoccupied the Crown lawyers of Spain. Such questions as how to defend their rights against territorial claims by other nations, or how to put relations with the Indians on a legal basis, did not crop up or were not raised. Early accounts like Captain John Smith's *True Travels, Adventures, and Observations* from Virginia, or William Bradford's *History of Plymouth Plantation* from Massachusetts, confine themselves to factual descriptions of local conditions, enquire into the specific circumstances and prospects of life overseas, and describe the natural products, the fauna, and the manners and customs of the native inhabitants.[10] These documents lack the literary skill, the brilliance, and the emotional rhetoric of the conquistadors' narratives, but they are attractive because of their simplicity and the often astonishing precision of their observations.

Having sketched the historical background, it is now time to turn to Pennsylvania, one of the most interesting and successful colonies founded in the seventeenth century. Its exemplary character, especially as regards the regulation of relations with the Indians, has repeatedly attracted the attention of posterity.[11]

Of all the privately founded colonies in America, Pennsylvania was the one whose early history bore the firmest imprint of a single personality. William Penn was born in the south of England in 1644. His father, the admiral of the same name, had distinguished himself in the naval battles between England and Holland.[12] Coming from a well-to-do background, and sent by his ambitious father at an early age to study at English and French universities, Penn could have risen high in the service of his country. In 1667, however, he joined a Christian community, the 'Society of Friends', or Quakers, which had been brought into being ten years earlier by George Fox, as a highly personal and internalized form of religious observance opposed to the Established Church.[13] In the next few years Penn wrote polemical pamphlets on Catholic, Anglican and Puritan doctrines, but also argued that people should have absolute liberty to practise any form of religion, thus earning himself several terms of imprisonment. His missionary journeys covered large areas of England, the Netherlands and Germany, where he and his friends laid the foundations for the later emigration of fellow believers from the northern Rhineland and Westphalia.

The idea of creating a new home for the members of the Society of Friends and other religious minorities threatened by persecution seems to have occurred to Penn about 1676. In the spring of 1680 he approached King Charles II with a request to be assigned a territory on the Delaware River. Not only was Penn on good terms with the royal house, but his request enabled the Crown to pay off an old debt to his father: this may be why the charter confirming the allocation of land was prepared with astonishing speed.[14] As with other privately founded colonies, this charter laid down the relations between the Crown and the colony and confirmed the validity of English law overseas. The powers granted to Penn, who is repeatedly described in this document as 'the true and absolute proprietary', were virtually unlimited. The King also insisted on calling the colony Pennsylvania after its proprietor. Great care was taken to determine the border separating the new territory west of the Delaware River from the neighbouring colonies of New Jersey and Maryland, though the area was still so inadequately mapped as to make this difficult. Relations with the Indian population are mentioned at two points in the charter. Firstly, Penn is given responsibility 'to reduce the Savage Natives by Gentle and just manners to the Love of civill Society and Christian Religion';[15] secondly, the proprietor is then authorized to raise troops in the event of 'Incursions as well of the Savages themselves, as of other Enemies, Pirates & Robbers'.[16] It is interesting, finally, that the King obviously took for granted the idea of the discoverer's rights, according to which territories discovered by English ships, whether or not they were already inhabited, became the property of the discoverers and could be handed on to vassals like a feudal fief. Later, as we shall see, Penn acknowledged the Indians' prior rights to their land by purchasing it from them with carefully worked-out treaties. By doing so he was, strictly speaking, opposing the orthodox legal doctrine of England.

In 1681 and 1682 Penn was busy devising a constitution for his colony. Some twenty draft constitutions have survived, and from reading them it is apparent that several legal advisers were consulted and that every phrase was disputed. The views of John Locke and Shaftesbury and the liberal, indeed utopian, tendencies associated with the Whig party are discernible in certain early drafts which transfer legal authority comprehensively to the Grand Assembly, a parliament to be elected by the land-owning settlers. Its lower chamber was to pass laws and its upper chamber was to supervise their practice through various commissions. Pressure from worried investors, who felt that this Constitution gave the representatives of the people excessive authority, evidently caused it to be replaced by the Frame of Government, which came into force in May 1682. This version transferred governmental powers to the Governor and the Provincial Council, which replaced the previous upper chamber; the lower chamber, the Assembly, retained advisory functions. This increasingly oligarchical tendency ran counter to Penn's original plans. It was further strengthened by the fact that Penn, as the proprietor designated in the Charter, entrusted important posts in the Provincial Council to influential benefactors with whom he had close personal ties. The newly created Free Society of Traders was also based on a small group of prosperous Quaker merchants. At the outset, Penn may well have been reluctant to accept this growing concentration of political and economic power in a few hands; critics also pointed out to him that such a development was scarcely consonant with the spirit of the Society of Friends. However, Penn was himself too much of a business man, and knew too much about the founding of other North American colonies, not to be aware that the mere labour power of a group of pioneers was an insufficient basis on which to build a prosperous colony.

The Constitution did incorporate, without qualification, two of the main principles of the Society of Friends, which were to underpin the 'Holy Experiment'.[17] Emphasis is placed, firstly, on the idea that people are naturally good, and that, as God's deputies on earth, they must ensure that their system of government conforms to the divine imperative. Human existence in society is not ruled by fear and suspicion, as in Thomas Hobbes's conception of the state: there is no *bellum omnium contra omnes* that can be controlled only by absolutism. Rather, the Quakers conceive human society as naturally tending towards peace, reciprocal understanding, and mutual help among its members. The positive law created by humankind serves only to preserve this state; it is less concerned to punish misguided individuals than to guide them back to the right path.

Not only, however, are people basically good; within the limits set by Christian faith and positive law, they are also free. It is true that, unlike the framers of the American Declaration of Independence a century later, Penn saw no reason to offer any definition of civic freedom other than those already present in the English legal tradition, for example in the

Petition of Right (1628) or the Habeas Corpus Act (1679). There was, however, one respect, the guarantee of religious freedom, in which the Frame of Government went beyond contemporary English law. It provides 'that all Persons living in this Province, who confess and acknowledge the One Almighty and Eternal God, to be the Creator, Upholder and Ruler of the World, and that hold themselves obliged in Conscience to live peaceably and justly in *Civil Society*, shall in no wayes be molested or prejudiced for their Religious Perswasion.'[18] This article of toleration is a reaction to the bitter and prolonged persecution which religious minorities had suffered under the Stuarts; it was also largely responsible for the unique character of Penn's policy towards the Indians.

When Penn arrived in Delaware Bay on 24 October 1682, there were some two thousand Europeans, including Dutch, Swedish and Finnish settlers, and perhaps a hundred black slaves living in the region. The Dutch had first tried to settle there in 1632, though without success; a few years later, the Swedes founded Fort Christina and took up the fur trade. Their fierce commercial competition with the Dutch operating from New York soon turned into a military conflict. The English finally took control in 1664, without wholly eclipsing the Dutch and Scandinavian elements of the population. Between 1682 and 1685 over 100 ships with English settlers on board entered the mouth of the Delaware River. Some 8,000 emigrants are estimated to have reached the area of present-day Philadelphia during this period, a figure greater than the volume of immigration into Massachusetts in the 1630s; Virginia took all of thirty years to attract an equal number of settlers. There were several reasons for this unprecedented boom in emigration. The settlers had landed, fortuitously, at a spot particularly suitable for habitation; the Quakers were coming under increasing pressure from the English government; and from 1689 to 1713 England was almost continuously at war with France.

On the Delaware, as elsewhere, the original inhabitants, with the oldest rights of possession, were the Indians. The Lenni Lenape or Delaware Indians, to whom the land belonged, led peaceful and relatively prosperous lives in scattered hamlets: they grew maize, beans and pumpkins, and went hunting in winter.[19] They belonged to the same linguistic group as the Algonkins, who had already encountered the French on the St Lawrence River and the English in Virginia. The name Lenni Lenape means 'the true or original people', but despite the implication of special status, shared by other tribes as well, the Lenni Lenape did not behave in a warlike or domineering way. Their restraint in dealing with the Europeans, their equanimity in times of material hardship, their distinct aversion to resolving conflicts by military means, and the trustworthiness of their character, are all clearly registered in the first European accounts. Praise was regularly given, too, to the Lenni Lenape's liberal mode of conducting politics by communal discussion and consultation in their assemblies, rather than by the decree of a single authoritarian figure. Penn, who observed the Indians closely and described them in a short report to the Free Society of Traders in London, did not hesitate to declare them superior to the Europeans in numerous respects:

> I find them [the Indians] a people rude, to Europeans, in dress, gesture, and food; but of a deep natural sagacity, Say little, but what they speak is fervent and elegant; if they please, close to the point, and can be as evasive. In treaties, about land, or traffick, I find them deliberate in council, and as designing, as I have ever observed among the politest of our Europeans.[20]

Another early immigrant whose description of the Lenni Lenape has come down to us, the German Franz Daniel Pastorius, writes (around 1700) as follows: 'They are at pains to be sincere and upright, keep promises meticulously, neither deceive nor offend anybody; they are very hospitable and look after their guests devotedly.'[21] Elsewhere he writes:

> I must end this eulogy of my unsavage savages by adding that they have a great aversion to war and the shedding of human blood, but rather live in peace with everyone, whereas almost the whole of Christendom is armed and its people, with barbarous cruelty, both offensively and defensively, attack and rend one another much worse than the most abominable monsters.[22]

In material culture, however, the Lenni Lenape were far inferior to the Europeans. They were familiar with simple techniques of pottery, weaving and basket-making, made clothes and shoes from leather, carved wood, and recorded important historical events in drawings scratched on bark. They cultivated the soil by the primitive method of turning it over with a stick, and their harvests were consequently small; they caught fish with darts, bone hooks and nets. Their principal means of transport were portable canoes made of beech and elm bark; their settlements were connected by a system of footpaths, skilfully adapted to the configuration of the land. As currency they used 'wampum pearls', which were taken from sea-snails and mussels, bored through and strung on cords. These wampum strings or 'sewants', as they were called in Pennsylvania, were also in use among the Europeans, who acquired them from the Indians living along the New England coast and transported them south by sea. These pearls, together with European manufactured goods, firearms and gunpowder, were used for trading in furs and land. When the two cultures first came into contact, the Indians often put the whites' imported goods to inappropriate or impractical uses, and greatly overestimated the power of such goods to enhance their lives; while for their part they were astonished at the value the Europeans placed on animal skins and ownership of land.

The Lenni Lenape soon became accustomed to imported goods and learnt how to use them. Since, however, they themselves could not have made such goods even if they had wanted to, they became dangerously dependent on the Europeans. Alcohol, introduced to the region by the Dutch, was fatal in its effects: when drunk, Indians ceased to be peaceable and went berserk. Before the Europeans arrived, the weapons of the Lenni Lenape had been confined to wooden clubs and swords, besides bows and arrows: only later were imported firearms joined by the dreaded tomahawk, the small battle-axe with an iron blade. For the population size of the tribe in the seventeenth century, we have to rely on vague estimates. It is clear, however, that the population density on each side of the Delaware and around its estuary was very low: one observer, in 1670, speaks of no more than 1,000 men capable of bearing arms.[23] There can be no doubt that all these factors – the Indians' unwarlike mentality, feeble weaponry and low population density – made it possible for their relations with the Europeans to develop peacefully even before Penn's arrival.

When he reached Delaware Bay in October 1682, Penn, unlike the other English colonizers in North America, had definite notions about how to organize relations between settlers and Indians. We have already given a foretaste of these by quoting the favourable assessment of the Lenni Lenape in Penn's 1683 account of the Indians. There are, however, two documents written as early as 1681 which demonstrate the Quaker's readiness to extend to the Indians the toleration provided in the Frame of Government. On 16 October 1681 Penn composed an 'Address to the Indians' for his representatives to read to the coastal tribes. It begins:

> My Freinds [sic]
> There is one great God and Power that hath made the world and all things therein, to whom you and I and all People owe their being and wellbeing, and to whom you and I must one Day give an account, for all that we do in this world: this great God hath written his law in our hearts, by which we are taught and commanded to love. . . .[24]

Penn goes on to explain that it has pleased this great God, through the will of the King of England, to transfer to him this part of North America, and that he wishes to enjoy it with the 'love and consent'[25] of the Indians, with whom he means to live as a friend and neighbour. Penn further assures them that, unlike other colonists in the New World, he does not intend to seek his own profit at the expense of the indigenous population, and that his fellow settlers share his views. A second text contains specific instructions to his representatives, particularly about the founding of Philadelphia:[26] this likewise recommends a loving and understanding approach to the Indians, for, says Penn, 'we have their good in our eye, equall with our own interest.'[27]

These two early documents contain the essence of Penn's scheme for relations between Europeans and Indians, and also of the contradictions latent within his scheme. There is no mistaking the difference between Penn's 'Address to the Indians' and the *Requerimiento* of the Spanish Crown jurist Palacios Rubios, the hortatory declaration which the conquistadors used to read to the Indians of Central and South America. The *Requerimiento* proclaimed that the Pope had bestowed overseas territories upon the Kings of Spain, commanded the Indians to submit to Spain and accept Christianity, and warned that if they refused they would be subjugated by warlike means and set to forced labour. The Spaniards' anthropological notions followed the Aristotelian assumption that humanity was naturally divided into masters and servants, civilized people and barbarians.[28] Penn followed George Fox, the founder of the Society of Friends, in assuming that all people were to be regarded equally as God's creatures and hence that, irrespective of their religious beliefs and practices, they should be considered capable of apprehending the divine voice, 'the Christ within'.[29] As a child of God, the Indian belonged to the Christian community even before receiving the sacrament of baptism through the intermediacy of a priesthood. Biblical history seemed to provide additional evidence that the Indians were not all that distant from the Christian world. Both the Puritans of New England and the Quakers to the south were inclined to see the Indians as descendants of one of the ten tribes of Israel which had been defeated and taken captive by the Assyrians in 722 BC. This event, it was argued, meant that the Indian peoples had left the main avenue of historical development for a by-path, but had not dropped out of history altogether.[30] For Puritans and Quakers holding such views, the conversion of the Indians had implications very different from those present in the sixteenth-century Catholic doctrine of colonialism. On the English view, the question whether or not the inhabitants of overseas territories were converted had no bearing on their status as colonial subjects, and hence no tempers were raised in the discussion as to whether conversion should be performed by force, gentle persuasion, or not at all.

While the English colonists all agreed that the Indians were children of God and essentially akin to themselves, Quakers and Puritans neverthe-less held significantly differing views on one important matter. When the conduct of the Indians deviated from European standards, the New Englanders were disposed to interpret this as an aberration and to attribute it to diabolical possession, while the Quakers, in this matter as in others, were considerably more tolerant in their judgements. For example, the Indian dances, which both the Puritans and the French Jesuits in Canada roundly condemned as obscene, are judged with remarkable mildness in Penn's *Account of the Lenni Lenape*: 'Their Postures in the Dance are very Antick and differing, but all keep measure. This is done with equal Earnestness and Labour, but great appearance of Joy.'[31] Doubtless it was this tolerance that, along with other factors such as the absence of a firm ecclesiastical structure, gave missionary activity a low priority among the concerns of the Pennsylvania Quakers.

Not only were the Quakers unquestionably sincere in wishing to establish peaceful, indeed friendly relations with the Indians, as Penn's early remarks on founding the colony show; they attached no less importance to the hope of combining the Indians' good with the advancement of their own interests. In order to achieve this, Penn behaved with the utmost circumspection. The land transfer agreements concluded by the owner of the colony or his representatives adhered precisely to the English legal criteria of the day and assured the Lenni Lenape that they were being treated as equal partners as well as receiving appropriate and satisfactory payment. The Quakers also considered it important to give the Indians a full explanation of the content and implications of the agreements and to conclude them without exercising pressure, using unfair means of persuasion, or providing alcoholic drinks.[32] The accredited representatives of both parties authorized the agreements by signatures or signs; important discussions were recorded in memoranda; and the Indians acknowledged the receipt of goods and wampum strings equivalent in value to the land.

Penn was at pains to avoid the abuses that had emerged hitherto in dealings between Englishmen and Indians on the East Coast. Thus, as early as the spring of 1682, he forbade alcohol to be given to the Indians, renouncing what was generally seen as a highly effective source of influence because he recognized its corrupting results.[33] As was mentioned earlier, Penn's land transfer agreements went beyond the provisions of the Charter, which did not regard the Indians as legal owners of land. Occasionally, too, pieces of land already sold by the Indians to other settlers who had been prevented by circumstances from occupying or keeping them were acquired once more by Penn, in order to clarify the legal situation. He also arranged for the agreements, once concluded, to be read aloud again and thus renewed at regular intervals: this was a skilful way of acknowledging the importance of oral tradition among the Indians, and events were to prove that it established a tradition of friendly and neighbourly relations. Finally, the Indians were also assured of their right to bring disputes with white settlers directly to the Governor, and although this did not constitute an independent tribunal, it did permit the amicable settlement of many minor differences. The full instructions for his representatives that Penn composed in July 1681 recorded the conditions for the purchase of land in minute detail and reaffirmed his wish that the Indians should be treated justly and humanely. This remarkable document enjoins

> that noe man shal by any wayes or means in word or Deed, affront or wrong any Indian, but he shall Incurr the Same Penalty of the Law as if he had Committed it against his Fellow Planter . . . that the Indians shal have Liberty to doe all things Relateing to the Improvement of their ground and provideing Sustenance for their Familyes, that any of the planters shall enjoy.[34]

Despite such consideration, it was impossible to avoid certain ambiguities, which later helped to strain relations between Europeans and Indians. Thus, the parties to an agreement did not usually possess sufficient geographical knowledge to define the precise extent and value of the area that was to change hands. They took their bearings from landmarks such as tall trees or rock formations, and were often vague in specifying distances, especially inland in a westerly direction. A further difficulty arose from the fact that for a long time the Quakers were ill-informed about the social structure of the Lenni Lenape. Hence, it sometimes happened that treaties were concluded with individual Indians who had not received the necessary authority from their tribe, and a tendency developed among the Quakers' representatives to assume that anybody willing to sell must also be authorized to sell.

Most serious was the fact that the Indians, unacquainted with European notions of property and accustomed to frequent changes of residence, could never fully accept that these land transfer agreements were final. To Penn's credit it may be said that unlike the founders of other colonies, who disingenuously spoke of 'the right to use land' when they really meant acquiring it, he always explained his intentions openly to the Indians. Also, instead of expelling the original inhabitants from their settlements, he sought to devise acceptable transitional arrangements. However, even Penn did not fully understand how profoundly the relations between Europeans and Indians were being transformed by the new element, the colonial acquisition of land. He believed it possible to continue acting on the principles of reciprocity, of *do ut des*, which had so far governed the largely peaceful fur trade on the East Coast, and he hoped that by behaving in a more liberal, honest and understanding fashion than others, he would be able to integrate the acquisition of land into existing practice. His Christian paternalism did indeed manage to maintain the illusion of harmonious relations over a period of almost sixty years – something practically unique in the history of relations between cultures – but he misunderstood the significance of this historic process.

Penn's task, as he understood it before God and history, was to provide his co-religionists and other oppressed religious minorities with a new home across the Atlantic, and he measured the success of this enterprise primarily by the number of those who succeeded in constructing a better life on the Delaware. Although the relationship with another culture founded on the love of God and one's neighbour, postulated by Penn, was of considerable importance within the Quakers' view of the world, it was secondary to his main task. When the influx of settlers far exceeded all expectations, it never occurred to Penn or his successors to restrict immigration for the sake of the Indians whom it threatened, for to do so would have meant denying the governing idea of this colony, which was based on toleration of persecuted fellow Christians. To let these fellow believers settle and achieve economic security, to create a shared social and political ethos, and to develop a way of life which would permit the industrious to attain a level of material well-being sufficient to guarantee respectability and stability without any display of opulence: these were the priorities to which Penn, who was perfectly capable of hard-headed and profit-minded calculation, directed his attention.[35] Yet each European immigrant who saw the chance of making a new start for himself and his family in Pennsylvania thereby reduced the chances of the Indians. The Society of Friends, whose philanthropic sensibility was unquestionably sincere and exceptional for its time, was unable either to prevent this fateful development or to steer it in a direction that would have been acceptable to the Indians in the long run.[36]

The first treaty of friendship and land transfer between the Quakers and the Lenni Lenape was concluded in July 1682 by one of Penn's representatives, his cousin William Markham. The territory being transferred was in what is now Bucks County, in north-east Pennsylvania: its purchase price was a relatively high one, including 350 wampum strings, twenty rifles, two barrels of gunpowder, forty pairs of stockings, 200 knives, forty axes, various fabrics, tobacco, and − even then − some alcohol.[37] One of the earliest agreements with the Indians in which Penn was personally involved was made, probably in the spring of 1683, under a large elm tree in the Indian village of Shakamaxon, within the city boundaries of present-day Philadelphia. We have no written records of this event, but we do possess pictures by artists of Quaker origin which, though painted in the following century, do attempt to capture the spirit of the encounter, perhaps idealizing but not consciously distorting it. They include the famous painting 'Penn's Treaty with the Indians' (1771) by Benjamin West, who was born in Pennsylvania in 1738 and later attained fame in England. It portrays Penn amid his fellow Quakers, unarmed, dignified and clearly trustworthy, giving a roll of cloth to the Lenni Lenape and Tamanend, one of their chiefs. The Indians, in their nakedness, posture and facial expression, comply with the neoclassical demand for 'noble simplicity and calm grandeur' formulated by the German art critic Winckelmann, whom Benjamin West had met in Rome. West's painting is obviously intended as something more than the record of a historic moment; it becomes an allegory of friendship between nations, a symbol of how God's gift of all-embracing love can overcome the differences of race, manners and levels of civilization produced by geography and history.[38]

A series of paintings by Edward Hicks (1780–1849) alludes to the encounter under the Shakamaxon elm tree in a quite different but no less impressive manner. Like West, Hicks was a Quaker from Pennsylvania, but far from imitating West's ascent to academic honours and the position of court painter, he tried to supply his material needs by painting inn-signs and his spiritual needs by preaching. Hicks was one of the most important naïve painters in the history of American art. Under the title 'A Peaceable Kingdom' he painted Pennsylvanian landscapes transfigured by Utopian radiance. Over fifty versions survive, which suggests that these paintings were much in demand. Following Isaiah's prophecy that the time is at hand when the wolf shall dwell with the lamb and the sucking child shall play on the hole of the asp,[39] Hicks, awkwardly and movingly, recreated the lost paradise in his paintings, where wild beasts sport peacefully with the children of Pennsylvanian settlers. The background never fails to show Penn, surrounded by Indians, as though elevated to a higher but still human plane. From their very different social viewpoints, both painters, West and Hicks, evoke a phase of relations between Europeans and Indians which perhaps never existed in that form, and certainly did not exist in their time. Nonetheless, their paintings demonstrate that Penn's longing to establish the European–Indian relationship in undisturbed harmony was still very much alive in the late eighteenth and early nineteenth centuries.

Historical development, however, followed a more arduous course. During the two years of Penn's first visit to North America, from 1682 to 1684, he certainly succeeded in establishing relations with the Indians on a firm basis of mutual trust. Chief Tamanend promised, in a much-quoted speech: 'We will live in love with Ona [the Indian name for Penn] and his children as long as the creeks and rivers run, and while the sun, moon, and stars endure.'[40] It did indeed look as though Penn's meetings with various Indian delegations had founded a lasting agreement, 'the only treaty', as Voltaire later wrote admiringly, 'that was never sworn and never broken.'[41]

Yet it must not be forgotten that Penn's Indian policy was only a part of the activities that he pursued tirelessly during his brief first visit: for example, the colony's founder attached scarcely less importance to planning its capital, Philadelphia. The original intention was to clear 10,000 acres of land between the Schuykill and Delaware Rivers for this purpose. This area soon had to be reduced to some 1,250 acres, roughly the extent of the present-day city centre; nonetheless, until the American Revolution Philadelphia was still the city with the largest population and the greatest cultural importance in the entire British Empire. Its founder wanted Philadelphia to be 'a greene Country Towne',[42] a spacious, well-ordered, peaceful city laid out on a grid pattern, in which even the smallest plot of land would still have room for a modest house with a front garden. The peaceful intentions of the city's inhabitants were to be demonstrated by the absence of any fortifications on the perimeter, and its broad avenues, still today known simply by the names of indigenous trees, were expressly designed to allow traffic and social encounters, but not parades and processions.[43]

For the most part, the problems of demarcating the territory and founding the city could be satisfactorily solved, thanks to Penn's expertise, oratorical powers, and charm, as well as his co-religionists' selfless support. However, his constitutional projects and his method of allotting land soon met with resistance. It was chiefly the colonists who did not belong to the Society of Friends, and who had settled in this region before 1682, who opposed the extensive privileges conferred on the Governor and Provincial Council by the Frame of Government. As early as April 1683 Penn was obliged to agree to a modification of his Constitution. Thereafter the members of the Assembly incessantly criticized the supremacy vested in the Governor, demanding that they should not only be consulted about draft legislation but have the right to propose legislation themselves. Moreover, the less well-off colonists, Quakers among them, accused Penn of allocating land in an arbitrary and partisan way, and instances of patronage did demonstrably occur.

Complications also arose in dealings with the proprietor of neighbouring Maryland, Lord Baltimore, who considered himself the rightful owner of land that was also claimed by Penn. Although both parties to the dispute liked to refer to their own piety, the surviving correspondence shows that they, like other people, had difficulty in reconciling their principles with their interests.[44] It was this conflict that made Penn abandon his original plan of taking up permanent residence in Philadelphia and return home in August 1684, in order to bring his frontier disputes with Lord Baltimore before the English courts.

By 1690, if not earlier, it was obvious that the Holy Experiment was in jeopardy and that the beliefs of the Society of Friends were better suited to private life than to government. One reason for its collapse was the Quakers' ultimate failure to convince other denominations of their high claims to civic integrity; but another, however paradoxical it may sound, was that the Quakers took their moral scruples to excess and thus disqualified themselves from government, by the standards both of English law and of political realities.[45] In the long run, for example, the right to refuse to take an oath, which had been demanded by the Society of Friends and included in the Frame of Government, proved incompatible with English law, which required an oath to be taken by an official on the latter's admission to office and by anyone testifying in court. It was admittedly possible for some time to conduct the business of government by replacing the oath with such formulae as 'in the presence of Almighty God': later, however, the more punctilious Quakers were increasingly excluded from positions of responsibility. The Quakers displayed an equal lack of realism in their resolute pacifism, which meant, among other things, refusing to form military units even for purposes of self-defence. After 1732, as relations between Indians and Europeans rapidly deteriorated, this attitude left settlers on the borders of Pennsylvania defenceless against attacks and enabled enemy warships to enter Delaware Bay unopposed during the naval conflicts between England and France. This state of affairs angered many colonists and was unacceptable to the Crown. Accordingly, William III, who had ascended the British throne after the 'Glorious Revolution' of 1688, found himself compelled to deprive the colony temporarily of its autonomy and order the Governor of New York to ensure that it was defended by military forces.

Penn fought for the survival of his Holy Experiment until his death in 1718. In 1699 he again crossed the Atlantic in order to reconcile the various factions that were at loggerheads over the form of government, the relation between religion and politics, and the allocation of land. In 1701, shortly before returning once more to England, Penn agreed to a new Constitution, known as the Charter of Privileges. By comparison with the Frame of Government of 1682 this revision was a clear move towards democratization, in that it assigned full legislative powers to the Assembly, sharply curtailed the rights of the proprietor, and reduced the influence of the Provincial Council, which retained only an advisory function. The new Constitution, probably the most liberal to be found in any English possession across the Atlantic, was to remain in force until 1776.[46] Even if Penn ultimately failed to introduce into politics what he imagined as the uncompromising purity of the Christian life, much of the spirit of the Society of Friends survived, and not just among its devotees. A tolerant attitude towards different beliefs, and a tendency to judge political decisions by their ethical quality, have remained particularly influential in the history of the state of Pennsylvania. This disposition was probably crucial in enabling Philadelphia to become a centre of resistance against Britain during the turmoil of the War of Independence, and to appear the appropriate birthplace for a new democratic order.

Given the tensions among the settlers, as well as between them and the Crown, which characterized the colony's early decades, how did relations between the Europeans and the Indians develop? We have already pointed out that the accommodating, tolerant, but paternalistic manner of dealing with the Lenni Lenape, recommended and practised by Penn, ensured that the relationship remained virtually untroubled by conflict for almost sixty years, from 1682 to 1737 – a unique state of affairs in the history of European–Indian relations, and one to which historians have given due credit. From 1732 a profound change began to be discernible. Here as elsewhere, the fur trade supplied something of a guarantee that contacts would remain peaceful. Even by the turn of the century, however, owing to changes in European fashions, the trade in beaver skins was beginning to decline, while deer, though still in demand in Europe, had become rare or close to extinction in these regions. Subsequently, relations with the Indians were increasingly dominated by dealings in land. By 1720 Philadelphia had grown into a city of 10,000 inhabitants, in which trade, crafts and shipbuilding were flourishing, and the Lenni Lenape who lived and hunted between the Schuykill and the Delaware had been forced to move further to the north-west. A series of land transfer agreements, the most important being those of 1683, 1684, 1718, 1732, 1736 and 1737, extended the colony's territory as far as the Susquehanna River, about sixty miles west of Philadelphia: it is estimated that in 1720 roughly 19,000 white farmers, hunters and fur-traders were living in this area of settlement.[47] Although Penn's relatives and their capable adviser James Logan, who negotiated these purchases, continued to appeal to the spirit of their colony's founder, there was no mistaking the new energy and ruthless single-mindedness animating the settlers' expansionism. Although the letter of written agreements was still respected, verbal assurances, such as Penn's promise never to expel Indians from their homes by force, were forgotten, despite frequent appeals to them by the indigenous population.[48]

Another important factor in this process of change was connected with political developments within the Indian community. At the turn of the century the Lenni Lenape had become subordinate to the Iroquois federation of the Six Nations, which numbered 16,000 people among its constituent tribes and was thus the principal power among the native population of the east coast. It is no longer possible to reconstruct precisely how the Lenni Lenape became attached to the Six Nations, but we know that in 1712 they sent a delegation to deliver tribute to Onondaga (the present-day Syracuse), the capital of the Iroquois Federation.[49] It would also appear that the Iroquois, who were in the habit of referring contemptuously to the Lenni Lenape as 'women', made them painfully aware of their insignificance by forbidding them to wage wars or conclude treaties. These developments were closely followed by

James Logan, an experienced business man who was exceptionally well-informed about the Indians. He resolved to discuss Pennsylvanian affairs in future with representatives of the Six Nations directly. By this decision and through lavish gifts he gained the sympathy and support of the Iroquois but forfeited the friendship of the Lenni Lenape, who rightly felt that they had been cheated.

In trying to strengthen links with the Six Nations and their allies, Logan of course had the ulterior purpose of countering the threat posed by French settlement in North America. During the seventeenth century the French, established at the mouth of the St Lawrence, had reached the Great Lakes region and explored the Mississippi and its tributaries. Early in the following century they had established several forts at strategic points in the interior, particularly in the Ohio valley. Although with roughly 70,000 settlers they were far inferior to the English, whose colonists numbered some 1,650,000,[50] the French had for the most part managed to remain on the right side of the Indians, chiefly by concentrating on trade relations. The advance westward by the English colonists and the mounting hostility between Britain and France in Europe made it inevitable that conflict would also arise in the New World. Logan deserves credit for perceiving this pattern in good time and by ensuring, through his approach to the Iroquois, that the war would be fought from as strong a position as possible. On the other hand, there is no ignoring the fact that his far-sighted strategy reduced the Lenni Lenape, whose peaceableness, mildness and natural courtesy had been so highly praised by Penn and the first settlers, to mere pawns in the power game played over their heads for interests alien to them.

This was the situation when, in autumn 1737, there occurred that memorable incident which has gone down in North American history as the 'Walking Purchase'. Once again the settlers wanted more land: this time an area on the upper Delaware which the English claimed had been transferred to Penn by agreement several years before. Although the Lenni Lenape had good grounds for disputing this, they finally yielded to the massive pressure exerted by the colonists and declared their readiness to give up as much of the territory in question as a man could walk round in a day and a half.[51] The Indians assumed that a man walking over rough terrain would be able to cover no more than thirty miles, taking time off to hunt, rest and eat. What Logan organized, however, was not a march but a race. First, the chosen route was cleared as far as possible of bushes and similar obstructions; then three outstandingly strong and well-trained runners were sent out, one of whom actually covered a distance of almost seventy miles. Realizing that they had been swindled, the Lenni Lenape resolved not to evacuate their dwellings without resistance; but voices were also raised among the Quakers and in the

Assembly to demand fair treatment for the Indians. Thereupon, Logan, with Penn's descendants and some prosperous Quakers, turned to the Iroquois. By distributing lavish presents this faction succeeded in gaining the support of the Six Nations and inducing them to bring pressure to bear on the Lenni Lenape, their subjects. In 1742 the Iroquois sent a spokesman to the council of the Lenni Lenape who told the latter in no uncertain terms that they were women, wholly incapable of concluding treaties, and should clear off immediately without any further debate or argument.[52] This menacing command, uttered not by white settlers but by one of their kinsmen (albeit at the Europeans' instigation), finally forced the Lenni Lenape to submit. Most of them, accompanied by the Shawnee Indians who lived to the north-west, migrated to the Ohio River region, where the French greeted them as welcome allies.

The Walking Purchase was the end-result of long-standing latent incompatibilities and misunderstandings, and also of a deliberate change of policy towards the Indians which had been carried out within a few years. It thus marks the conclusion of a promising phase of inter-cultural relations. As often happens in historical processes which reflect the growing estrangement of two groups, it was left to chance to decide when and how the final rupture became manifest. Under different circumstances, an incident like the Walking Purchase could just as well have occurred a few years earlier or later. There is no doubt that the growing mutual estrangement of the Europeans and the Lenni Lenape entered a critical phase when the 'proprietorial party', led by Logan, realigned its policy towards the Indians by seeking an alliance with the Iroquois. This realignment resulted in turn from an increase in hostility between Britain and France, both in Europe and the New World, which was astutely judged by the colonists.

It is indisputable that after the day of the Walking Purchase, 19 September 1737, the innocence and hopefulness which had marked the first encounter between Quakers and Indians had vanished, never to return. The Utopia of the Holy Experiment was lost for ever. The spring of 1754 saw the first clashes between Virginian militia and French troops at Fort Duquesne, the present-day Pittsburgh, and in the following year the French and their Indian allies inflicted a defeat on General Braddock, who was fresh from England and unfamiliar with conditions in America. Thereupon, the Lenni Lenape and Shawnee Indians, egged on by the French colonists and by their own thirst for revenge, began to attack the farms in western Pennsylvania, killing the inhabitants and laying waste the fields. The frontier settlers were defenceless against these attacks, since the Assembly, dominated by punctilious Quakers, was not prepared to abandon its pacifist policy and vote credits for raising a militia. Not until the end of 1755, at Benjamin Franklin's instigation, were the financial means made available for defence – a historic decision, since it marked the exact point at which the Quakers' political influence ceased to control the destinies of Pennsylvania. The undeclared frontier war in North America, known to American historians as 'the French and Indian war', spread to Europe in May 1756 and led to the Seven Years' War, which Winston Churchill was not far wrong in calling 'the first world war'.[53] As was only to be expected, at least in the overseas territories, the Seven Years' War, despite initial French successes, ended with a decisive British victory, and in the Peace of Paris (1763) France handed over Canada and all her possessions east of the Mississippi to Britain. At the peace negotiations there was no mention of the Lenni Lenape, who had so unluckily forfeited the support of either side. Later, in the War of Independence, they were once more drawn into the white men's wars. Their scattered remnants still survive on reservations in Oklahoma and Ontario.

One may speculate about what might have become of the Indians of Pennsylvania if Penn's conception could have been given a permanent form. The immense influence exerted by Penn's personality during only two short visits to America remains astounding. The purity and humanity of the colonists' intentions may sometimes have been praised by historians in unduly glowing terms, but have never been seriously questioned. The first trustworthy biographer writes: '[ . . . ] if the fable of the *golden age* was ever verified, or a *paradisical state* introduced on earth, in reality, it has been universally acknowledged, they must have borne the nearest resemblance to that of *Pennsylvania!*'[54] A modern authority also arrives at a similar judgement: 'Pennsylvania came nearest of all the English colonies to a just and sensible handling of the problem. Until the middle of the eighteenth century, relations here between Indians and Europeans were, on the whole, cordial.'[55]

It would nevertheless be wrong to attribute the final collapse of this relationship solely to the new alliances sought by Logan and to the tensions preceding the French and Indian War. Although Penn never suspected it, the seeds of future conflict were already present in the very process of colonization. The acquisition of land, to take just one example, had fateful consequences because the Lenni Lenape's conception of property and their semi-nomadic way of life were ignored and because the goods offered as recompense made them dependent on European commerce. Daniel J. Boorstin has convincingly shown that Penn's paternalism failed to comprehend the historic importance and the implications of this procedure, and that instead of foreseeing and forestalling the profound conflict that was in the making, Penn tried to handle individual incidents on a day-to-day basis with the help of civilized manners and Christian charity.[56] A really serious policy of dealing with the Indians would have had to take precedence over the needs of the settlers, but this was ruled out by the godly plan on which this colonial enterprise was based. Such an Indian policy would have needed, first and foremost, to take account of the destabilizing effect which contact with Europeans exerted on the Lenni Lenape's own culture. The tradition that has come down to us testifies repeatedly to the settlers' lofty moral aspirations, but shows also that they were astonishingly imperceptive about the more indirect consequences of their encounter with the Indians. True, they recognized the corrupting influence of alcohol, and endeavoured to counteract it; true, they constantly urged their fellow colonists to behave themselves impeccably, hoping that this good example would be imitated. Yet the Quakers were strangely blind to the less obvious changes caused by their presence among the Indians. Not only did they fail to perceive the extent to which their own way of life, with their technological superiority and efficiency, undermined the cultural self-confidence of the Lenni Lenape, infecting this peculiarly sensitive people with doubt, disquiet, new expectations and new needs; they also paid little attention to the personality changes affecting the prominent Indians who functioned as intermediaries. This is a process of considerable interest to social psychologists, and one which has been described by Anthony Wallace, an authority on the encounter of cultures in Pennsylvania, in his biography of the important chief Teedyuscung, who remained to the last on peaceful terms with the Europeans:

> The individual Indian was finding that the equable and polite way of life, which had worked so well in the old days, was not rewarding when he dealt with Europeans, who regarded this equability merely as a fortunate lubricant for their own commercial machinery. The old techniques of social behavior were thus useless, and the Indian felt tricked and resentful, confused and bitter. In his uncertainty, with the whites before him as examples of successful brigands and also as punishing 'fathers' or 'brothers' (as they were collectively termed), he began to display 'white' personality characters – aggressiveness and ingratiation – which he acquired partly by conscious imitation and partly by the more subtle process of identifying himself with these punishing father-figures.[57]

The Quakers cannot have failed to notice that friendly dealings with the Lenni Lenape became more difficult as the years went by; but the astonishment with which they commented on this change shows how little they understood its causes.

Specific questions about the future conduct of relations with the Indians were seldom discussed by the Pennsylvania Quakers. Although Penn tried to avoid expelling the Lenni Lenape from their homes and to smooth the transition, he was very far from advocating social integration. Nor were any projects devised in Pennsylvania for resettling the Indians in reservations or 'reductions', like those developed by the Jesuits in South America. While the Quakers maintained the goal of Christianizing the Indians, they were easily discouraged by initial failures and never displayed any such theological zeal as the Spaniards had shown. If asked whether they intended to assimilate or subjugate the Indians, the Quakers would certainly have defended the idea of assimilation, but their actual conduct was evasive: thus, they were at pains to avoid discussing the topic of racial mixing. In the final reckoning, therefore, one must conclude that despite their undeniable resolve to treat the Indians peaceably and tolerantly, the Quakers did not understand the problem of cultural encounter in its historical setting, any more than they coped with it in practice. The principal concern of Penn and the Quaker settlers was to establish a community of the just in a territory which they had taken away from other people. The failure of the Holy Experiment was already implicit in this paradox. Thus it came about that the English colonists' cheerful certainty of performing the wishes of Divine Providence was finally matched among the Indians by an identity crisis, visions of decline, and passive fatalism interrupted occasionally by abrupt acts of violent resistance – a tragic nexus to which, in retrospect, there seems no possible solution.

# The 'Controlled Relationship'
## *The Europeans in China*

The colonial system developed by the Portuguese in the Eastern hemisphere in the fifteenth and sixteenth centuries was based on a loose network of trading stations on the edge of the ocean: it may be precisely defined as a maritime empire, and, given Portugal's limited resources, it could have been nothing else. These bases tended to be very much alike, with their fortifications and warehouses, with small contingents of Portuguese and the larger class of native middlemen, interpreters and officials; but the manner in which the Portuguese dealt with members of non-European cultures was not everywhere the same. It has been said of the Portuguese, perhaps too epigrammatically, that 'in the Atlantic they were explorers, in the Indian Ocean they were conquerors, and in the Far East they were businessmen.'[1] In fact, their voyages along the east and west coasts of Africa were dominated by problems of navigation and cartography, reinforcements and supplies. They did their best to avoid military involvement, seldom advancing into the interior or attempting colonization. Trade, and the cultural encounters it required, did not proliferate until the seventeenth century, when the growth of plantation colonies in Brazil and the Caribbean created an increasing need for African slaves. In the Indian Ocean, however, the Portuguese collided spectacularly with the Arab naval forces which controlled the area. In a small number of brilliant sea-fights, described by chroniclers with all the rhetoric of the Crusading tradition, they managed to break the Muslims' monopoly and to enter into mutually profitable relations with the coastal population. Finally, in the Far East, first in China and later in Japan as well, the encounter between Portuguese and non-Europeans had a different character again. The former found their freedom of action limited both geographically and socially: it was the Chinese and Japanese who decided where the two cultures should meet, who should take part, and which outside influences would be admitted. Subject to drastic controls, trade was tolerated, even welcomed; but the hosts made it plain that they did not need foreign trade and wanted to decide the terms of the encounter. It is this form of 'controlled relationship' between cultures that will be examined in the present chapter, taking China as an example.

The main source of information about the Middle Kingdom that was available to the Portuguese before they passed the Cape of Good Hope was Marco Polo's account of his travels, the *Book of the Wonders of the World*.[2] The Venetian had visited the Far East in the late thirteenth century, had spent seventeen years in the service of the powerful Mongol ruler Kublai Khan, and had travelled through much of his empire. Many of the marvels that Polo reported from 'Kitai' (China) have been confirmed by modern research. For his most famous readers, Henry the Navigator and Christopher Columbus, the book provided stimulus and guidance for their own projects. When the rumour spread through Europe that Columbus, contrary to his own assertions, had not found the sea route to Kitai after all,[3] the ambition of the Portuguese explorers was roused. In Calicut, Vasco da Gama's followers had heard how other foreigners, presumably Chinese, had visited the Indian coasts a few decades before their own arrival; these people were a kind of 'white Christians' who 'wore their hair long, like Germans, and had beards only around their mouths, like the cavaliers and courtiers of Constantinople.'[4] In Malacca, where the Portuguese arrived as early as 1509, Europeans and Chinese again encountered each other, almost two centuries after Marco Polo. When Afonso de Albuquerque's fleet anchored here in 1511, there were five Chinese junks in the harbour, whose crews, on reaching home, gave a favourable account of the approaching strangers. The Sultan of Malacca, who paid tribute to the Emperor of China, was less pleased by the appearance of the Portuguese. After vainly requesting military support from Peking, he capitulated to the newcomers.

It was probably in 1514 that the first Portuguese voyagers sighted the south China coast near what is now Hong Kong, and claimed sovereignty by erecting a pole with a coat of arms attached to it.[5] Detailed information about the first encounter comes from the letters of two Italians in the service of the Portuguese. One of these describes the Chinese as follows:

> They are people of great skill, and on a par with ourselves but of uglier aspect, with little bits of eyes. [ . . . ] During this last year some of our Portuguese made a voyage to China. They were not permitted to land; for they [the Chinese] say 'tis against their custom to let foreigners enter their dwellings. But they sold their goods at a great gain, and they say there is as great profit in taking spices to China as in taking them to Portugal.[6]

Similar hopes were inspired by the report of another visitor to China, who reached the Bay of Canton in 1515 and declared on his return that 'the Chinese wanted peace and friendship with the Portuguese and that they were a very good people.'[7]

Two years later the first official Portuguese embassy arrived in the Bay of Canton, bearing a letter from King Manuel to the 'King of China'. The leader of this delegation, Fernão Peres d'Andrade, asked the commander of the Chinese coastguards for permission to sail up the Pearl River to Canton, and, after some delaying manoeuvres, he was supplied with pilots. At the end of September 1517 Fernão Peres arrived with his ships in Canton, where he hoisted flags in greeting, and terrified the Chinese, to whom this custom was unknown, by firing a salute. When the city authorities remonstrated indignantly that he had entered by force and behaved improperly, the Portuguese replied apologetically, declaring that he had come to pay tribute; he also agreed, together with his followers, to await the arrival of the Governor-General of Kwang-si province and to practise the ceremonial which was indispensable for meetings with Chinese dignitaries. After discussions had proceeded satisfactorily, the Portuguese were permitted to land and engage in trading. The Governor-General promptly informed the Emperor of this unprecedented event, the appearance of a hitherto unknown nation, and requested further instructions; the Portuguese for their part left an authorized agent, the courageous apothecary Tomé Pires, in Canton, with directions to go to Peking as soon as he received the requisite permission.

The impression made by the first naval visit by Europeans to Canton was described by a Chinese official as follows:

In the year Chengte *ting-ch'ou* [1517], when I was secretary of the provincial government in Canton, and was acting as deputy for the commissioner in charge of merchant shipping, there suddenly appeared [one day] two large sea-going ships, which sailed in towards Canton, right up to Huaiyüan-i. They said that they brought tribute from the land Folangchi. The person in charge of their ship was called Chiapitan [Captain]. The crew all had prominent noses and deep-set eyes. Their heads were all wrapped round with a white cloth, like the dress of the Mohammedans. I immediately made a report to the Governor General [of the provinces of Kuangtung and Kuangsi] Lord Ch'en Hsi-hsüan, with the personal name Chin, who was staying at Canton. Since these people did not know the rites, I arranged that they should be practised in the ceremonies for three days in Kuanghsiao-szu [a mosque] and then be led to the audience [with the Governor-General]. As it is not laid down in the *Collected Statutes of the Ming Empire*, that this land brings tribute, I submitted a complete report on the matter to the throne.[8]

In 1520, with immense pomp and some not unfounded expectations of opening up lucrative trade relations, Tomé Pires and a few Portuguese companions set off on the long road to Peking, but their reception at the hands of the supreme dignitaries of the Empire was the most ungracious imaginable. Pires was not admitted to an audience with the Emperor: the authorities burnt the letter from the King of Portugal, refused to accept presents, and showered the delegation with reproaches. This response was probably due to incidents which had occurred meanwhile on the coast and had been reported to Peking. In August of the previous year a brother of Fernão Peres d'Andrade, a domineering character devoid of diplomatic skill, had arrived before the Bay of Canton and caused general alarm by his bullying manner. Simão Peres d'Andrade refused to pay the Chinese the usual customs duties, administered justice according to his own whims, and began building fortifications in the teeth of opposition: indeed, it was even rumoured that the Portuguese kidnapped the children of noble Chinese families in order to roast and devour them. For the time being, Andrade's foolish behaviour put paid to any prospect of continuing the relationship between Portuguese and Chinese, despite the promising start that had been made. Tomé Pires's embassy was conducted back to Canton under guard and imprisoned there; Pires died in captivity in 1524. The Chinese were no longer prepared to co-operate, nor could they be compelled to do so by Portuguese arms. After 1522 European seafarers were forbidden on pain of death to enter Chinese coastal waters.

The behaviour of the Chinese, during these first contacts and subsequently, only becomes intelligible if some fundamental facts about the political and conceptual structure of their powerful empire are borne in mind. What was novel about the encounter between the Chinese and the Portuguese was that both their cultures possessed a long historical tradition of unquestioned ethnocentrism. China regarded itself as the centre of the inhabited world, to a more exclusive degree than Western Christendom had ever done. It was thanks to internal colonization by the Romans that Europe, laboriously and amid constant perils, had begun to develop a certain cultural self-awareness; but Chinese texts reveal that long before this the Middle Kingdom already considered itself the heartland from which all refinement and culture radiated to the states outside, whose importance diminished in proportion to their distance from the heartland. The figure of the Emperor, whose actions are sanctioned by Heaven and who is consequently called the 'Son of Heaven', symbolizes and underpins this claim to global priority. After Mongol rule was swept away in 1368 by the founder of the Ming dynasty, Chu Yüang-chang, this old-established sense of superiority became linked with a distinct national awareness. Under the Ming dynasty (1368–1644) order and internal cohesion were restored, apart from a few local disturbances. The unity of China was strengthened by administrative reform and by carefully defining the responsibilities of the central and provincial authorities. In relation to the outside world, the rebuilding and partial extension of the Great Wall became a symbol of national revival, as did the fifteenth-century maritime expansion – something exceptional in Chinese history – which explains why the Portuguese found Chinese already settled in Malacca. Internal conquests, mainly to the north-east of the Empire, laid the territorial foundations for present-day China; and the Chinese mustered enough strength to oppose the notorious attacks by Japanese pirates on their coastal regions more effectively than before, though without lasting success.[9]

It was this gigantic empire, with a highly developed economy generated by the improvement of communications and the creation of new centres of production, that the Portuguese stumbled on in 1514. The arrival of these strangers gave China no reason to hope for any benefits; nor (apart from the private interests of the trading population on the coast) had the Chinese any need to build up their foreign trade. Besides, as we have seen, the insolence of the Portuguese was not exactly calculated to arouse sympathy. In the Chinese sources the European voyagers are called 'Folangchi' or 'Feringhi', a word with distinctly pejorative overtones. A high court official expressed the general opinion when he summed up the earliest dealings with the Portuguese as follows:

> The Feringis are most cruel and crafty. Their arms are superior to those of other foreigners. Some years ago they came suddenly to the city of Canton, and the noise of their cannon shook the earth [ . . . ] Now if we allow them to come and go and to carry on their trade, it will inevitably lead to fighting and blood shed, and the misfortune of our South may be boundless.[10]

The word 'Folangchi', meaning 'Franks', probably became current through its use by Muslims staying at the imperial court: it is hardly surprising that these Muslims had no reason to employ the word as a compliment. The term 'Folangchi' was still in use in the seventeenth century, when the Dutch and English began to penetrate the Portuguese monopoly of trade in this part of the world. It is typical of the undiscriminating character of such verbal stigma that the Chinese seldom made any effort to distinguish individual European nations or to identify the people employed in the service of the Portuguese.

While the word 'Folangchi' still referred, though vaguely, to the regions from which the European voyagers came, other terms were in use which merely conveyed the gulf between the newcomers' level of civilization and that attained by the denizens of the Middle Kingdom. All these terms may be translated with reasonable precision as 'barbarians'; occasionally an attribute was added to distinguish European 'barbarians' from others, such as the Japanese or the Mongols.[11] These 'barbarians' were marked out by their inability to write Chinese and hence to gain access to the culture of the Empire and the full humanity shared by all cultivated Chinese; they should think themselves fortunate to be graciously received by high officials and dignitaries who deigned to accept their tribute. In Chinese there were various terms for 'barbarians' – some focusing on the external features distinguishing foreign nations, and some which laid more stress on their moral and personal inferiority. Thus the notion of 'Yi-ti', which had been current since long before the Christian era, emphasized that the barbarian defined himself by not being a Chinese ('Chu-hsia'); he could only lose the stigma of barbarism by forgetting his origins and becoming completely assimilated. The Cantonese word 'Fangim' was used similarly, as a Dominican traveller explained: 'Now they [the Chinese] hold not commerce with us under the name of Portugal, neither went this name to the Court when we agreed to pay customs; but under the name of *Fangim*, which is to say "people of another coast".'[12] The same source mentions another Chinese term for 'barbarians', apparently referring primarily to negative characteristics, when he writes: 'they suffered not a Portugal in the country, and for great hatred and loathing called them *Fancui*, that is to say "men of the devil".'[13]

The pronounced Sinocentrism variously expressed by the concepts of 'Folangchi', 'Fangim' or 'Fancui' had a visual counterpart in the ceremonial surrounding the payment of tribute. By appearing at the Imperial court at regular intervals in order to deliver their tribute, members of alien cultures expressed their obedient submission to the Chinese world order. This custom was already practised before the Christian era among the steppe peoples of Central Asia, and in the course of time it had developed into an elaborate ritual. Foreign visitors were obliged to wait until they had been instructed in the correct performance of this ritual. It centred on the 'kotow', in which the tribute-bearer knelt down three times and bowed his head to the ground nine times. Western visitors tended to interpret this 'kotow' as an act of submission which detracted from the authority of the rulers who had dispatched them. They did not sufficiently realize, of course, that it was a gesture of court etiquette with which everyone complied; the Emperor himself performed the 'kotow' before his symbolic ancestors in heaven and before his parents or their monuments. For the rest, the foreigners who visited the Emperor's seat to deliver their tribute were treated with great respect and courtesy. No efforts were spared to make their long journey as pleasant and as safe as possible. Visitors were invited to use the sedan-chair as a comfortable mode of transport, and were offered accommodation in the best inns along the way. The tributary gifts expected of them were mostly objects or goods of no great value which merited a place in the Imperial treasury as 'curiosities'. The presents given by the Emperor in return, mostly silks, were incomparably more precious, showing that the central government set greater store by prestige than by profit. Foreign embassies, on the other hand, were chiefly interested in the commercial opportunities which the payment of tribute might open up. Such commerce was permitted by an act of Imperial grace which must not be misinterpreted as a movement towards free trade based on natural law. The tribute system was instead an aspect of China's internal affairs, as is underlined by the unconcern of the Chinese about sending embassies or traders abroad: indeed, such forms of contact with the outside world were liable at times to be severely punished.

Yet the cultural arrogance of the Chinese should not be blamed for the failure of early trading contacts. The rupture of mutual relations in 1522 was principally the fault of the Portuguese. They had behaved insolently, refused to pay customs duties, and treated the local laws, customs and religion with disrespect. Presumably the Portuguese expected to succeed by the same tactics that had worked in India and, naturally, on the ill-defended Spice Islands.[14] In the case of China, they not only overestimated the extent of their own power; they also lacked any precise conception of the size of the country and failed to realize that here, in contrast with India, there was no prospect of exploiting local conflicts for their own ends.

For over thirty years, from 1522 to 1554, the Portuguese were officially excluded from trade with China. Admittedly a certain amount of smuggling went on, though its centre moved from the province of Kwangtung north-eastwards to the coastal waters of Fukien and Chekiang, where numerous offshore islands provided hiding-places. Many among the local population undoubtedly profited from such commerce and frustrated the efforts of officials to carry out the instructions they received from the central government, while European seafarers often collaborated with Japanese merchants and freebooters.[15] Since the Japanese, like the Chinese, were forbidden to go to sea and engage in foreign trade, the Portuguese enjoyed a remarkably complete monopoly and had a largely free hand in determining prices. After their accidental discovery of Japan in 1542, where the thunder of their cannon had aroused admiration (in contrast to the reaction of the Cantonese) and their more cautious behaviour had awakened goodwill, they had a new and exceedingly lucrative market. Until 1610, when the Dutch began to outstrip them in Japan, the Portuguese brought spices from India and the Moluccas to China, where they acquired silk and porcelain for Japan. The Japanese paid for these commodities in silver, which in turn could be disposed of in China for high prices. This Far Eastern trade triangle, of which C. R. Boxer has given a masterly description,[16] was to be crucial for the resurgence of Sino-Portuguese relations, once the Middle Kingdom had relaxed its ban on trade.

This occurred in 1554. For some time previously the provincial officials of the coastal districts had reported to Peking that the economy was sharply declining and the population was being reduced to poverty. Their enquiries whether the situation might be remedied by reopening Canton harbour met with a negative response from the central government. One such petition for the resumption of trade survives from the year 1530. The customs revenues that might be expected as the result of such measures, wrote the Provincial Governor, would not only bring his accounts into the black and make funds available for campaigns against pirates, but would increase the supply of the spices which were so much in demand at court. Admittedly, this petition expressly ruled out any dealings with the Portuguese and other Europeans accompanying them, and recommended an especially strict guard on the coasts near the mouth of the Pearl River.[17] Not until 1554 was the prohibition on Portuguese trade with China officially relaxed. Neither a Chinese nor a Portuguese version of the treaty survives (assuming such a treaty was actually drawn up). We do, however, possess a letter from Captain Leonel de Souza recounting how he managed to bring the prolonged negotiations with the Navy Superintendent in Canton to a satisfactory conclusion.

> In this manner [writes Souza] I concluded peace arrangements, and settled the affairs of the trade in China, whereby many have engaged in business and numbers accepted the opportunity of going safely to the City of Canton and other places, carrying on business freely, without hindrance. [ . . . ] All this entailed a great deal of trouble, far more than I can explain in writing, but there was no other way.[18]

If Leonel de Souza was dreaming of unrestricted trade and direct access to Canton harbour, then of course he was deluding himself. First, the Portuguese were assigned some islands at which they might land: only in 1557 were they permitted to establish a permanent settlement on the peninsula of Macao, west of present-day Hong Kong and about ninety miles from Canton.

We have given the name 'controlled relationship' to the type of cultural contact that developed in Macao from 1557 onwards, leading to considerable prosperity for both partners between 1580 and 1600. The name is intended to convey that one of the partners – China – was always in a position to determine the conditions and nature of relations between the two, with military force available as a last resort, while the other partner – Portugal – had to accept the terms offered. This did not, of course, prevent the subordinate partner from using every possible tactical device, from bribery to blackmail. Thus, it was clear from the outset that in allowing the Portuguese to settle on the Macao peninsula, China was in no way yielding its sovereignty over this territory – and the Portuguese knew this. It is true that in later centuries patriotic inhabitants of Macao have tried to use the scanty source material on the city's early history to reconstruct a formal cession of territory, and have claimed that Macao was acquired by conquest or given to the Portuguese in gratitude for their help in combating piracy.[19] It may be true that the Portuguese rendered good service in the fight against Japanese pirates, but this had no territorial results. To dispose of land, even for a suitable price, would have been wholly out of the question, if only because such a step was forbidden both by the instructions from the Imperial court regarding foreign policy and by the conception of the state held by the higher officials. It is also interesting to note that for many years Peking was kept in the dark about the first Portuguese settlers on Macao, obviously from fear that the action would be censured and countermanded by the Emperor, and that foreign trade would thus be nipped in the bud.[20]

The Chinese were strict in ensuring that the Portuguese remained incapable of fortifying Macao or capturing it by force. For a long time munitions and weapons were not allowed on land, or permitted only on a very small scale, and it was only after a Dutch attack in 1622 that permission was given to secure the base by a wall and to equip it with artillery.[21] Such concessions could, however, be revoked at short notice if orders to that effect arrived from Peking or if the simultaneous appearance of several ships gave the provincial government cause for concern. In such an event the Chinese might well order the fortifications to be razed.

The Chinese also showed who was master when they fixed the dues which the Portuguese had to pay. Besides a regular rent, which was increased from time to time, they demanded heavy customs duties and harbour dues; and officials' palms also had to be greased, as need and circumstances might dictate. A Spanish traveller reported in 1582:

> [The Portuguese of Macao] are still nowadays without any weapons or gunpowder, nor justice, having a Chinese mandarin who searches their houses to see if they have any such. And because it is a regular town with about five hundred houses and there is a Portuguese governor and a bishop therein, they pay every three years to the incoming viceroy of Canton about 100,000 ducats to avoid being expelled from the land, which sum he divides with the grandees of the household of the king of China. However, it is constantly affirmed by everyone that the king has no idea that there are any such Portuguese in his land.[22]

The control exercised by the Chinese over the relationship was particularly apparent in the restrictions placed on the settlers' freedom of movement. The peninsula was an inhospitable place, previously inhabited only by a few fishermen, and it was easily kept under surveillance from the mainland. Commercial dealings were confined as far as possible to Macao and its immediate surroundings; Chinese customs officials, very few of whom probably lived in the town itself, served as intermediaries. High Portuguese officials were occasionally invited to Canton for talks, but were allowed to spend only one day there. In 1565 an embassy that tried to set out for Peking to deliver tribute was turned back. In 1574, when the number of colonists had risen to over 10,000, the provincial government decided that the time had come to erect a wall, manned by guards, on the isthmus between the settlement and the mainland. The Portuguese who occasionally ventured into the interior had to provide themselves with a pass and go under an arch on which was inscribed the admonition: 'Dread our Greatness and Respect our Virtue.'[23]

This *Porta do Cerco* was opened chiefly when markets were held in Macao, about once a week; afterwards the door was again locked and sealed with strips of paper bearing official stamps. Since this was the only access to the mainland, and the channel through which the town was supplied with food, the Chinese could put the Portuguese under pressure, for whatever reason, simply by ordering the *Porta do Cerco* to be shut. The Dominican monk Navarrete writes in 1670:

> At a quarter of a League distant from that City, where the narrow part of that neck of land is, the Chineses [sic] many years ago built a Wall from Sea to Sea, in the middle of it is a Gate with a Tower over it, where there is always a Guard so that the People of Macao may not pass across, nor the Chineses to them. The Chinese have sometimes had their liberty, but the Portugueses were never permitted to go up the Country. Of late Years the Gate was shut; at first they open'd it every five days, when the Portugueses bought Provisions; afterwards it grew stricter, and was only open'd twice a Month. Then the rich, which were but very few, could buy a Fortnights Store; the Poor perish'd, and many have starv'd.[24]

This isolationist policy was not inconsistent with allowing the inhabitants of Macao self-government within their town boundaries, where they remained largely unmolested so long as they did not infringe the Chinese laws. Similar self-government by unassimilated marginal populations had been successfully tried out in China for hundreds of years, as in the case of the Arab and Persian trading settlements which were established at points along the south coast of China between the eighth and twelfth centuries. The Chinese did not regard self-government as a special privilege granted to or claimed by the foreigners. This concession was rather a mark of their contempt for the 'barbarians', who were considered incapable of understanding, let alone imitating, the cultivated manners of the Chinese, and who therefore might as well go on living in the barbarian fashion they were used to.

Little is known for certain about the beginnings of self-government in

Macao. We know that at the outset neither the Chinese government nor the Viceroy of Goa took the trouble to define the legal status of this outpost. Since its foundation an important supervisory function had been assigned to the *Capitão Mór da Viagem do Japão*, the General Captain of the Japan Fleet, who inspected the government on his visits to Macao.[25] Around the year 1560 a kind of mercantile republic began to develop, governed by a town council elected by those free subjects of the King of Portugal who had either been born or settled in Macao. The town council included the local commander (*Capitão da Terra*), a supreme judge (*Ouvidor*) and a bishop, supported by numerous officials: among the latter was a *Procurador* who was responsible for public works and had the important task of maintaining relations with the Chinese provincial government.

In 1582 doubts arose in Canton about this system of government, and the Chinese Governor-General summoned a delegation of the city fathers to discuss the matter. After some hesitation the town sent to Canton a judge with experience of dealing with mandarins, and a Jesuit priest. The two delegates were obliged to listen to severe reprimands, which they managed to appease by tactful speeches and costly presents. It is at this time that the Portuguese are thought to have received the first official guarantee of permission 'to live in the town, provided that they observe the laws of the Empire.'[26] Two years later the Emperor finally deigned to take note of what had been happening in Macao. He showed his interest by conferring on the *Procurador* the title of a mandarin of the second degree, thus incorporating him more closely into the Imperial system of government. In the official correspondence on these matters the *Procurador* is addressed as 'I-mu', literally 'Eye of the Barbarians',[27] which referred to what the Chinese considered his dual function of keeping an eye on his compatriots while simultaneously looking to their trading partner. At the same time, in 1586, the form of municipal government that Macao had adopted was also approved by the Viceroy of Portuguese India in Goa. Thereafter, Macao enjoyed a remarkable degree of independence both from the Viceroy and from the authorities in Portugal. The decisions of the aristocratic officials, the Fidalgos, carried little weight in Macao: influence remained in the hands of the local Portuguese mercantile class with their close-knit web of contacts and interests and their familiarity with the realities of Far Eastern trade and the Chinese mentality. Obviously, people in Goa and Lisbon were content so long as business in Macao went well and tax revenues arrived regularly: *dirigiste* intervention could only have done harm.

Kept at arm's length by Peking, keeping itself remote from Goa, Macao developed after 1580 into a community with a distinctive character and very marked self-confidence. Everything, not only politics but also personal relationships, was dominated by trade, and the resulting profits were reflected in the magnificence of the public buildings and the churches. Though hardly on a par with the buildings of Spanish Manila, these still astounded visitors, not least because of the town's impressive position on high ground. At the start of contact with the Portuguese the Chinese had already shown a demand for the goods which they promised to deliver. Demand continued to mount, not only for spices of all kinds from India and the Malay Archipelago, but also for precious luxury articles such as ivory, aromatic oils, exotic wood and European fabrics, especially velvet. Conversely, an increasing range of Chinese goods came to be sought overseas. Alongside silk, which in varying quality was disposed of mainly to the Japanese market, there were ornaments and trinkets, lacquered objects and painted porcelain, medicinal drugs and musk.[28] The variety of European and Oriental goods that passed through Macao was reflected in the appearance of the better-off townspeople, giving their clothes and the interiors of their houses a colourful and flamboyant tone which newly arrived travellers found very arresting.

It must be admitted that even in a flourishing period like the one that began around 1580, the relations between Chinese and Portuguese officials remained chilly and formal, even though both sides were well aware that their relationship was mutually profitable. Europeans regarded the mandarins' demeanour as markedly condescending, stiff and puppet-like, and the sources mention with some annoyance the inspection of ships and their cargoes, which was obviously conducted with a ritualized thoroughness that was doubly irritating.[29] A seventeenth-century Spanish observer, still under the sway of the conquistador mentality, was astonished that the Portuguese submitted so meekly and unresistingly to Chinese procedures.[30]

In other areas of contact, however, encounters between members of the two cultures were much less strained, sometimes even friendly. Within a 'controlled relationship', the opportunities for such informal exchanges occurred chiefly in connection with food supplies and the fitting-out of ships. Both these areas involved Chinese peasants, market traders and artisans who knew the habits of the Portuguese and were able to converse with them in 'Pidgin Portuguese'.[31] Outside the town there had developed agricultural enterprises where the Chinese grew European vegetables for the Portuguese, who did not like eating rice: these vegetables often found their way on to Chinese menus as well.[32] There were of course also small plantations, run by the Portuguese themselves with the help of imported black slaves; but the Chinese continued to find vegetable-growing attractive, since the colonists paid considerably higher prices than their fellow countrymen did. Though some provincial governors disapproved of this local trade and of the bustling markets in which it was carried on, they had to recognize that this also served the interests of the indigenous population. For whenever Peking sent renewed instructions to keep a sharper eye on the foreigners or to shut the land route to Macao, hardship resulted also for the Chinese in the district. Hence a provincial governor, in a particularly tense situation, wrote as follows to the Imperial court: 'If we maintain this strict supervision in Macao, then where will our people, once they have lost their livelihoods, find the money to buy our rice – assuming that we have rice to sell them? In the opinion of your humble servant, the people will be worn out within a few years and will starve to death.'[33]

No less so than with these peasants were the Chinese concerned with the upkeep and fitting-out of the ships and with supplying food for their crews. Transporting goods and people to and from the ships lying in the harbour, producing provisions, and performing running repairs all required a large number of workers, and native labourers and artisans soon managed to make themselves indispensable. It is not surprising that contacts with Chinese women sometimes led to marriage; what is surprising is that the Church sanctioned and supported such connections. In these cases the Chinese woman adopted the Catholic faith on getting married, but occasional conversions took place for other reasons. On baptism, the convert's Chinese name was replaced with a Christian one, and some converts also took up residence in Macao. It could likewise happen that Portuguese families adopted Chinese children, since it was considered an act of charity to provide young heathens with a Christian upbringing. For domestic service, black slaves seem to have been preferred; but Chinese servants, bought in their youth, were not uncommon. Within a few generations, these close contacts produced a largely mixed-race population, entirely free from racial prejudice, whose looks were admired by aesthetically inclined travellers. The Englishman Peter Mundy, who visited the town in 1637, gives a vivid description of this state of affairs when, after being invited to the home of a high Portuguese magistrate, he notes:

[ . . . ] wee were here served with weomen Maides, Chineses of his own household, boughtt by him, whereof every housekeeper here hath Many who are accompted among their household stuffe or Meanes; and by report but one woman in all this towne thatt was borne in Portugall; their wives either Chinesas [sic] or of thatt Race heretoffore Married to Portugalls.

[ . . . ] There were att thatt tyme in the house 3 or 4 very pretty Children, Daughters to the said Senor Antonio and his kindred, thatt except in England, I thincke not in the world to be overmatched For their pretty Feature and Complexion, their habitt or Dressing beecomming them as well, adorned with pretious Jewells and Costly apparrell, their uppermost garmentts beeing little Kimaones, or Japan coates, which graced them allsoe.[34]

The economic and cultural life of Macao, like its diplomacy, were dominated by the clergy, and especially by the Jesuit order, whose influence could be discerned in the subtlest social ramifications of town life. As early as 1562, ten years after Francis Xavier, one of the order's founders, had died within sight of the Chinese coast, the Jesuits built a simple wooden church and a hospice; in 1602 they completed the Cathedral of St Paul, whose magnificent façade has survived to the present day. It is true that the decades following Matteo Ricci's first visit to Peking in 1598 are the great age of the Jesuit mission in China; but the base from which their work started, Macao, was solidly established as their headquarters before the beginning of the seventeenth century. This is not the place to describe the Jesuit mission to the mainland, to show how the Fathers succeeded in exploiting such freedom of action as the 'controlled relationship' left them, or to follow the controversies that ultimately brought their missionary work to an end. All these matters have been dealt with in an extensive scholarly literature.[35] Some indication must be given, however, of how the order operated in Macao itself and of the close connection between business and politics that characterized their operations in China.

When one considers the Jesuit missions in other parts of the then known world, such as Paraguay or Canada, the extent to which they were affected by material, worldly desires is open to argument. Here, however, there is no question that the Jesuits of Macao were adroit dealers in a double sense. They not only invested vigorously in the China and Japan trade, but also succeeded in gaining the goodwill of business magnates whose donations they needed for their charitable work. The Crown did make several attempts to prevent the Jesuits from investing money and to transfer such activities to the Viceroy of Goa, but in vain. As the mission on the mainland grew in importance during the seventeenth century, the Jesuits extended their commercial commitments even further. They were, after all, often the only Portuguese who formed links with the Chinese and who had mastered the lofty art of knowing when to deliver tribute, administer bribes, serve as intermediaries and pocket their share of the profits. No wonder their business acumen, based on a close study of the Chinese mentality, aroused criticism from members of other orders. Thus, a Dominican monk from Manila, who as a Spaniard was in any case not particularly well disposed to the Portuguese, wrote as follows:

At Macao in China, where they had a theological college, a store was operated next door with direct communication to the college, so that the presiding Padre whose commercial acumen was considerable, could conveniently go backwards and forwards. [ . . . ] They speak of the dried radish-leaves which they consume for their nourishment, but make no mention of the very delectable chicken which follows.[36]

Peter Mundy, whom we have already met, was also struck by the symbiosis of money and spirit camouflaged by hypocrisy: 'For here these Padres trade in shipping, goodes, and building, alleadging the necessity off itt, as the greatt charge they are att in sending their breatheren to sundry ports where they have residences, with their Maintenance, etts. there.'[37] However, although he was an Englishman and a Protestant, Mundy was evidently very taken by the urbane life-style and entertainments offered by the Jesuits: he enjoyed dining in their stimulating company, never missed a theatrical production that they directed, and was impressed by the influence of Chinese culture apparent in numerous performances, such as children's dances. Ultimately, no doubt, it was the Jesuits' worldly sophistication, along with their readiness to meet an alien culture with tactful and polite interest, that made them best qualified to carry on the difficult dialogue with the learned officialdom of the Chinese Empire.

Early in the seventeenth century Macao's star began to sink. The principal reason for the decline in its economic prosperity was the intrusion of Dutch trading fleets, soon followed by English ones, into Asia. The annihilation of the Spanish Armada in 1588 was a severe blow not only for Spain but also for Portugal, which since 1580 had been annexed to the Spanish Crown under Philip II. Neither country was now in a position to guarantee the security of its Asian bases and the trade routes connecting them. From 1602 the Dutch began to gain a firm foothold in the Malay Archipelago, where they seized control of the spice trade and set up a powerful organization by founding the East India Company. In 1619 they founded Batavia (Jakarta) and made the 'Queen of the Eastern Seas', as the city proudly called itself, into the region's most important trading centre. In 1622 an attempt by its energetic governor, Jan Pieterszoon Coen, to conquer Macao came very close to succeeding. A Chinese source comments with apprehension and disquiet on the appearance of the 'red-haired barbarians', as the Dutch were called:

> They are covetous and cunning and have good knowledge of valuable commodities and are clever in seeking profits. They spare not even their lives in looking for gain and go to the most distant regions to trade. [ . . . ] Moreover, they are very ingenious people; the sails of their ships are like spider's webs so that they can be turned in all directions for wind, and go any where they want. If one meets them in the high seas, one is often robbed by them. [ . . . ] Wherever they go, they covet the rare commodities, and contrive by all means to take possession of the land.[38]

The Dutch and English continued to pose a threat even after the unsuccessful attempt at military conquest in 1622. Macao found itself obliged to demand support from Manila and Goa – reluctantly, because it thus increased its dependence on other colonies – and also built new fortifications in feverish haste. This illegal fortification in turn aroused the suspicion of the Chinese, who, having been further disquieted by malicious rumours, were afraid of an invasion, and even thought they already knew the name of the Jesuit priest who was to replace the incompetent rulers of the declining Ming dynasty on the Imperial throne. In the town itself there was unrest among the Chinese population, leading to temporary closure of the access routes and consequent starvation. Even before these events, the Chinese policy on foreign trade had vacillated between lenience and severity; now, as the Dutch and English appeared off the coast, anxious to participate in commerce, the situation became still more confused. On the one hand, the Chinese were inclined to form even closer links with the Portuguese so that they might confront further developments jointly; on the other, inhabitants of the coastal provinces were well aware of the advantages to be gained from breaking the Portuguese trade monopoly. From the account left by Mundy, whose English trading company arrived off the coast in 1637 with a proposal to open unrestricted commercial relations, one can discern what frantic diplomatic activity was unleashed by his ship's visit and by the new balance of power in the region.

Another major reason for Macao's commercial decline was the loss of the lucrative Japan trade. We have already mentioned the friendly reception given to the first Portuguese who reached Japan in 1542. A flourishing trade rapidly developed, and the expansion of missionary activity convinced the Jesuits that they had found their principal sphere of action at the extremity of the known world. About the year 1580 the total number of baptized Japanese Christians was estimated at 150,000, an enormous success in comparison with the twenty or so Chinese converts of which Macao could then boast.[39] In Japan, as later in China, the Jesuits concentrated on the higher levels of society, and they managed to convert several local rulers (Daimyô) to Christianity. In 1587, however, one of the most powerful of these rulers, Hideyoshi, unexpectedly turned against the missionaries and sought contact with the Dutch, who promised to deliver goods without saving souls as well. Members of the Jesuit order suffered savage persecution, as did the Japanese converts, thousands of whom were martyred. Commercial relations with Macao deteriorated drastically. Even today the reasons for this sudden change of mood by the Japanese are not known for certain. A later traveller whose impartiality can be relied on, the Swede Thunberg, cannot be far wrong in asserting that the Portuguese were dazzled by their astounding initial successes and treated the Japanese in an increasingly insolent and bullying fashion.[40] It is also likely that Hideyoshi, whose power base was insecure, correctly perceived that Christianity embodied a politically subversive force and that he could gain the sympathy of a majority of the population by attacking it. In 1639 all Portuguese were expelled from the country and all trade links broken off. The relevant edict runs: 'If a Portuguese ship should ever again enter a Japanese harbour, for whatever reason, be it dangerous seas or stormy weather, then the entire crew shall be executed to the last man.'[41]

In Macao, however, people were not yet willing to accept that the Japanese meant what they said. A new embassy was sent to Japan the following year, and received a terrible welcome: the leaders, and over fifty others, were beheaded after the briefest of trials, while the rest were set free so that they might report the event to Macao. Subsequently the Japanese confined their dealings to Portugal's arch-enemy, the Dutch, though strictly within the limits of a 'controlled relationship'. The Dutch were permitted to set up a trading-post on the artificial island of Deshima in Nagasaki harbour, just as clearly separate from the mainland as Macao was from China. However, the story of Dutch–Japanese trade, which was carried on very successfully for the next two centuries, belongs elsewhere.[42]

Macao's misfortunes abroad were accompanied by internal difficulties. Now that it had ceased to enjoy economic success, serious differences arose within the administration of the town. There had always been tension between rival monastic orders, and it now turned into open conflict. Artillerymen egged on by the Jesuits did not hesitate to fire at the Dominican monastery. The Viceroy of Goa tried unavailingly to restore peace. Although the news of the installation of the Duke of Braganza as King of Portugal in 1640 was celebrated with effervescent enthusiasm by both the Portuguese and the Chinese sections of the population, it did not lead to reconciliation. In the same year, the important base of Malacca fell into the hands of the Dutch, and diplomatic ineptitude caused a breach with the Spanish in Manila. Thereafter, Macao was overtaken by decline. The Spanish Dominican monk, Navarrete, who stayed in Macao about the year 1640, eloquently laments its political and moral disintegration, and concludes: 'The miserable State and wretched Condition the Portuguese do now, and have liv'd for some Years in these parts, might make them sensible, if Prejudice did not blind them, that their own Sins, and not those of others, have brought all these Misfortunes upon them.'[43] At all events, whether the townspeople or others were to blame, Macao's economic ascendancy was finally over. The town declined into comparative insignificance, though this very insignificance may well have helped to ensure its survival until the present day.

A final question: during the sixty or so years in which the Portuguese enjoyed satisfactory and often highly profitable relations with the giant Empire of China, what opinions did they form about that country and its inhabitants? It can be stated straight away that European sources hardly ever describe the Chinese as 'barbarians' or 'savages'. Obviously, the most superficial impression sufficed to remove any doubt that this was a civilized nation, whose manners might be strange and alien, but certainly not crude or unpolished. Accounts of China contain no hint of the condescending tone and the compassionate sympathy which so often govern the judgements of European travellers in Africa and Asia. It is true that many eye-witnesses felt superior to the Chinese in military strength, and, since they had no idea of the extent and populousness of the Empire, even talked of conquering it without difficulty. Thus, one of the earliest Portuguese accounts, by Tomé Pires, who had a weakness for hasty judgements and fanciful descriptions, declares that the Chinese are so weak and so easy to defeat that ten ships provided by the Viceroy of Goa would suffice to capture the entire southern coast.[44] In an essay on Portugese and Spanish projects for colonizing South-East Asia, C. R. Boxer draws attention to the extravagant, conquistador-like fantasies entertained by European voyagers and traders, and comments on 'this overweening self-confidence, which, if it involved the Spaniards and Portuguese in many disasters, was also largely responsible for many of their successes.'[45] It was not until fifty years after Pires that the Augustinian canon Martín de Rada provided a detailed and factual account of the military strength of the Chinese people, commenting not only on the inferiority of their artillery and fortifications, but also on the immense numerical superiority of their army.[46]

In social intercourse with the Chinese, however, the Portuguese often had a feeling of inferiority. Although they had ample social experience and were not behindhand in arranging pomp and ceremony, the Portuguese had to confess that in these matters the Chinese were far ahead of them: for instance, they had much to learn about etiquette. Many commentators arrived at judgements similar to that of the Dominican missionary Gaspar da Cruz, who writes: 'The Chinas [sic] are very courteous men. The common courtesy is, the left hand closed, they enclose it within the right hand, and they move their hands repeatedly up and down towards the breast, showing that they have one another enclosed in their heart; and to this motion of the hands, they join words of courtesy.'[47] Admittedly Gaspar da Cruz then adds that the customary greeting among Chinese is 'Ch'ao-fan', which means 'Have you eaten or not?', and points out the great importance attached to eating in China.

All other accounts concur in this judgement, but none of them mentions over-indulgence or rude manners, let alone gluttony or cannibalism, which so often feature in contemporary reports from Africa and America. In China, by contrast, it is the polished table manners and the care taken in preparing food that arouse the astonishment of travellers. Gaspar da Cruz writes:

> And presently there were two small sticks, very fine and gilt, for to eat with, holding them between the fingers; they use them like a pair of pincers, so that they touch nothing of that which is on the board with their hand. Yea, though they eat a dish of rice, they do it with those sticks, without any grain of the rice falling. And because they eat so cleanly, not touching with the hand their meat, they have no need of cloth or napkins. All comes carved and well ordered to the table. They have also a very small porcelain cup gilt, which holdeth a mouthful of wine, and only for this is there a waiter at the table. They drink so little because at each mouthful of food they must take a sip of drink, and therefore the cup is so small.[48]

We owe to Martín de Rada a vivid description of a great banquet, such as the Chinese liked to give on festivals or for any other pretext. He tells of a highly elaborate welcoming ceremony that continued until the guests were seated; of geese and ducks, capons and chickens, gammon and bacon, decoratively arranged on large tables, as well as many kinds of exotic fruit, exquisitely prepared; and entertainment was not lacking, for an orchestra played table music and actors and acrobats displayed their skills.[49]

After this, it goes virtually without saying that Chinese hospitality is commended. Once again it was Rada who acquired experience of this, through accompanying an embassy to the seat of the Governor-General. The Augustinian canon writes: 'We journeyed by the same cities through which we had come, everything necessary being given to us with the same punctuality as on our coming, and even more bountifully. Everywhere we went, they came out to receive us with great pomp, and served us very splendid banquets.'[50] It was remarkable, too, how inquisitively the Europeans were questioned about all manner of things, each time they arrived at a staging-post. The Governor-General in person asked a number of questions through his interpreter. He was very surprised to learn that Europeans could read and write, and, as proof of this extraordinary fact, he caused a printed book to be shown to him, constantly declaring that the invention of printing was an achievement of the Chinese alone. The Governor-General showed great interest in pictures of Christ on the cross, the Virgin Mary, and the saints, which the monks used as book marks. Rada writes optimistically:

> He kept them, and sent to tell us that he would hold them in great respect. The Viceroy also asked which were the most devout and familiar prayers

among us. We told him the Pater Noster, and the Ave Maria, and the Creed. He asked for them to be explained to him, and showed great pleasure in hearing them, making a show of learning them from memory.[51]

If one seeks some order in the information about China and the Chinese supplied by travellers, one finds that their observations follow a pattern that does not greatly differ from that found in European travel narratives from other parts of the world. Pride of place is given to remarks on external differences, in appearance, garb, hair-style or manners, between Chinese and Europeans, with attention being paid chiefly to members of the higher levels of society. Next come moral judgements on the national character: thus, high praise is given to the industry, dexterity and ingenuity of the artisans and the modesty and virtue of Chinese women, but at the same time traders are censured for their craftiness and the poorer people for their thievishness. We also find comparative judgements such as the remark that poverty is less marked in China than in Portugal.[52] It is much rarer for travellers to provide insight into such social processes as the working of the administration, the career structure of officials, or family life, no doubt because the 'controlled relationship' made it difficult to gain access to such information. Yet even here there are exceptions which prove the rule. Thus, Galeote Pereira, writing about the year 1500, gives a detailed and critical description of the higher officials who at that time formed China's dominant class, and Gaspar da Cruz deals thoroughly with justice and punishment. There is only scanty information about the country's geography and natural products, a topic which was of extreme interest, for example, to the first English settlers in North America. The lack of interest shown by the inhabitants of Macao must be due to the fact that the idea of further settlement in China was soon abandoned and their freedom of movement on the mainland was in any case very restricted.

The Portuguese felt unquestionably superior in one respect – in adhering to the one true religion. As mentioned earlier, the term 'barbarian' is hardly ever used in Portuguese travel narratives; if it does occur, then, amusingly enough, it is applied to the Dutch and English. The Chinese are more often referred to as 'heathens' or 'idolaters'. No observer doubts that the Chinese are intellectually capable of accepting Christ's message, and, moreover, that their desire for knowledge and their ready receptiveness virtually predestine them to become Christians. The travellers constantly ask how the gospel could have remained unknown to the Chinese until the coming of the Portuguese. An explanation often repeated by other travellers is given by Gaspar da Cruz when he speculates that the Apostle Thomas, while in India, may have visited China and left some missionaries there, who worked successfully in the early Christian period. It may be, Cruz goes on, that Buddhism, which has spread through China since the second century AD, incorporated certain elements of Christianity and preserved them in a distorted form. Thus, he recounts a visit to a Buddhist monastery in Canton, inhabited by 'their sort of priests', where he came upon a statue that looked remarkably similar to an image of the Virgin Mary:

> It might well be the image of Our Lady, made by the ancient Christians that Saint Thomas left there, or by their occasion made, but the conclusion is that all is forgotten. It might also be some heathen image. As the greatest God they have is the Heaven, so therefore the letter that signifieth it is the principal and the first of all the letters. They worship the sun, the moon and the stars, and all the images they make without any respect.[53]

The intelligence, curiosity and alertness of the Chinese, and their attitude of apparent negligence towards their religious rituals, misled the Portuguese missionaries into thinking that conversion might proceed without encountering insuperable obstacles. In contrast with West Africa and parts of India, there was no competition here from Muslims, though Gaspar da Cruz observes that they had no chance in any case, as the Chinese were too fond of pork.[54] The Dominican voices the prevailing opinion when he says:

> There is a very good disposition in the people of this country for to become converted to the faith; one reason being that they hold their gods and their priests in small esteem, whereby when they learn of the truth they esteem it, which is not the case with any of the peoples in all the regions of India. Another reason is that they greatly like to listen to the doctrine of the truth, and they harken to it with great attention, as I found in them several times from my own experience, preaching to them on occasion in the public street, where crowds gathered to look as if at some new thing or new form of dress, until there was no room for any one to pass. As I saw that many people had gathered I preached to them, and they greatly rejoiced to hear me and asked questions that formulated their doubts very well. And being satisfied with my answers, they said that what I told them was very good, but that hitherto they had not had any one who told them thereof. This was the answer which I always received from them, both in public preaching as in private conversation.[55]

The same confidence in the willingness of the Chinese to be converted was felt by Martín de Rada, who ends his account of his travels with the following sentence: 'Finally, the land is very fruitful, abundant and populous, although with people who are heathen and thus suffer from the evils which afflict those who do not know God, to whom be honour and glory for evermore, and may He convert and bring them to the knowledge of Himself. Amen.'[56] Yet neither Cruz nor Rada, nor any member of any other order, was destined to spread the Gospel successfully on the mainland. In the mid-sixteenth century the Middle

Kingdom was still impenetrable within the armour-plating of its voluntary isolation, and the ethnocentric traditionalism of its people was far too powerful for conversion to be possible. These are also the main hindrances of which Gaspar da Cruz warns his readers when he apologizes for not having remained longer in China.[57]

Until the eighteenth century the Jesuits remained the most important sources of information about China. While Rousseau's disciples devoted themselves to different versions of the cult of the noble savage, Voltairians, free-thinkers and perfectibilists turned longingly to the Middle Kingdom, which aroused Utopian fantasies through the inaccessibility which seemed to place it on a different level of reality. Those features criticized in the Jesuit reports were now reinterpreted in a positive light. Thus, Leibniz, one of the earliest Sinophiles in Europe, attributed the country's presumed military weakness to a pacifist disposition which he imagined to be widespread there and which he associated with Christian thinking.[58] To Voltaire, the hierarchy and centralism of the Chinese political system seemed expressions of a wise concern for the common good, such as was embodied in the benevolent despotisms of the Enlightenment.[59] Soon afterwards, decorative elements and new techniques of Far Eastern art were readily adopted by the Rococo style, giving 'Chinoiserie' a greater influence on interior design than any non-European culture had exercised since Islam. This fashion, however, did not stimulate any serious intellectual engagement with the cultures of the Far East.

# Cultural Contact as a Scientific Challenge

## *The English and French in the South Seas*

---

The discovery and exploration of the Pacific is unique among the enterprises of the early colonial period, inasmuch as the prospects that normally attracted Europeans – the acquisition of land and territory for settlement, the extension of trade and the discovery of gold and silver – here played only a minor role. For centuries the vast distances separating the Pacific from Europe permitted only brief contacts, and the interest they aroused was predominantly scientific in character. There were three fields, geography, botany and ethnology, which received a powerful impetus from contact with Pacific cultures; and it is with these aspects of cultural encounter that our final chapter will deal.

By the mid-eighteenth century the map of the world had assumed the form with which we are now familiar, at least as far as the coastlines of the continental land masses were concerned. The interiors, especially of Africa and Asia, remained largely inaccessible; but the sea, which had always been far easier for explorers to traverse, had been reconnoitred all over the globe. The South Pacific was still little known and little visited. In 1513 Balboa had been the first to cross the Panama isthmus and see before him the largest of all the oceans, to which he gave the name 'Mar del Sur'. In the usual rhetorical style of the conquistadors, the chronicler Oviedo recounts how Balboa approached this vast expanse of water from above the Bay of San Miguel, and, wading to and fro along the beach, delivered a solemn oration in which he took possession of the sea in the name of the King of Spain.[1] Seven years later, the Portuguese Fernão de Magalhães (better known as Magellan), circumnavigating the globe in the service of Spain, passed through the straits named after him and entered the almost motionless southern ocean which he called the Pacific; though later voyagers, better acquainted with this ocean's storms, have more often called it the 'South Sea'. By drifting too far northwards, Magellan missed the groups of Pacific islands which could have offered provisions and staging-posts for his ships and their crew. His sailors suffered torments from famine and disease, especially scurvy. In a much-quoted passage from his shipboard journal, Pigafetta recounts: 'We ate only old biscuits turned to powder, all full of worms and stinking of the urine which the rats had made on it, having eaten the good. And we drank water impure and yellow. We also ate ox hides which were very hard because of the sun, rain and wind.'[2] After three months' sail, in which only two islands, both barren and uninhabited, were sighted, Magellan's three ships anchored off the islands of Guam and Rota in the Marianas group. They called them 'Islas de Ladrones', islands of thieves, because the local population, wholly unacquainted with European notions of property, stole everything on board that was not nailed down. Otherwise the Spaniards were given a kind and friendly reception, to which they responded with brute force: seven islanders were killed and about fifty of their houses were burnt down. Pigafetta's account discloses the natives' surprise on finding their hospitality and curiosity rewarded in such a way: 'And know that whenever we wounded any of those people with a shaft which entered their body, they looked at it and then marvellously drew it out, and so died forthwith.'[3]

The Pacific voyages undertaken between Magellan's great voyage and George Anson's circumnavigation of the globe in 1740–4 added little to scientific knowledge.[4] Half a century after Magellan, Alvaro de Mendaña sailed from Peru and ventured into the expanses of the Pacific. Fancifully combining Inca legends with his own knowledge of the Bible, he hoped to discover the land of Ophir from which King Solomon imported gold. Although Mendaña did find a group of Melanesian islands which, logically enough, he called the Solomons, he found no gold: he came upon peace-loving islanders and waged war upon them. In 1606 the New Hebrides were discovered by Pedro de Quiros, but his plans for colonizing and Christianizing them came to nothing, like the similar plans formed earlier by Mendaña. The expedition of Isaak Le Maire and Willem Corneliszoon Schouten, the first Dutchmen to enter the Pacific via Cape Horn, likewise had few results to boast of. More successful was the voyage of Abel Janszoon Tasman, who sailed in 1642 from the Dutch settlement of Batavia, discovered the island south of Australia which now bears his name, and reached the west coast of New Zealand. After a clash with the Maoris, Tasman turned north-eastwards, sighting several islands of the Tonga and Fiji groups on his return voyage. Thus, in the course of his ten months' journey, he had sailed round Australia in a wide arc for the first time, though the coastline of this continent could not yet be charted. Even in one of Tasman's later voyages he succeeded only in charting stretches of the north coast of Australia. Another sailor who, like Magellan, circumnavigated the globe was the English freebooter William Dampier. On his voyage, of which he wrote a valuable account, he managed in 1699 to shed light on the geography of the region to the west of New Guinea. In 1722 the Dutchman Jacob Roggeven discovered Easter Island. Soon afterwards Vitus Bering, a Dane in the service of Russia, explored the northern Pacific beyond Kamchatka and the Aleutian Islands; while in 1765 John Byron, on his way round the world, took formal possession of the Falklands on behalf of Great Britain, but made no noteworthy discoveries in the Pacific region.

In this context mention should be made of the regular sailings across the Pacific from Acapulco to Manila which the Spaniards maintained from the sixteenth century until the end of the eighteenth. Between 1570 and 1780 the 'Manila Galleon' carried some 5,000 tons of Mexican silver to the Philippines, where it was used mainly to buy silk from China.[5] No discoveries were made on these journeys; indeed, it may be noted as a curious fact that none of these galleons touched at Hawaii or was driven there by adverse weather.[6]

Many of these Pacific voyages and the contacts with other cultures to which they led were stimulated by the hope of coming across a still unknown continent, the Terra Australis, in the extreme south of the globe. The belief in the existence of this southern continent may be described as one of the most fruitful errors in the history of geography. It goes back to Ptolemy's *Cosmographia*, where the Indian Ocean is portrayed as an inland sea with land on all sides. This notion of the world was widely disseminated by German printers and publishers around 1500 and believed in by the explorers of the Renaissance, their credulity increased by vague hints in Marco Polo. Seventeenth-century cartographers, such as the Dutchman Ortelius, depicted the southern continent in their atlases as a land mass stretching southwards from Cape Horn and the Cape of Good Hope.[7] The persistence of this conjecture for centuries is all the more astonishing, since it received scarcely any support from the findings of expeditions to this region. The voyages of Mendaña, Quiros, Le Maire, Tasman and Roggeven provided no substantial indications that a southern continent actually existed. Yet the hope of landing one day on the coast of Terra Australis was undiminished. In 1700 Dampier was inclined to identify the actual Australia with the legendary southern continent, and in 1740 Anson assumed that the island of Juan Fernandez, off the coast of Peru, signified the presence of a nearby continent. One immediately recalls the idea of a north-west passage, a direct link between the Atlantic and the Pacific, which persisted no less obstinately in the seafarers' minds; but while special expeditions were sent out to find the north-west passage at a very early period, it was only in the second half of the eighteenth century that a systematic search was made for the southern continent.

In the period from Anson's return (1744) to James Cook's first voyage round the world (1768), the debate on the southern continent became one of the principal concerns of geographical theorists. In 1744 the English mercantilist John Campbell, in the preface to an edition of travel narratives, drew attention to travellers' reports of a Terra Australis Incognita and urged his fellow countrymen to lose no time in opening up trade relations with these distant regions, so as to ward off competition from the Spanish, Dutch and French.[8] In 1756, the year in which the outbreak of the Seven Years' War put paid to French hopes of founding a North American empire, the French geographer Charles de Brosses put forward his theory of the existence of a southern continent in his *Histoire des navigations aux terres australes*.[9] In addition, in 1770 Alexander Dalrymple published his *Collection of Voyages to the South Seas*, in which he asserted the existence of a southern continent even more enthusiastically than his predecessors. He declared apodictically that this continent must be *'equal in extent to all the civilised part of ASIA, from TURKEY to CHINA inclusive'* with a population of fifty million.[10]

How, it may be asked, could so many publications appear on a subject whose relevance had never been clarified, and this, moreover, in an epoch which prided itself on consulting only experience? Part of the explanation lies in the pattern of international politics. About the year 1755 the conflict between Britain and France in non-European regions had reached crisis point. Contemporary observers could not but perceive that William Pitt's energetic imperial policy left France with little prospect of extending her colonial possessions in North America and India. As de Brosses emphasized, the Terra Australis Incognita seemed to offer new terrain for colonial activities, though as a trading partner rather than as a place of settlement. After the Peace of Paris in 1763, the French actually expected the southern continent to compensate them for the setbacks they had suffered in Europe, and Choiseul, the French foreign minister, began to concern himself with the subject, though he was at pains to represent his nation's interest in it as primarily commercial and scientific. Earlier, after her colonial and maritime defeats in the War of the Spanish Succession (1701–13), France had gambled on the profits which, according to the Scottish speculator John Law, could be gained from the legendary riches of Louisiana: similarly, she now hoped that the Terra Australis Incognita would prove a winning card. It is likely that the British interest in the southern continent evinced by Dalrymple's work ought not to be interpreted primarily as a reaction to de Brosses: he and Dalrymple corresponded as fellow scholars, and Dalrymple copied so much from de Brosses that he could hardly have polemicized against his

French colleague. However, Dalrymple shared the spirit of his age. He took for granted the global pre-eminence which his country had achieved with the Peace of Paris, though he also wanted to avoid any future conflict with France. As a solution he envisaged a liberal system of international trade under the paternalist supervision of Great Britain. For Dalrymple, as for others, the question of the southern continent owed its fascination to the political situation; though he regarded the Terra Australis Incognita not as a consolation prize but as a possible testing-ground for new colonial strategies based on free trade.

The importance which the question of the southern continent acquired from the mid-century onwards cannot, however, be interpreted solely in terms of the political situation, but must also be related to the Enlightenment's peculiar conception of the world. Since Descartes and Locke, deists, pantheists and materialists had all assumed that the earth must be a balanced system of interacting forces, an organism within which every object derived its meaning from the whole and vice versa.[11] This view, also held by de Brosses and Dalrymple, meant that anyone contemplating the globe must find it puzzling that the continental land masses mainly covered the northern hemisphere. It was impossible, wrote de Brosses, that such an extensive region of the globe should not contain somewhere an extensive mass of land which helped to maintain the balance of the earth as it rotated.[12] Dalrymple likewise saw an obvious necessity for the existence of a southern continent, if only to equalize the 'comparative quantity of land in the two hemispheres'.[13] These philosophical arguments, which would now be the province of physical geography, also took into account the notion of a pre-established harmony among the winds. They were rational and persuasive, and since the savants of the Enlightenment were inclined to identify the logical necessity of their reasoning with the necessity of natural laws, anything that they considered logical must have a counterpart in nature.

There was something of a time-lag before the theoretical discussions of the Terra Australis Incognita were followed by practical enquiries. The secret instructions given by the British Admiralty to Samuel Wallis, who discovered Tahiti in 1767, were the first to include specific orders to resolve the question of a southern continent. The instructions from the King of France to Louis-Antoine de Bougainville, who left Europe on his voyage round the world a year after Wallis, included the remark: 'Since our information regarding these islands, or continent, is still very slight, it would be very desirable to perfect it.'[14] Neither Wallis nor Bougainville succeeded in finding a non-existent continent, and Bougainville added the following comment:

> I agree that it is difficult to imagine such a large number of low-lying islands and half-submerged pieces of land without assuming the existence

of a nearby continent. But geography is a science of facts; if one yields to the systematizing impulse while sitting in one's study, one risks falling into the greatest errors, which can sometimes only be corrected at the cost of sailors' lives.[15]

Finally, James Cook, who set out on his first voyage round the world a year after Bougainville, received detailed additional instructions from the Admiralty directing him to search for the southern continent: its discovery was said to be the most important object of this expedition, along with the observations of the transit of Venus across the sun which were to be made on Tahiti. The instructions read as follows:

> Whereas there is reason to imagine that a Continent or Land of great extent, may be found to the Southward of the Tract lately made by Capt$^n$ Wallis in His Majesty's ship the Dolphin (of which you will herewith receive a Copy) or of the Tract of any former Navigators in Pursuits of the like kind;

> You are therefore in Pursuance of His Majesty's Pleasure hereby requir'd and directed to put to Sea with the Bark you Command so soon as the Observation of the Transit of the Planet Venus shall be finished and observe the following Instructions. You are to proceed to the southward in order to make discovery of the Continent above-mentioned until you arrive in the Latitude of 40°, unless you sooner fall in with it. But not having discover'd it or any Evident signs of it in that Run, you are to proceed in search of it to the Westward between the Latitude before mentioned and the Latitude of 35° until you discover it, or fall in with the Eastern side of the Land discover'd by Tasman and now called New Zeland.[16]

The additional instructions for Cook's first voyage also require him, in the event of discovering the continent, to explore its coastline as minutely as possible, to make an exact survey of its landscape and natural products, to record the temperament, character, abilities and number of its population, and, 'with the Consent of the Natives',[17] to take possession of suitable territories in the name of the King of England. However, Cook too failed to find the legendary southern continent. He remarks firmly though somewhat apologetically in his journal: 'Certain it is that we saw no visible signs of land, according to my opinion, neither in our rout to the Northward, Southward or Westward untill a few days before we made the east Coast of *New-Zeland*.'[18] Thus, the controversy was finally resolved, and although Dalrymple obstinately adhered to his thesis in his subsequent writings, this merely resulted from his personal character and a private feud with Cook which he thought it necessary to maintain. After Cook's second voyage (1772–5) the Terra Australis Incognita was no longer on the scholarly agenda. The article on 'Terres australes' in the 1779 edition of Diderot's *Encyclopédie* shows an enlightened freedom from illusions: 'It is the business of seafarers, who may be carried by the orders of their employers or the hazards of their profession into these regions of the globe, to tell us what they find there. It is not the business of geographers to anticipate their discoveries with conjectures which cannot stand the test of experience.'[19] From then on the chimerical southern continent was to be the preserve of authors of imaginary voyages in the wake of *Robinson Crusoe*, such as Restif de la Bretonne, who in a novel of 1781 made a party of Europeans fly to 'Megapatagonia' and discover a human republic on an island there.[20]

Although the question of the southern continent was finally answered in the negative, it suggests some general conclusions about the history of geography in the Enlightenment. Firstly, it must be stated that eighteenth-century geography was essentially maritime geography; its English and French practitioners rightly described themselves as hydrographers. It was not until after Cook's third voyage that scholarly interest turned to the exploration and mapping of the interiors of the continents. It is astonishing how precisely developments in different parts of the world run parallel to each other: in the early nineteenth century Mungo Park visited the Upper Niger on behalf of the London African Association; Lewis and Clark, starting from the Mississippi, reached the Pacific, and Alexander von Humboldt explored the Amazon basin; soon afterwards, explorers became distinctly more active in Central Asia and Australia. The nineteenth century was to be the age of great inland journeys.

Eighteenth-century geography was not unpolitical, though it often liked to appear so. It received essential stimuli from the historical situation of the two nations, England and France, where the study of geography was principally carried on. It is true that geographers, and indeed all propagandists for exploration, advised against the creation of overseas settlements; the transportation of British convicts to Botany Bay was an exception. Both rival sea powers had had discouraging experiences with overseas settlements: France in Canada and Louisiana, Britain with its rebellious North American possessions. However, the distinct priority accorded from 1781 onwards to commercial relations and free trade did not mean that power struggles were no longer being conducted overseas. The instructions given to voyagers make it evident that aspirations for the extension of national power had remained largely intact. Thus, Bougainville was ordered to identify newly discovered territories by erecting coats of arms on poles, as the Portuguese had done in the fifteenth century, and 'to make a documentary record of such acquisitions in the name of His Majesty, but without leaving anyone behind to found a colony.'[21] Crews were still required to keep their sea-routes and the results of their discoveries a close secret, although when official accounts of voyages were published, a more liberal attitude was adopted, in keeping with the Enlightenment demand for the free exchange of information within the European republic of letters. The seafarers' code of conduct also included observing the activities of rival powers, and spying on them when possible: thus, when La Pérouse landed at Madeira, he was directed to 'procure information about the garrison maintained there by the Portuguese Crown, also about the island's trade with the English and other nations.'[22] There can be no doubt that, despite their pretence of disinterested scholarship, the eighteenth-century explorers were chiefly concerned with the enhancement of national prestige. The directions given to Cook observe that the success of his voyage would 'redound greatly to the Honour of this Nation',[23] and all the instructions issued to explorers contain similar formulations.

In the late eighteenth century, geographers were more sharply aware than ever before of the gulf separating the theorist, the armchair geographer, from the practitioner, the person who actually went on voyages. Hence the long-term effect of the controversy over the Terra Australis Incognita: people were obliged to admit that it was no longer sufficient to summarize and collate other people's reports, as geographers had done since the mid-sixteenth century. After Bougainville's voyage (1767) it became customary to have scientific specialists on board, not only those who had been assigned geographical and astronomical tasks, but also botanists, zoologists and (if the term can be used at this date) anthropologists. This type of voyage of discovery was a French speciality. La Pérouse took seventeen scholars on his expedition to the South Seas (1785), while the voyages of D'Entrecasteaux and Baudin (1791 and 1800) were accompanied respectively by ten and twenty of these 'naturalists', as they were generally termed.[24] It was of course not always easy to integrate these specialists into shipboard life, and even a commander with the social experience of James Cook had a hard time of it with the academics. As far as science was concerned, however, the inclusion in the ship's company of a team of scholars, often backed up by gardeners and draughtsmen, proved a valuable innovation. On these voyages a vast quantity of minerals and plants was collected, all kinds of animals caught and preserved, and specimens of archaic art were transported to Europe. The interdisciplinary co-operation of the specialists on board freed geography from its one-sided link with the history of exploration and brought it into fruitful contact with other disciplines such as geology, botany and zoology – a development which culminated in Darwin's famous voyage round the world in 1831–6. Research teams of the kind devised by Bougainville and Cook remained a characteristic feature of the voyages of the nineteenth and early twentieth centuries, which were principally intended to explore the Arctic and Antarctic. On the other hand, it is interesting to note that on the long and often extremely demanding expeditions made in the nineteenth century in the interiors of Africa, Asia and America, the usual type of explorer was still the robust individual with as diverse a training as possible.

The fleeting contacts between cultures in the Pacific had a fruitful influence not only on geography but also on the natural sciences. The eighteenth century was the period when Linnaeus's international fame was at its height.[25] Since the non-European world was still little known to botanists, a handy system of classification by sexual features and the brilliant and equally accessible idea of binary nomenclature could not fail to encourage people to set about botanical research there with unprecedented enthusiasm. There is space to mention only a few of the pupils of Linnaeus who were exploring the world at that time: Peter Kalm, who travelled through North America and left an account of his travels, including interesting remarks on politics; Adam Afzelius and Andreas Sparrman, who collected botanical specimens in Africa; Karl Peter Thunberg, who visited Japan and took a remarkably open-minded interest in Japanese culture; and Carl Solander, who accompanied Cook on the latter's first voyage. Historians of science have also noted, however, that Linnaeus's influence encouraged a merely additive accumulation of material and gave a new and deplorable lease of life to such artificial ordering principles and static concepts as the 'great chain of being' or the 'constancy of species'.[26] The South Sea voyager Solander is a prime example of the scholar whose anxiety to garner specimens distracts him from the task of interpreting his materials scientifically.[27] The physiological and morphological study of tropical flora had to wait for nineteenth-century botanists who could base their work on the insights of Jussieu, De Candolle and Darwin.

Eighteenth-century botanists set great store by transplanting tropical growths to Europe and other parts of the world. In 1773 Joseph Banks, who accompanied Cook on his first voyage round the world and later became President of the Royal Society, established a living herbarium in the Royal Botanic Gardens at Kew in which to rear plants from all regions of the British Empire, including the South Seas. By the late eighteenth century the Jardin des Plantes in Paris, which had originally been a herb garden known as the 'Jardin du Roy', could provide a superb conspectus of tropical flora. A gardener from the Jardin des Plantes sailed on La Pérouse's expedition. These botanical gardens, with their hothouses containing exotic plants, attracted scholars from all over the world. One of the most distinguished, Alexander von Humboldt, once remarked in passing that it was the sight of a 'colossal dragon-tree' (*Dracaena draco*) in the Botanical Garden at Berlin that gave him the first impetus to travel overseas.[28] Natural products had of course been transplanted from one continent to another in earlier centuries. To name only a few examples, manioc, maize, the sweet potato and the tomato were disseminated across the globe as early as the period of the Portuguese and Spanish voyages.[29] Not until the eighteenth century, however, do we find maritime expeditions whose main purpose was the transplantation of natural products. Here, too, Joseph Banks played a significant part, for in 1787 he advised the Admiralty to have bread-fruit trees transported from Tahiti and the neighbouring islands to the West Indies.[30] The bread-fruit was to provide a reliable food supply for slaves on the British plantations, where food shortages had become notorious since the United States had become independent and reduced their imports. The task of fetching the bread-fruit trees was entrusted to William Bligh. His first attempt failed because of the famous mutiny on board his ship, the *Bounty*, but a few years later he did succeed in bringing these plants to Jamaica. Admittedly, the success was only partial, since the trees flourished in the West Indies but their fruit never became a popular part of the local diet. Two other projects instigated by the indefatigable Banks either came to nothing or were translated into action only after his death. The plan to export hemp fibres from New Zealand to the Australian convict settlement at Botany Bay sank into oblivion. His other project, the transplantation of tea from China, where it originated, to India, was to be taken up by the East India Company in 1836, with lasting consequences for the world economy.[31] It may be added that the English were far from being pioneers in the systematic transplantation of tropical products. As early as 1750 the French naturalist Pierre Poivre had managed to procure nutmeg and clove seeds from the Moluccas, then in Dutch hands, and take them to Mauritius. In 1769 and 1771 two French expeditions brought more spices from the Malay Archipelago to Mauritius. Subsequently, Mauritius became an important centre for the exchange of tropical plants in what was left of the French colonial empire.[32]

The projects of Banks and Poivre went beyond the bounds of mere scientific experiment: by aiming to modify the world economy, they assumed a political dimension. Both naturalists remained loyal to strongly mercantilist principles. Their efforts were not designed to foster international trade, but to bring raw materials closer to their home countries, by transporting spices to Mauritius and tea to India. Mercantilist thinking also lay behind Banks's plan to secure the sugar supply from the West Indies by making the slaves' diet, and hence their capacity for work, dependent on the importation of a foreign product. Banks's writings contain no trace of the obvious enough idea of reducing the plantation islands' concentration on a single crop and guaranteeing their self-sufficiency by encouraging them to produce their own foodstuffs. Nor does he challenge the slave economy, though at the very time when the *Bounty* set off on its voyage the activities of the British anti-slavery movement were approaching their first peak.

We have seen that in the case of the Pacific, comparatively few and brief contacts sufficed to sustain the interest of geographers and naturalists. The same applies to ethnographers.

If one examines the instructions given to eighteenth-century Pacific voyagers, one is struck by the urgency with which they are adjured to maintain peaceful relations with alien peoples. As early as 1764, when John Byron embarked on his voyage round the world, he was ordered to 'endeavour by all proper means to cultivate a Friendship with the Inhabitants, if you shall find any, presenting them with such Trifles as they may value, and showing them all possible civility and respect.'[33] Almost identical words are used in the instructions to Cook: 'You are to endeavour by all proper means to cultivate a friendship with the Natives, presenting them such Trifles as may be acceptable to them.'[34] And La Pérouse is told to instruct his crews as follows: 'He shall order all the members of his crews to live on harmonious terms with the natives, [ . . . ] and he shall forbid them, on pain of the most condign punishments, ever to use force to deprive the inhabitants of anything which they refuse to surrender voluntarily.'[35] If the instructions came not from an official source but from private individuals or scientific societies, they were liable to contain even more strongly worded exhortations to treat members of alien cultures tolerantly. The recommendations given to Cook on his first voyage by the President of the Royal Society are interesting in this respect, especially as they clearly undermine the primacy previously accorded to claiming newly discovered territories for the Crown. Cook is reminded:

> To have it still in view that sheding the blood of those people is a crime of the highest nature: – They are human creatures, the work of the same omnipotent Author, equally under his care with the most polished European; perhaps being less offensive, more entitled to his favor.
>
> They are the natural, and in the strictest sense of the word, the legal possessors of the several Regions they inhabit.
>
> No European Nation has a right to occupy any part of their country, or settle among them without their voluntary consent.
>
> Conquest over such people can give no just title; because they could never be the Agressors.[36]

Such exhortations to maintain peaceful relations undoubtedly reflect a transformation in the attitude of Europeans to members of other cultures. The formula 'the consent of the inhabitants' had been included by the English in the seventeenth century in the land transfer treaties which they concluded with the North American Indians: here, however, it is used in a deeper sense, since it assumes that the other party has the power of decision. The humanitarian viewpoint may have been reinforced by the absence of any plans to colonize the Pacific region, if only because of the enormous distances involved. Such advice was also based on sound common sense. On prolonged voyages it was vitally important for seafarers to stay out of conflicts which might reduce the numbers of the crew and weaken morale on board; and there was also a danger that the ship's supplies might be reduced by being used for barter. It is obvious, too, that in the Enlightenment such grave losses as those suffered by Anson's crew during his voyage round the world could affect national prestige. Hence, the instructions to La Pérouse say that 'His Majesty would consider it an outstanding achievement by this expedition if the voyage could be completed without the loss of a single life.'[37] Admittedly, exhortations to treat the South Sea islanders peacefully were often accompanied by warnings to exercise caution in dealing with them. Thus, Cook was told before setting out on his second voyage that, while treating the natives with friendship and consideration, he should also be on his guard against surprise attacks.[38] Similar admonitions accompanied La Pérouse on his voyage. After the inhabitants of Samoa had attacked some sailors and killed De Langle, one of his captains, La Pérouse noted in his journal: 'He fancied that he could keep them [the islanders] under control without needing to shed blood, and thus he became a victim of his humane views.'[39]

The new climate of inter-cultural tolerance which, intellectually at least, governed relations between Europe and the rest of the world in the later eighteenth century had various causes, the interactions of which are difficult to unravel. In recent years a plethora of scholarly studies and literary essays have dealt with these themes under the rubric 'the noble savage', disclosing certain utopian, exotic and erotic yearnings characteristic of our own century which have not always done much to advance our knowledge of intellectual history.[40] Here we shall single out only a few important aspects of this cluster of problems.

This change of mood was crucially influenced by two books, composed about the middle of the eighteenth century by writers whose temperaments and outlooks had little in common: Voltaire's *Essai sur les mœurs* (1756) and Jean-Jacques Rousseau's *Discours sur l'origine de l'inégalité parmi les hommes* (1754). Voltaire's compendious historical work was the first to leave the beaten track of a Christocentric history of the world and to focus on the plurality of cultures. Chinese and Islamic culture gained the author's particular respect because of their high level of civilization. While Voltaire remained under the sway of Enlightenment progressivism, according the age of Louis XIV the place of honour in the course of world history, Rousseau helped to imbue Europeans with a lasting sense of cultural insecurity by turning his gaze to pre-literate, 'uncivilized' phases in the development of mankind. Rousseau's hypothetical fiction of the 'natural man' arose from the individualist's irritation with the absolutist, courtly society of the Rococo era; his installation of the counter-image of the *homme naturel*, with his economic independence, political liberty and moral purity, was a declaration of war on all the forces that seemed to make for constriction, corruption and self-alienation in Rousseau's epoch. The suggestion that the traveller, in traversing space, was simultaneously on a voyage of discovery back to his origins and to happier phases in human development, was an original and important idea which was taken up enthusiastically in the writings of Rousseau's followers.

The extension of spatial and temporal horizons by Voltaire and Rousseau is dialectically related to the increased emphasis on inner, emotional experience which became discernible, especially among marginal religious groups, in the later eighteenth century. These currents of feeling, derived from the benevolent emotions underpinning charitable endeavours, were crucial in encouraging Europeans to recognize the shared humanity of people of different races and cultures and to base relations with alien peoples on a feeling of evangelical responsibility which renounced any claim to political sovereignty. The effects of this new internalization of religious feeling on relations between Europe and the rest of the world are shown most impressively from 1770 onwards in the origins of the British anti-slavery movement, in which Methodists took a decisive part. Pietist tendencies, in turn, helped significantly in the establishment of Protestant missionary societies, such as the London Missionary Society, founded in 1795, whose initial activities, as we shall see, were concerned with the Pacific region. Finally, the revolt of Britain's North American possessions should be seen as another major impetus to the self-critical revision of attitudes to the non-European world. The salutary shock of these events prevented Britain from repeating all the mistakes made in America when building up her 'second Empire' in the Eastern hemisphere.

It was intellectual sources like these that fostered the demand for peaceful dealings with native peoples which we have found in the instructions to voyagers in the late eighteenth century. Occasionally this feeling yielded to a radical anticolonialism. Thus, in the wake of the Pacific voyages the view was sometimes uttered that it would have been better if the Europeans had never discovered these Edenic regions and never exposed their innocent inhabitants to the risks of European influence. When Bougainville brought a Tahitian named Auturu back to

Paris, he provoked opposition from intellectuals. It was irresponsible, they argued, to snatch a young man who had enjoyed the privilege of growing up in the South Seas from his ancestral home and expose him to the corrupting influence of a European metropolis. Bougainville found himself forced on the defensive, emphasizing that the islander had accompanied him to Europe entirely voluntarily.[41] Voices were raised to urge that Auturu should be taken back to Tahiti as soon as possible, and in 1771 the Ministry of Marine instructed the seafarer Marion-Dufresne accordingly. Auturu, however, fell ill and died on the voyage. Similar criticisms were to be heard in Britain when James Cook brought the Polynesian Omai back from his second voyage. Omai too was dispatched to his home on Cook's third voyage, but our information suggests that he failed to reintegrate himself into the society from which he had originally come.[42]

The fear that contact with Europeans might have fatal effects on the Pacific islanders also governed the heated debate between the French and British as to which of them had introduced venereal diseases into the Society Islands. In the account of Cook's second voyage by Georg Forster, perhaps the most valuable source we possess for the history of Pacific exploration, the pros and cons of European influence are weighed up and the resulting moral conflict formulated. Forster concludes:

> It were indeed sincerely to be wished, that the intercourse which has lately subsisted between Europeans and the natives of the South Sea islands may be broken off in time, before the corruption of manners which unhappily characterises civilized regions, may reach that innocent race of men, who live here fortunate in their ignorance and simplicity. But it is a melancholy truth, that the dictates of philanthropy do not harmonize with the political systems of Europe![43]

Benevolent interest in non-Europeans was also the basis for the questionnaires which eighteenth-century Pacific voyagers took with them. The practice of asking travellers specific questions and thus encouraging them to observe alien peoples closely goes back to earlier centuries, just as the demand for peaceful approaches to other nations is hardly a pioneering achievement of the Enlightenment. However, much evidence suggests that in the sixteenth and seventeenth centuries such instructions arose exclusively from the wish to establish a profitable relationship. A revealing document in this respect is the set of instructions which the governor of the English trading company, the Merchant Adventurers, gave in 1553 to some seafarers who were trying to reach China by the north-east passage, rounding the North Cape. From Marco Polo's account it was already known that China was a powerful empire whose princes were confident of their authority; the journey thither was laborious and required considerable resources, so that the instructions inevitably had to recommend caution in dealing with foreigners. Hence they say: 'Item every nation and region is to be considered advisedly, and not to provoke them by any disdaine, laughing, contempt, or such like, but to use them with prudent circumspection, with al gentlenes, and curtesie.'[44] There then follow directions to observe foreign cultures closely, paying particular attention to the possibility of opening up trade relations:

> Item the names of the people of every Island, are to be taken in writing, with the commodities, and incommodities of the same, their natures, qualities, and dispositions, the site of the same, and what things they are most desirous of, and what commodities they will most willingly depart with, and what mettals they have in hils, mountaines, streames, or rivers, in, or under the earth.[45]

In the late sixteenth century there appeared several printed guides for travellers, known as 'apodemics', intended for upper-class young men who were travelling to complete their education. These apodemics urged their users to observe the world around them by personal inspection and by systematically noting down whatever seemed worthy of record.[46] There do not seem to have been any such apodemics to form the minds and characters of people travelling outside Europe: a comparable function was performed by the instructions provided by Admiralties or by the learned societies which emerged in the seventeenth century. Thus, the very first number of the *Philosophical Transactions*, the organ of the Royal Society founded in 1600, contained a list of questions for travellers entitled 'General Heads for a Natural History of a Country, great or small'.[47] For the rest, the immense collections of travel narratives which appeared in the seventeenth century, like Purchas's *Hakluytus Posthumus* and Dapper's *Naukeurige Beschrijvinge der Afrikaensche gewesten*, were at pains to present their information systematically. An early instance of this kind was Bernhard Varenius's *Geographia Generalis* of 1650, in which descriptions of alien peoples followed a sequence which was much imitated subsequently: the natives' external appearance, their origins, their food; commerce and crafts; virtues and vices; marriage customs and funeral ceremonies; language; system of government; the most important localities of the country; historical traditions; prominent personalities among the people in question.[48]

The ethnographic questionnaires of the eighteenth century went further in their attempts to acquire and systematize information, especially as the scholars who drew them up were familiar with the current state of research and asked questions specifically designed to confirm or extend their knowledge. A characteristic example is the catalogue of questions which was compiled by the German Orientalist Johann David Michaelis in 1762 on behalf of the Learned Society of

Göttingen and given to Carsten Niebuhr when he set out on his Arabian expedition.[49] As far as Pacific exploration is concerned, it is worth looking closely at the copious scientific instructions which accompanied La Pérouse on his voyage. Fifteen printed pages were taken up by the questions supplied by the *Académie de Médicine* alone, which were appended to these instructions. Taking a typically Enlightenment stand against superstition and prejudice, the medical questionnaire abjures any myth-making: 'We do not speak here of giants, dwarfs, mermaids, etc., because these alleged freaks of nature have never been observed by anyone except the prejudiced or ignorant travellers in whose overheated imaginations they existed.'[50] Taking the present state of knowledge as their starting-point, the *Académie*'s questions proceed according to such patterns as these: 'Dampier says that the inhabitants of Van Diemen's Land [Tasmania] lack two teeth. Do they lack them naturally, or do they pull one another's teeth out?'; or: 'Do the inhabitants suffer from leprosy? Are the painless swellings which Cook observed on the arms and legs to be considered a feature of this disease?'[51] In this way the doctors' catalogue of questions deals with the anatomy and physiology of the human body, hygiene and the spread of disease, and the alien peoples' remedies and curative methods. It is admittedly striking that the object of study, the inhabitant of non-European territory, scarcely ever figures as a social being, even when the discussion concerns topics like living conditions, life expectancy and the age of puberty, which would seem liable to provoke social questions. This applies, moreover, to the entire body of scientific instructions issued to La Pérouse. It is no less striking, finally, that none of the instructions given to him includes any discussion of research methods — that is, the means by which the desired information is to be obtained.

A book with a profound and lasting influence on the development of ethnography was *Considérations sur les diverses méthodes à suivre dans l'observation des peuples sauvages* (1800), by the French naturalist Joseph-Marie de Gérando. We know that these recommendations were invited by the *Société des Observateurs de l'Homme*, founded in December 1799, a short-lived precursor of the anthropological societies that were to be founded from 1835 onwards in France, Britain, the United States and Germany. In 1883 the *Considérations* were rediscovered and published in the *Revue d'anthropologie*. At present they are most readily available in an English edition.[52]

From the point of view of the historian interested in contacts between European and non-European cultures, de Gérando's work is most revealing when it criticizes previous methods of ethnographic observation. After some introductory remarks which stress the urgent need for people to study humankind and indicate the author's belief in monogenesis and the unity of the human race, he reproaches voyagers for devoting too little time to ethnographic studies and, in particular, for failing to learn the languages without which it is impossible to grasp the essential character of other cultures. De Gérando is astute enough to realize that the arrival of a European ship must throw the natives into a state of astonishment, terror or unease, which makes it difficult to assess their normal behaviour. This circumstance alone suggests that anyone engaged on more serious research should spend a longer time among them. It was not new to propose that Europeans should have prolonged and intimate contact with the natives and communicate with them in their own language: the Jesuit missionaries in Paraguay and Canada had made the same demand at the beginning of the seventeenth century, and had furnished their narratives with glossaries in order to assist communication.[53] However, the missionaries' efforts were aimed primarily at making themselves understood and only secondarily at understanding their interlocutors: the purpose of their work was to convey a message. De Gérando's conception of communication, which included sign language, gesture and mime, went well beyond what the missionaries had attempted, as is made clear by the following passsage from the *Considérations*:

> The main object, therefore, that should today occupy the attention and zeal of a truly philosophical traveller would be the careful gathering of all means that might assist him to penetrate the thought of the peoples among whom he would be situated, and to account for the order of their actions and relationships. This is not only because such study is in itself the most important of all, it is also because it must stand as a necessary preliminary and introduction to all the others. It is a delusion to suppose that one can properly observe a people whom one cannot understand and with whom one cannot converse. The first means to the proper knowledge of the Savages, is to become after a fashion like one of them; and it is by learning their language that we shall become their fellow citizens.[54]

'To become after a fashion like one of them': this also implies that the observer has to become conscious of the relativity of his or her own standpoint. Hitherto, writes de Gérando, travellers have succumbed too easily to the temptation to judge the customs of primitive peoples by analogy with their own, to ascribe to them their own dispositions and desires, and to make them reason in a European fashion.[55] In making this criticism, he comes close to the conception of culture formulated thirty years before in Germany by Johann Gottfried Herder in the famous sentence: 'Every nation has its centre of happiness in itself, as every sphere has its own centre of gravity'[56] – a sentence which could have provided a suitable epigraph to Forster's *Voyage Round the World*. It would, however, be incorrect to see de Gérando as initiating a radical historicism based on empathy. Rather, the author of the *Considérations* is very close to Voltaire: he supports the latter's critique of prejudice and the pluralistic view of other cultures set out in the *Essai sur les mœurs*; and, like Voltaire, he never doubts that human destiny is to advance steadily in progress and civilization, or that it is in the best interests of other cultures to emulate the high level of civilization attained by Europe. Like Voltaire, de Gérando denounces the misdeeds of European colonial powers who used their overseas expansion solely for exploitation and enslavement; and from their guilt he argues – showing himself here less sceptical than the author of the *Essai sur les mœurs* – that civilized Europe has an inescapable moral obligation to guide other cultures in a kindly and humane manner towards civilization. 'Columbus put in the New World only greedy conquerors', writes de Gérando; 'and you are proceeding towards the peoples of the South only as pacifists and friends. The cruel adventurers of Spain brought only destruction before them, and you will spread only good deeds.'[57] He agrees with Dalrymple and de Brosses, and also with the Scottish economist Adam Smith, in regarding commercial relations as the best means not only of preserving international peace but also of promoting civilization and hence universal happiness.

> A philosophical traveller would be much more far-seeing. He would see in this trade a means of leading the people to civilization. In fact, our help is almost indispensable in this process; and only need can bring them close to us. So initial barter will make early communications easier; these contacts will perhaps serve to inspire in the Savage some new desires which will bring him still closer to us. Always well received, well treated, witness of our happiness, of our riches, and at the same time of our superiority, he will perhaps attach himself to us from gratitude or interest, will join in some alliance with us, will call us among his people to teach them how to reach our own condition. What joy! What a conquest, if some hope were open to us of exercising a gentle and useful influence on these abandoned Peoples [ . . . ][58]

If one tries to sum up the attitude of late eighteenth-century Europe to the development of relations with the newly discovered peoples of the Pacific region, one is immediately struck by the desire to keep these relations free from conflict. It is certainly true that this desire resulted not only from the new sense of human responsibility which had emerged in Europe about the mid-century, but also from solid calculation. Voyages across such distances with their logistical problems denied the seafarers the support of military strength. However, the scientific aims which formed the overriding purpose of Pacific voyagers in the later eighteenth century also made it imperative for contact to proceed peacefully. This of course applied particularly to ethnographic research. During the exploration of the South Seas a more deliberate attempt was made than ever before to animate, correct and extend scholarly discussions at home by means of observations made on the spot. Information was subjected to closer historical and critical scrutiny, specialists in various disciplines worked together more intensively, their contact with the authorities responsible for colonial policy was broadened, and their researches were brought to the attention of an ever-increasing reading public. Towards the end of the century the method by which ethnographic information was acquired itself became the object of critical scrutiny. Demands were made for voyagers to spend longer periods studying non-European peoples and to master their languages in order to approach them without prejudice. Non-European peoples themselves no longer figured in the European consciousness principally as sources of valuable raw materials and cheap labour, or as souls thirsting for conversion, but as creatures with the same origins and the same rights, who were to be understood within their historical and social environment. After examining the instructions and directions issued to Bougainville, Cook, La Pérouse or Baudin, it seems perfectly justified to say that relations between Europe and the non-European world had undergone a decisive intellectual reorientation. The 'prehistoric age of anthropology' was nearing its end, and the first intimations of field research were becoming visible.[59]

Nevertheless, the interest that eighteenth-century Europeans took in the South Seas remained largely material. The link established in international law between discovery and appropriation remained in force, or at least was not explicitly dissolved, even if the resulting claims were of a theoretical nature and primarily intended to fend off European competitors. Travel accounts and instructions were already sketching the outlines of a new colonial relationship founded on trade. Based on the concept of 'trusteeship', this relationship was to be that of a guardian to his charge. It was hoped, no doubt sincerely, that such tutelage would guide non-Europeans to civilization and happiness.[60]

The methodological considerations, the perceptive advice and questions, set out by de Gérando in his *Considérations* could not be used by Nicolas Baudin's expedition, for which they were intended. This enterprise was ill-starred from its inception. Sickness and squabbles induced some of the crew and the accompanying scholars to leave the ship at Mauritius; later the captain himself fell gravely ill; and the quarrels on board became unendurable. The expedition did manage to collect considerable botanical material, to locate some islands more precisely, and to chart a hitherto unknown stretch of the South Australian coastline; but the bad working atmosphere and the impossibility of spending a long period on land meant that little could be achieved in the way of ethnographic research. The sumptuously produced scholarly account of the voyage, published in 1807 by its leading naturalist, François Péron, could not disguise the failure of the enterprise.[61]

If one attempts a summary description of the approximately thirty years of Pacific voyages from Wallis in 1767 via Bougainville, Cook, and La Pérouse to Baudin in 1803, and the phase of cultural contact which they constituted, then one has to emphasize their peacefulness. Warlike clashes certainly occurred on some islands, such as New Zealand, and even relations with Tahiti were occasionally overshadowed by serious incidents; but the dominant note was one of mutual harmony, to an extent very seldom seen in the entire course of colonial history. It was, however, the South Sea islanders, as well as the Europeans, who helped to prevent bloodshed on any large scale. European visitors to the Pacific testify repeatedly to the islanders' friendly approaches and to their willingness to perform services for the newcomers. The image of joyful and excited islanders rowing out to the European ships in canoes laden with fruit has become a symbol of such encounters. From among many witnesses, let us quote a gifted writer, Georg Forster:

> It was one of those beautiful mornings which the poets of all nations have attempted to describe, when we saw the isle of O-Taheitee, within two miles before us. The east-wind which had carried us so far, was entirely vanished, and a faint breeze only wafted a delicious perfume from the land, and curled the surface of the sea. [ . . . ] Having perceived the large vessels on their coast, several of [the inhabitants] hastened to the beach, launched their canoes, and paddled towards us, who were highly delighted in watching their occupations.
>
> The canoes soon passed through the openings in the reef, and one of them approached within hale [sic]. In it were two men almost naked, with a kind of turban on the head, and a sash round the waist. They waved a large green leaf, and accosted us with the repeated exclamation of *tayo!* which even without the help of vocabularies, we could easily translate into the expression of proffered friendship. The canoe now came under our stern, and we let down a present of beads, nails, and medals to the men. In return, they handed up to us a green stem of a plantane, which was their symbol of peace, with a desire that it might be fixed in a conspicuous part of the vessel.[62]

Forster's description points back three centuries to the report in which Columbus recorded his arrival in the Bahamas. Both voyagers entered the long-sought harbour in the radiance of early morning, beheld friendly natives as naked as God made them, and were astonished to realize the natural wealth of the newly discovered region. In the West Indies, as in the South Seas, the Europeans were regarded on their arrival as gods and accorded divine honours. The literary tradition of Hawaii has preserved a characteristic account of Cook's first arrival there. We are told how dumbfounded the Hawaiians were as they stood on the shore watching the approach of the sailing-ships, which seemed to them like a forest floating across the sea. When a cannon was fired on board, all realized that they were receiving a visit from superhuman beings. The islanders' account continues:

> And in this night the gun was fired, and the shot flew up, and they believed it was a god, and gave him the name Lonomakua. And the people of the island thought that there would be a war. Then an old woman of high rank named Kamakalehi, the mother of Kauuali'i, said: 'Let us not fight against our god, but rather be pleasant to him, so that the god may be kindly disposed to us.'[63]

As a rule the islanders did all they could to win over the white newcomers or gain their favour. They showered the Europeans with information and advice about whatever they wished to know, and helped them in every possible way. They did their best to supply the provisions of which the seafarers often wanted huge quantities. They readily bestowed their young women on the visitors, even after noticing that venereal disease was beginning to spread. Even deserters, who were wholly at the islanders' mercy, had nothing to fear from them. It was certainly possible for the mood to change to hostility when the Europeans, often unwittingly, violated a taboo or disappointed the islanders' expectations. An example is the incident, often described despite the scanty documentation, which occurred on 14 February 1779 and ended in the death of Captain Cook at the hands of the Hawaiians.[64] Yet the way in which Charles Clerke, Cook's successor in command, reacted to this killing showed how much times had changed. If a leader of the Spanish conquistadors in the New World lost his life in battle or through assassination, his followers responded with the most brutal reprisals, such as random killing, the murder of hostages, and the pillage and burning of the natives' homes. Clerke, on the other hand, retained his self-control, though some of his crew could not understand his restraint, and managed to restore good relations.[65]

The Pacific region did not witness any warlike collision of cultures ending in the liquidation of the indigenous population; but even here it proved impossible to develop the early contacts into a form of reciprocal encounter capable of guaranteeing the independence and integrity of the alien culture. Merchants and missionaries, though at first only in small numbers, followed in the wake of the discoverers. From 1785 onwards Hawaii, thanks to its situation, became an ideal base for fur-traders who visited the Alaskan coast: in Alaska they hunted sea otters or bartered them from the Indians, later disposing of the pelts in China. Initially a British preserve, this trade passed into American hands after the War of Independence, letting the Americans stake their claim to a commercial and foreign policy of their own in the Pacific. In the early nineteenth century the trade in sea otter pelts gradually declined and was replaced by the trade in sandalwood: once again the principal consumer was China, where the wood brought from Fiji, the Marquesas and Hawaii was used for precious carvings and as a source of aromatic oils. By about 1850 the whaling industry, conducted by the ships of various nations, had become the most important in the Pacific, and it has rightly been said that it was the whalers, not the explorers, whose lengthy voyages brought to light the last coastal regions of the great ocean.[66] The South Sea islanders were generally prompt and willing to adapt to the lucrative trade in skins, wood and other natural products, not to mention pearls and whale-oil, and they began to specialize in the tasks and skills required for equipping, maintaining and supplying ships. At anchorages and in the burgeoning ports the relations between whites and islanders produced a mixed-race population, the islanders' social order and customs underwent a far-reaching transformation, and corrupting influences took their toll, aided here as elsewhere by the fatal effects of brandy. As early as 1792, during his second visit to Tahiti, Captain William Bligh noted in a distinctly disillusioned tone that the local population included 'a set of ragamuffins with whom it is necessary to observe great caution'.[67]

Equally profound changes were brought about by the activities of European missionaries. After the foundation of the London Missionary Society in 1795, missionaries began to land, first in Polynesia, then on other archipelagos. The initial difficulties arising from inadequate preparation and from the clergymen's inability to adapt to native ways were rapidly overcome, and Christianity prevailed almost everywhere. The first aim of the London missionaries was to 'civilize' the islanders, in other words to encourage seemly behaviour and respectable clothing, to root out pagan rituals and customs, and to combat cannibalism and infanticide wherever these might occur. They directed their first attentions to the families of prominent chiefs, who also embodied sacred power in traditional society, and the conversion of the upper ranks had its due effect on the mass of the people. This procedure can be observed particularly clearly on Tahiti, where the missionaries formed an alliance with the chief, Pomare II, and did not hesitate to advance his political interests in order finally to win him and his subjects over to the true faith.[68]

In 1821, when two inspectors of the London Missionary Society examined the progress made in converting the heathen on Tahiti, they saw every reason for optimism. They wrote in their report:

> While we see, with great satisfaction, all these islands living under just and humane laws, and blessed with all the institutions of the gospel, in full

operation, we rejoice in beholding the progress which civilization has made in islands so lately in the depths of barbarism and the grossest superstition. That, in so short a period since the downfal [sic] of idolatry, so many of the people should have become acquainted with the arts of reading, writing and arithmetic – so many excellent places of divine worship and numerous comfortable dwelling-houses built, and articles of furniture made – such a complete change effected in the manners of the people, from gross sensuality to the greatest decency and good behaviour – a people degraded by crime below any other people upon the face of the earth, but now the most generally, and the most consistent, professors of Christianity of any nation under heaven: – these are to us facts so singular that we are at a loss for words to express our gratitude to God.[69]

The South Sea missionaries of the nineteenth century deserve credit for taking the islanders' side against most of the excessively ruthless commercial or political intervention by Americans and Europeans.[70] Their arrival in this region, however, brought the phase of mere cultural contact to a definite end and also destroyed the illusion cherished by earlier voyagers in the Pacific that the paradise they seemed to have discovered might be preserved as it was. The German writer and naturalist Adalbert von Chamisso foresaw this when he visited the South Seas in 1817 as a member of a Russian expedition. After landing on Hawaii he wrote in his diary: 'On O-Taheiti, on O-Waihi, the handsome bodies have been concealed under shirts provided by the mission, song and dance have fallen silent, and the taboo of the Sabbath descends quietly and sadly upon the children of joy.'[71]

# Notes

CHAPTER 1 TYPES OF CULTURAL ENCOUNTER: CONTACTS, COLLISIONS
AND RELATIONSHIPS

1 L. C. Wroth, *The Voyages of Giovanni da Verrazzano, 1524–1528* (New Haven, 1970), pp. 137–8.
2 *The Journal of Christopher Columbus*, tr. C. Jane, revised by L. A. Vigneras (London, 1960), p. 23.
3 See A. T. Vaughan, *New England Frontier: Puritans and Indians*, 1620–1675 (New York, 1965), p. 65.
4 On these problems, see I. Eibl-Eibesfeld, *Die Biologie des menschlichen Verhaltens* (Munich, 1984), p. 421.
5 A. Pigafetta, *Magellan's Voyage: a narrative account of the first navigation*, ed. R. A. Skelton (London, 1975), pp. 91–4.
6 B. Hilder, *The Voyage of Torres* (Nedlands, Queensland, 1980), p. 28.
7 J. Smith, *The General Historie of Virginia* (1627) in *The Works of Captain John Smith*, ed. E. Arber (London, 1884), p. 446.
8 See, for example, the instructions given to Torres, which he disregarded: *La Austrialia del Espíritu Santo*, vol. I, ed. C. Kelly (Cambridge, 1966), pp. 144–7.
9 See S. de Madariaga, *Christopher Columbus* (London, 1939), p. 212.
10 See G. Fernández de Oviedo, *Historia general y natural de las Indias*, vol. III (Madrid, 1959), pp. 212–13.
11 J. A. Williamson, *The Cabot Voyages and Bristol Discovery under Henry VII* (Cambridge, 1962), p. 212.
12 B. de Sahagún, *Florentine Codex: general history of the things of New Spain*, Book 12 (Santa Fe, New Mexico, 1975), p. 47.
13 A. Núñez Cabeza de Vaca, *Relation of Núñez Cabeza de Vaca* (March of America Facsimile Series, no. 9, Ann Arbor, 1966), p. 151.
14 *The Voyages of Cadamosto*, ed. G. R. Crone (London, 1937), p. 49. In some instances the natives' desire to touch the Europeans can be interpreted as sexual foreplay – for example, the behaviour of the Tahitian women: 'Elles me dépouillèrent aussi de mes habits. La blancheur d'un corps européen les ravit', quoted from *Journal de Charles-Othon de Nassau-Siegen*, in *Bougainville et ses*

*compagnons autour du monde*, vol. II, ed. E. Taillemite (Paris, 1977), p. 396.

15  *The Journals of Captain James Cook on his Voyages of Discovery, 1776–1780*, ed. J. C. Beaglehole, vol. III: *The Voyage of the* Resolution *and* Discovery, *1776–1780* (Cambridge, 1967), p. 267.

16  Father P. Le Jeune, *Brief Relation of the Journey to New France* (1632), in *The Jesuit Relations and Allied Documents*, ed. R. G. Thwaites, vol. V (Cleveland, 1897), p. 121. The original runs: 'les messagers rapporterent à leur maistre que c'estoient des hommes prodigieux & espouuantables' (p. 120).

17  R. Otto, *The Idea of the Holy* (London, 1926), pp. 12–24.

18  See now N. Wachtel, *The Vision of the Vanquished: the Spanish conquest of Peru through Indian eyes, 1530–1570* (Hassocks, 1977), pp. 13–32.

19  M. León-Portilla, *Rückkehr der Götter*, ed. R. Heuer (Munich, 1962), p. 32. Cf. the original Aztec account in Sahagún, *Florentine Codex*, Book 12.

20  Sahagún, *Florentine Codex*, p. 26.

21  Titu Cusi Yupangui, *Relación de la conquista del Perú y hechos del Inca Manco II* (1570), quoted in Wachtel, *The Vision of the Vanquished*, p. 22.

22  See M. J. Herskovits, *Man and his Works: the science of cultural anthropology (New York, 1948), pp.* 68–9. Similar phenomena in black African mythology form the subject of the detailed study by the anthropologist H. Baumann, *Schöpfung und Urzeit des Menschen im Mythos der afrikanischen Völker* (Berlin, 1936). While the Cherokees' myth, quoted above, served to strengthen their cultural self-image, most African creation and culture myths reveal a resigned acknowledgement of the superiority of the white men as more perfect products of creation: see Baumann, *Schöpfung und Urzeit*, p. 333.

23  See, for example, J. Höffner, *Kolonialismus und Evangelium* (Trier, 1972).

24  See R. Konetzke, *Entdecker und Eroberer Amerikas* (Frankfurt, 1963), pp. 45–6.

25  The European image of the native has been discussed in numerous publications: see, for example, F. Chiappelli (ed.), *First Images of America: the impact of the New World on the Old* (Berkeley, 1976), and K.-H. Kohl (ed.), *Mythen der Neuen Welt: Zur Entdeckungsgeschichte Lateinamerikas* (Berlin, 1982).

26  Wroth, *The Voyages of Giovanni da Verrazzano*, p. 135.

27  Quoted in *New American World: a documentary history of North America to 1612*, vol. V, ed. D. B. Quinn (New York, 1979), p. 269.

28  G. Forster, *A Voyage Round the World*, ed. R. L. Kahn (Berlin, 1968), pp. 155–6.

29  J. de Léry, *Journal de bord* (Paris, 1957), p. 271.

30  See G. R. Crone, *The Discovery of America* (London, 1969), p. 106.

31  See K. and J. Bakeless, *Explorers of the New World* (London, 1957), p. 142.

32  J. Verken, *Molukken-Reise 1607–1612*, in *Reisebeschreibungen von deutschen Beamten und Kriegsleuten im Dienst der Niederländischen West- und Ost-Indischen Kompagnien, 1602–1797*, vol. II, ed. S. P. L'Honoré Naber (The Hague, 1930), p. 83.

33  The most careful reconstruction of the incident is given by G. Kennedy, *The Death of Captain Cook* (London, 1978), pp. 37–80. See also M. Sahlins, *Islands of History* (Chicago, 1985).

34   Quoted in B. W. Sheehan, *Savagism and Civility: Indians and Englishmen in Colonial Virginia* (Cambridge, 1980), p. 172. In what follows I rely on Sheehan's analysis of the events.

35   See the fascinating discussion by W. Cronon, *Changes in the Land: Indians, colonists, and the ecology of New England* (New York, 1983).

36   *The Jamestown Voyages under the First Charter, 1606–1609*, ed. P. Barbour (Cambridge, 1969), p. 110.

37   On the situation in the Congo, see Georges Balandier, *Daily Life in the Kingdom of the Kongo from the Sixteenth to the Eighteenth Century* (London, 1968), pp. 42–85. On the West African situation and the shifts in power brought about by the Europeans, see the case study by A. F. C. Ryder, *Benin and the Europeans, 1485–1897* (London, 1969).

38   An example of English intervention in the dynastic succession in seventeenth-century Malacca is provided by the traveller Peter Mundy. See *The Travels of Peter Mundy in Europe and Asia, 1608–1667*, vol. III, ed. R. C. Temple (London, 1919), p. 120. Cf. H. Furber, *Rival Empires of Trade in the Orient, 1600–1800* (Minneapolis, 1976), pp. 310–14.

39   This can be documented for Virginia as well as New England. See Sheehan, *Savagism and Civility*, pp. 149–50, and F. Jennings, *The Invasion of America: Indians, colonialism, and the cant of conquest* (Chapel Hill, 1975), pp. 58–104.

40   See J. Fisch, 'Tod in Nagasaki. Die Hinrichtung einer portugiesischen Gesandtschaft im Jahre 1640', *Neue Zürcher Zeitung*, 7 March 1981.

41   See J. Axtell, *The European and the Indian: essays on the ethnohistory of colonial North America* (New York, 1981), pp. 16–35.

42   For a detailed account, see Jennings, *The Invasion of America*, pp. 160–8.

43   Quoted in Sheehan, *Savagism and Civility*, p. 173. See also H. C. Porter, *The Inconstant Savage* (London, 1979), pp. 459–83.

44   See Sheehan, *Savagism and Civility*, pp. 181–2.

45   See Vaughan, *New England Frontier*, pp. 319–20.

46   G. Friederici, *Der Charakter der Entdeckung und Eroberung Amerikas durch die Europäer*, vol. I (Stuttgart, 1925), p. 548.

47   N. Wachtel, 'The Indian and the Spanish Conquest', in *The Cambridge History of Latin America*, ed. L. Bethell, vol. I: *Colonial Latin America* (Cambridge, 1984), p. 213.

48   See Jennings, *The Invasion of America*, p. 26.

49   Ibid., p. 27.

50   Ibid., pp. 23, 27; cf. Axtell, *The European and the Indian*, p. 249.

51   Quoted in Cronon, *Changes in the Land*, p. 90.

52   It is estimated that in the space of twenty years the population of Polynesia was literally decimated by disease. See B. Danielson, 'La Polynésie', in *Ethnologie générale*, vol. II, ed. J. Poirier (Paris, 1982), p. 1318.

53   See K. G. Davies, 'The living and the dead: white mortality in West Africa, 1684–1732', in *Race and Slavery in the Western Hemisphere*, ed. S. L. Engerman and E. D. Genovese (Princeton, 1975). Cf. P. D. Curtin, *The Image of Africa* (London, 1965), pp. 73–4, 483–7.

54   Konetzke, *Entdecker und Eroberer Amerikas*, pp. 32–3.

55   On this topic see R. Konetzke, *Süd- und Mittelamerika*, vol. I (Frankfurt,

1965), pp. 173–219, and Wachtel, 'The Indian and the Spanish conquest', p. 220.

56 There is an often-repeated legend to the effect that the Dominican Bartolomé de Las Casas introduced the slave trade into the Caribbean: see J. von Stackelberg, '"Primero el clérigo Casas . . .": zur Legende vom *Apostel der Indios* als Initiator des Negersklavenhandels', *Iberoromania*, 13 (1981), pp. 30–46.

57 Most of these figures come from A. Wirz, *Sklaverei und kapitalistisches Weltsystem* (Frankfurt, 1984), pp. 35ff. This book provides an outstanding survey of the current debate on slavery.

58 On regional variations, see the article by C. N. Degler, 'Slavery in Brazil and the United States: an essay in comparative history', *American Historical Review*, 75 (1970), pp. 1004–28, which summarizes much previous research.

59 On working conditions and life on the slave plantation, see K. M. Stampp, *The Peculiar Institution: slavery in the Antebellum South* (New York, 1956). In the United States this book initiated a heated discussion of the problem of slavery, drawing on such novel methods as oral history and cliometrics. Outstanding contributions to this controversy include: S. Elkins, *Slavery: a problem in American institutional and intellectual life* (Chicago, 1959); E. D. Genovese, *Roll, Jordan, Roll: the world the slaves made* (New York, 1974); R. W. Fogel and S. L. Engerman, *Time on the Cross: the economics of American negro slavery* (Boston, 1974); N. I. Huggins, *Black Odyssey: the Afro-American ordeal in slavery* (New York, 1977). A major source is the nineteen-volume collection edited by G. P. Rawick, based on oral interviews, *The American Slave: a composite autobiography* (repr. Westport, Conn., 1972); the first volume offers a general survey of life on the plantation. On the situation in Brazil, see K. M. de Queirós Mattoso, *Ser Escravo no Brasil* (São Paulo, 1973), now available in English as *To be a Slave in Brazil* (New Brunswick, NJ, 1986).

60 It is understandable that a scholarly literature which tried to soften the facts of slavery should have guaranteed particular publicity for such exceptions and encouraged black authors to recount their own experiences accordingly. See the critical account by M. Plessner, *Onkel Tom verbrennt seine Hütte: Die literarische Revolution der schwarzen Amerikaner* (Frankfurt, 1963).

61 *Autobiography of the Reverend Josiah Henson* (Reading, Mass., 1969), p. 18.

62 Elkins, *Slavery*; for a criticism of this view, see E. D. Genovese, *In Red and Black: Marxian explorations in Southern and Afro-American historiography* (New York, 1971), pp. 73–101. There is an immense literature on the mixed-race societies that have emerged from the slave economy, especially on the 'special case' of Brazil. A good introduction to the problems involved is provided by P. Baxter and B. Sansom (eds), *Race and Social Difference: selected readings*, (Harmondsworth, 1972). Some publications, such as those by G. Myrdal and D. P. Moynihan, have also influenced political developments in the USA.

63 H. G. Gutman, *The Black Family in Slavery and Freedom, 1750–1925* (New York, 1976). Gutman took issue with the quantitative research of Fogel and Engerman in an earlier work, entitled *Slavery and the Numbers Game* (Urbana, Ill., 1975).

64 On the black contribution to North American culture, see the classic work

by C. S. Johnson, *The Negro in American Civilization* (London, 1931). On the specific role of religion in the formation of a black identity there are now historical case studies, for example, C. Joyner, *Down by the Riverside: a South Carolina slave community* (Urbana, Ill., 1984), pp. 141–71.

65  R. Bastide, *The African Religions of Brazil* (Baltimore and London, 1978), p. 95.

66  Mattoso, *Ser Escravo no Brasil*, p. 155.

67  See Wirz, *Sklaverei und kapitalistisches Weltsystem*, p. 164. Cf. also E. Montejo, *The Autobiography of a Runaway Slave*, ed. M. Barnet (London, 1968).

68  See J. D. Fage, 'Upper and Lower Guinea', in *The Cambridge History of Africa*, vol. III, ed. R. Oliver (Cambridge, 1982), pp. 512–13.

69  C. Jannequin, *Voyage de Lybie au Royaume de Sénégal* (Paris, 1643), pp. 43–4. Silent trade is described as early as Herodotus, *The Histories* (Harmondsworth, 1972), p. 336.

70  'Richard Eden's Account of John Lok's Voyage to Mina, 1554–5', in *Europeans in West Africa, 1450–1560*, vol. II, ed. J. W. Blake (London, 1942), p. 343.

71  Quoted in K. G. Davies, *The Royal African Company* (London, 1957), pp. 367–8.

72  J.-B. Labat, *Nouvelle relation de l'Afrique occidentale*, vol. 3 (Paris, 1728), p. 221.

73  Even so early a source as Jean de Léry's *Journal de bord*, describing conditions in mid-sixteenth-century Brazil, tells of Frenchmen who joined the Tupis and took part in their cannibalism. Those who joined the Muslims aroused particular disapproval; see, for example, J. Verken, *Molukken-Reise 1607–1612*, pp. 107–8: 'he took a white handkerchief from his pocket, tied it to a stick, and with this he ran along the seashore to a boat full of Moors that he had seen lying there; he was taken on board and carried to the island of Banda, where on the following day he was circumcised and made into a Turk.' In North America in 1770, the trapper James Adair writes: 'Many of the traders at present are lost and degenerate white savages.' See S. C. Williams, *Adair's History of the American Indians* (Kingsport, 1930), p. 306.

74  On the *coureurs de bois*, see M. Béland, *Chansons de voyageurs, coureurs de bois et forestiers* (Quebec, 1982); also U. Bitterli, *Schriftsteller und Kolonialismus* (Zürich, 1973).

75  *The Embassy of Sir Thomas Roe to the Court of the Great Mogul, 1615–1619*, ed. W. Foster, vol. I (London, 1899), p. 92; *The Voyages of Nicholas Downton to the East Indies, 1614–15*, ed. W. Foster (London, 1939), p. 31.

76  On this cluster of problems, see K. A. Wittfogel, *Oriental Despotism* (New Haven, 1957), esp. pp. 152–4, 305–6.

77  *The Travels of Peter Mundy*, vol. III, p. 111. Cf. p. 141.

78  Missionary activity will be discussed in Chapter 4, taking Canada as an example; further references to secondary sources will be given there.

79  The rites controversy was provoked around the year 1630 by the question of the extent to which the Jesuits could adapt Catholic ceremony and terminology to

the Confucian tradition. The Jesuits' conduct of their mission was condemned by the Papal Bull *Ex illa die* of 1715. See Etiemble, *Les Jésuites en Chine: la querelle des rites* (Paris, 1966).

80 The commercial involvement of Jesuit monks in China and on Macao is criticized both in Dominican texts and in the work of the Puritan traveller Peter Mundy. See *The Travels of Peter Mundy*, vol. III, ed. Temple, p. 293. On the same group of problems in Canada, see B. G. Trigger, 'The French presence in Huronia: the structure of Franco-Huron relations in the first half of the seventeenth century', *Canadian Historical Review*, 49 (1968), pp. 107–41.

81 See W. G. McLoughlin, *Cherokees and Missionaries, 1789–1839* (New Haven, 1984), pp. 33–4.

82 This is dealt with in U. Höner, *Die Versklavung der brasilianischen Indianer* (Zürich, 1980), who is very critical of the missions. Cf. the discussion in W. Reinhard, 'Gelenkter Kulturwandel im siebzehnten Jahrhundert: Akkulturation in den Jesuitenmissionen als universalhistorisches Problem', *Historische Zeitschrift*, 223 (1976), pp. 529–90.

83 This has recently been convincingly demonstrated, using Chinese source-material, by J. Gernet, *Chine et christianisme: action et réaction* (Paris, 1982), translated into English as *China and the Christian Impact* (Cambridge, 1985).

84 See Reinhard, 'Gelenkter Kulturwandel', pp. 574–85.

85 See K. S. Latourette, *A History of the Expansion of Christianity*, vol. V (London, 1943), pp. 198–263. See also H. Bingham, *A Residence of Twenty-one Years in the Sandwich Islands* (repr. New York, 1969), pp. 179–80.

86 See McLoughlin, *Cherokees and Missionaries*, pp. 82–101.

87 Herskovits, *Man and his Works*, p. 523, quoting from a memorandum issued in 1935 by the Social Science Research Council. On the historical relevance of the problem of acculturation, see also A. Dupront, 'De l'acculturation', in *XII$^e$ Congrès international des sciences historiques*, vol. I (Vienna, 1965), pp. 7–36; N. Wachtel, 'L'acculturation', in *Faire de l'histoire*, vol. I, ed. J. Le Goff and P. Nora, (Paris, 1974), pp. 124–45.

88 See C. Wissler, 'The influence of the horse in the development of Plains culture', *American Anthropologist*, 16 (1914), pp. 1–25.

89 The concept of cultural lag was introduced by W. F. Ogburn, *Social Change with Respect to Culture and Original Nature* (New York, 1923).

90 The effect of 'challenge and response' in the creation of cultures is discussed by A. J. Toynbee, *A Study of History*, vol. XII: *Reconsiderations* (London, 1961), pp. 254–63.

91 G. Balandier, *Ambiguous Africa* (London, 1966), pp. 168–95.

92 R. Bastide, *Le proche et le lointain* (Paris, 1970), p. 143.

93 See R. A. Billington, *America's Frontier Heritage* (New York, 1966).

CHAPTER 2   THE SYSTEM OF LIMITED CONTACTS: THE PORTUGUESE IN AFRICA
AND ASIA

1 On the structure of Portuguese society at this time, see V. Magalhães Godinho, *Estrutura da antiga sociedade portuguêsa* (Lisbon, 1977), pp. 71ff.

2  On cultural relations between the Iberian peninsula and Islam, see S. Hunke, *Allahs Sonne über dem Abendland* (Frankfurt, 1965) and J. Van Esse (ed.), *Das Vermächtnis des Islams* (Zürich, 1980). On relations with African culture, see C. Verlinden, *Les Origines de la civilisation atlantique* (Neuchâtel, 1966).

3  See F. de Almeida, *O Infante de Sagres* (Oporto, 1894); C. R. Beazley, *Prince Henry the Navigator*, new edn (London, 1968); and the detailed study by G. Hamann, *Der Eintritt der südlichen Hemisphäre in die europäische Geschichte* (Vienna, 1968).

4  *The Chronicle of the Discovery and Conquest of Guinea, written by Gomes Eannes de Azurara*, tr. and ed. C. R. Beazley and E. Prestage (London, 1896–9).

5  A lucid overview of Portuguese knowledge about the rest of the world is given in J. H. Parry, *The Age of Reconnaissance* (London, 1963). Some important travel narratives are reprinted in R. Hennig, *Terrae Incognitae: Eine Zusammenstellung und kritische Beurteilung der wichtigsten vorkolumbischen Entdeckungsreisen an Hand der darüber vorliegenden Originalberichte* (Leiden, 1936–9). The classic scholarly edition of Marco Polo is *The Book of Ser Marco Polo the Venetian concerning the Kingdoms and Marvels of the East*, tr. and ed. H. Yule, 3rd edn revised by H. Cordier (London, 1903). See also *Mandeville's Travels*, ed. M. C. Seymour (Oxford, 1967); *The Travels of Ibn Battuta*, ed. H. A. R. Gibb (Cambridge, 1958–71); and *Die Entdeckung und Eroberung der Welt*, ed. U. Bitterli (Munich, 1981).

6  Quoted in Beazley and Prestage (eds), *The Chronicle of the Discovery and Conquest of Guinea*, vol. I, pp. 27–8.

7  Ibid., p. 28.

8  Matthew 28: 18–20. On the part played by missionary activity in Portuguese colonial politics, see the useful survey by F. Blanke, 'Mission und Kolonialpolitik', in *Europa und der Kolonialismus*, ed. M. Silberschmidt (Zürich, 1962). See also H. Jedin, 'Weltmission und Kolonialismus', *Saeculum*, 9 (1958), pp. 393–404.

9  Beazley and Prestage (eds), *The Chronicle of the Discovery and Conquest of Guinea*, vol. I, p. 29.

10  On Prester John, see H. Baudet, *Paradise on Earth* (New Haven and London, 1965), p. 17. Baudet supplies an illuminating account of Utopian aspirations in the history of European colonialism. See also *Europeans in West Africa, 1450–1560*, ed. J. W. Blake, vol. II (London, 1942), p. 340.

11  These questions of international law are discussed in their context by H. Gollwitzer, *Geschichte des weltpolitischen Denkens*, vol. I: *Vom Zeitalter der Entdeckungen bis zum Beginn des Imperialismus* (Göttingen, 1972), pp. 36–43. Relevant documents are reprinted in E. Reibstein, *Völkerrecht: Eine Geschichte seiner Ideen in Lehre und Praxis*, vol. I: *Von der Antike bis zur Aufklärung* (Freiburg and Munich, 1958). See also R. Konetzke, *Süd- und Mittelamerika*, vol. I (Frankfurt, 1965), pp. 27–41; P. Chaunu, *L'Expansion européenne du XIIIᵉ au XVᵉ siècle* (Paris, 1969), pp. 207–10.

12  The Portuguese voyages of discovery are among the most popular subjects in the history of colonization. The account by O. Peschel, *Geschichte des Zeitalters der Entdeckungen* (Stuttgart, 1858), is very valuable, though dated. The following may also be recommended: J. Cortesão, *Os descobrimentos portu-*

*guêses* (Lisbon, 1960–2); Parry, *The Age of Reconnaissance*; B. Penrose, *Travel and Discovery in the Renaissance, 1420–1620* (Cambridge, Mass., 1952); Hamann, *Der Eintritt der südlichen Hemisphäre*; E. Prestage, *The Portuguese Pioneers* (London, 1933); E. Samhaber, *Geschichte der Entdeckungsreisen* (Munich, 1955), pp. 104–40. One of the best short accounts of Portuguese discoveries and settlements is C. R. Boxer, *Four Centuries of Portuguese Expansion, 1415–1825* (Johannesburg, 1961). Recent research is summarized in W. Reinhard, *Geschichte der europäischen Expansion* (Stuttgart, 1983).

13  On the invention of the caravel, see Chaunu, *L'Expansion européenne*, pp. 284–8, and B. Landström, *The Ship* (London, 1961), pp. 106–7.

14  L. Vaz de Camoens, *The Lusiads* (Harmondsworth, 1952), canto 4.

15  On the political implications of military technology, see C. M. Cipolla, *Guns and Sails in the Early Phase of European Expansion, 1400–1700* (London, 1965).

16  On the history of cartography, see the standard work by L. Bagrow, *History of Cartography*, revised by R. A. Skelton (London, 1964). On Portugal in particular, see A. Cortesão, *Cartografia portuguêsa antiga* (Lisbon, 1960); *Estudos de cartografia antiga* (Lisbon, 1979).

17  On the history of navigation, see E. G. R. Taylor, *The Haven-Finding Art: a history of navigation from Odysseus to Captain Cook* (London, 1956); G. Coutinho, *A náutica dos descobrimentos* (Lisbon, 1951–2).

18  On economic questions, see the standard work by V. Magalhães Godinho, *Os descobrimentos e a economia mundial*(Lisbon, 1963–5); for this particular topic, vol. I, p. 163.

19  On the Portuguese slave trade, see C. Verlinden, *L'Esclavage dans l'Europe médiévale* (Bruges, 1955); id., 'Les Débuts de la traite portugaise en Afrique, 1443–1448', *Studia Historica Gandensia* (1967); F. Mauro, *Le Portugal et l'Atlantique au XVII$^e$ siècle* (Paris, 1960); M. Goulart, *Escravidão africana no Brasil* (São Paulo, 1950).

20  This figure is given by A. F. C. Ryder, *Benin and the Europeans* (London, 1969), p. 36. Godinho, referring to contemporary sources, suggests a somewhat higher estimate: see *Estrutura*, pp. 83ff.

21  See C. R. Boxer, *The Portuguese Seaborne Empire, 1415–1825* (London, 1969), p. 104.

22  On the history of missions in Africa, see C. P. Groves, *The Planting of Christianity in Africa*, vol. I (London, 1948). In this connection important information about Africa and Asia is provided by the numerous editions and monographs by J. Wicki and G. Schurhammer; also J. Didinger and R. Streit, *Bibliotheca Missionum*, vols. XV–XVIII (Fribourg, 1951–3).

23  Quoted in G. Balandier, *Daily Life in the Kingdom of the Kongo from the Sixteenth to the Eighteenth Century* (London, 1968), pp. 52–3.

24  On India before and during Portuguese colonization, see R. Thapar, *A History of India*, vol. I (Harmondsworth, 1966), and A. T. Embree and F. Wilhelm (eds.), *Indien: Geschichte des Subkontinents von der Induskultur bis zum Beginn der englischen Herrschaft* (Frankfurt, 1967); also the competent surveys by D. Rothermund, *Grundzüge der indischen Geschichte* (Darmstadt, 1976), and the report on recent research by D. Rothermund *et al.*, 'Indische

Geschichte vom Altertum bis zur Gegenwart: Literaturbericht über neue Veröffentlichungen', *Historische Zeitschrift*, 1982: Sonderheft 10, pp. 229–49. On trade relations between Portugal and India, see especially A. R. Disney, *Twilight of the Pepper Empire: Portuguese trade in southwest India in the early seventeenth century* (Cambridge, Mass., 1978); also G. Schurhammer, *Die zeitgenössischen Quellen zur Geschichte Portugiesisch-Asiens und seiner Nachbarländer* (Leipzig, 1933); E. Zechlin, 'Die Ankunft der Portugiesen in Indien, China und Japan als Problem der Universalgeschichte', *Historische Zeitschrift*, 157 (1937–8), pp. 491–526.

25   Quoted in B. W. Diffie and G. D. Winius, *Foundations of the Portuguese Empire, 1415–1580* (Minneapolis, 1977), p. 181. According to other sources the Portuguese were greeted enthusiastically: 'Welcome to you all! Praise to God for guiding you to the richest land in the world!' (Quoted in Peschel, *Geschichte des Zeitalters der Entdeckungen*, p. 450.) If not due to the chroniclers' misinformation, such contradictions point to rivalry between different groups within the Indian coastal population.

26   Diffie and Winius, *Foundations of the Portuguese Empire*, p. 322.

27   The term 'thalassocratic', referring to colonial history, derives from Adolf Rein, who also speaks of 'potamic' colonization (i.e. spreading out along river systems). See A. Rein, *Die europäische Ausbreitung über die Erde* (Potsdam, 1931), p. 122.

28   On these topics, see C. R. Boxer, *Portuguese Society in the Tropics* (Madison, Wis., 1965), pp. 12–41.

29   Diffie and Winius, *Foundations of the Portuguese Empire*, p. 331.

30   Boxer, *The Portuguese Seaborne Empire*, p. 53.

31   Ibid., p. 219.

32   P. Chaunu, *Conquête et exploitation des nouveaux mondes* (Paris, 1969), pp. 288–90.

33   Ibid., p. 318.

34   G. Friederici, *Der Charakter der Entdeckung und Eroberung Amerikas durch die Europäer*, vol. II (Stuttgart, 1936), p. 90.

35   Quoted in J. Fisch, 'Der Niedergang des Abendlandes im Morgenland: Diogo do Couto (1542–1616) und die portugiesische Herrschaft in Asien', in *Niedergang: Studien zu einem geschichtlichen Thema*, ed. R. Koselleck and P. Widmer (Stuttgart, 1981), p. 163.

36   On Francis Xavier, see the extremely detailed biography by G. Schurhammer, *Francis Xavier: his life, his times* (Rome, 1973–82).

37   See the catalogue of the 17th exhibition of the Council of Europe, held in Lisbon in 1983.

38   See, for example, the studies by R. Bastide, *Brancos e Negros em São Paulo* (São Paulo, 1959) and *Le proche et le lointain* (Paris, 1970), pp. 15ff.

39   See G. Freyre, *The Masters and the Slaves* (New York, 1956).

40   Quoted in *The Voyage of Pedro Álvares Cabral to Brazil and India*, ed. W. B. Greenlee (London, 1938), p. 133. A masterly account of the Mediterranean in this period is given by F. Braudel, *The Mediterranean and the Mediterranean World in the Age of Philip II* (London, 1972).

41   On the development of the economic and political situation after 1600, see

H. Furber, *Rival Empires of Trade in the Orient, 1600–1800* (Minneapolis, 1976).

42   On the history of Brazil, see, in addition to the works of Gilberto Freyre, P. Calmon, *Historia do Brasil* (São Paulo, 1959); F. de Azevedo, *Brazilian Culture* (New York, 1950); C. R. Boxer, *The Dutch in Brazil, 1624–1654* (Oxford, 1957); T. O. Marcondes de Souza, *O descobrimento do Brasil* (São Paulo, 1946); Friederici, *Der Charakter der Entdeckung und Eroberung Amerikas*, vol. II, pp. 96–257. On relations with the Indians, see M. C. Kiemen, 'The Indian policy of Portugal in America, with special reference to the old state of Maranhão, 1500–1755', *The Americas*, 5 (1948–9), pp. 131–71, 439–61.

CHAPTER 3    CULTURAL COLLISION: THE SPANIARDS ON HISPANIOLA

1   P. Chaunu, *Séville et l'Amérique aux XVI<sup>e</sup> et XVII<sup>e</sup> siècles* (Paris, 1977), p. 81.

2   Columbus's geographical notions and their conflict with reality are discussed in detail by S. E. Morison, *The European Discovery of America: the southern voyages, AD 1492–1616* (New York, 1974), pp. 72–5. See also G. R. Crone, *The Discovery of America* (London, 1969), pp. 78–9. On the history of discoveries, see also F. Morales Padron, *Historia del descubrimiento y conquista de América* (Madrid, 1963); R. Konetzke, *Entdecker und Eroberer Amerikas* (Frankfurt, 1963).

3   On ethnography, see the standard work, J. H. Steward (ed.), *Handbook of South American Indians*, vol. 4: *The Circum-Caribbean Tribes* (Washington, 1948), pp. 522–39. On the geography of Hispaniola, see H. Blume, *Die westindischen Inseln* (Braunschweig, 1968).

4   Cf. Columbus's diary entry for 16 December, in *The Journal of Christopher Columbus*, tr. C. Jane, revised by L. A. Vigneras (London, 1960), p. 100. For the original, see the facsimile edition, *Diario de Colón*, ed. C. Sanz (Madrid, 1962), fols 37v–38v.

5   N. Wachtel, *The Vision of the Vanquished: the Spanish Conquest of Peru through Indian eyes, 1530–1570* (Hassocks, 1977). See also M. León-Portilla, *Die Aufzeichnungen der Azteken über den Untergang ihres Reiches* (Munich, 1965).

6   *The Journal of Christopher Columbus*, p. 101. In the original (*Diario de Colón*, fol. 38r): 'Después a la tarde vino el rey a la nao. El Almirante le hizo la honra que debía y le hizo decir cómo era de los Reyes de Castilla, los cuales eran los mayores príncipes del mundo. Mas ni los indios que el Almirante traía, que eran los intérpretes, creían nada, ni el rey tampoco, sino creían que venían del cielo, y que los reinos de los Reyes de Castilla eran en el cielo y no en este mundo.'

7   F. López de Gómara, *Historia general de las Indias*, vol. I (Madrid, 1941), p. 77: 'que supiesen cómo antes de muchos años vernían a la isla unos hombres de barbas largas y vestidos todo el cuerpo, que hendiesen de un golpe un hombre por medio con las espadas relucientes que traerían ceñidas.'

8   *The Journal of Christopher Columbus*, p. 111. In the original (*Diario de Colón*, fol. 42v): 'Finalmente, dice al [sic] Almirante, que no puede creer que

hombre haya visto gente de tan buenos corazones y francos para dar y tan temerosos que ellos se deshacían todos por dar a los cristianos cuanto tenían, y en llegando los cristianos, luego corrían a traerlo todo.'

9  *Select Documents Illustrating the Four Voyages of Columbus*, tr. C. Jane, vol. I (London, 1930), p. 6. The original runs: 'la Española es maravilla; las sierras y las montañas y las vegas y las campiñas, y las tierras tan fermosas y gruesas para plantar y sembrar, para criar ganados de todas suertes, para hedeficios de villas é lugares. los puertos de la mar aqué no havréa creencia sin vista, y de los rios muchos y grandes, y buenas aguas, los más de los quales traen oro' (ibid., p. 7).

10  *The Journal of Christopher Columbus*, p. 39. In the original (*Diario de Colón*, fol. 15v): 'Verdad es que, hallando adonde haya oro y especería en cantidad, me detendré hasta que yo haya de ello cuanto pudiere; y por esto no hago sino andar para ver de topar en ello.'

11  *The Journal of Christopher Columbus*, p. 117. In the original (*Diario de Colón*, fol. 44v): 'Nuestro Señor me aderece, por su piedad, que halle este oro [ . . . ]'

12  *Select Documents*, vol. II (London, 1933), p. 104. In the original: 'el oro es exçelentíssimo; de oro se hace tesoro, i con él, quien lo tiene, hace quanto quiere en el mundo, i llega á que echa las ánimas al Paraíso' (ibid., p. 103).

13  G. Friederici, *Der Charakter der Entdeckung und Eroberung Amerikas durch die Europäer*, vol. I (Stuttgart, 1925), p. 404.

14  *The Journal of Christopher Columbus*, pp. 101–2. In the original (*Diario de Colón*, fol. 38v): 'y así son buenos para les mandar y les hacer trabajar, sembrar, y hacer todo lo otro que fuese menester [ . . . ]'

15  On the difficult and much debated problem of Columbus's personality, see G. Hamann, 'Christoph Columbus zwischen Mittelalter und Neuzeit: Nachfahre und Wegbereiter', in *Europäisierung der Erde? Studien zur Einwirkung Europas auf die außereuropäische Welt*, ed. G. Klingenstein, H. Lutz and G. Stourzh (Vienna, 1980), pp. 15–38. Further C. Verlinden, 'Christoph Colomb: Esquisse d'une analyse mentale' in *Revista de Historia de América* (1980), and M. Torodash, 'Columbus Historiography since 1939', *Hispanic American Historical Review*, 46 (1966), pp. 409–28. On the theological background to Spanish colonial policy, see the brief account by S. Zavala, *Filosofía de la Conquista* (Mexico City, 1947), and, for more detail, J. Höffner, *Christentum und Menschenwürde: Das Anliegen der spanischen Kolonialethik im Goldenen Zeitalter* (Trier, 1947); H. Jedin, 'Weltmission und Kolonialismus', *Saeculum*, 9 (1958), pp. 393–404.

16  S. de Madariaga, *Christopher Columbus* (London, 1939), p. 192.

17  *The Journal of Christopher Columbus*, p. 58. In the original (*Diario de Colón*, fol. 22v): 'yo vi e conozco que esta gente no tiene secta ninguna ni son idólatras, salvo muy mansos y sin saber que sea mal. [ . . . ] Así que deben Vuestras Altezas determinarse a los hacer cristianos, que creo que si comienzan, en poco tiempo acabará de los haber convertido a nuestra Santa Fe multidumbre de pueblos.'

18  T. Todorov, *The Conquest of America: the question of the Other* (New York, 1984), p. 49.

19  The procedure of *pacificación* is discussed in detail by Friederici, *Der*

*Charakter der Entdeckung und Eroberung Amerikas*, vol. I, pp. 548–79. Cf. Zavala, *Filosofía de la Conquista*. The actions of the Spaniards on Hispaniola are described by Konetzke, *Entdecker und Eroberer*, pp. 26–43.

20  Quoted in Konetzke, *Entdecker und Eroberer*, p. 33.

21  On the *repartimiento* system, see R. Konetzke, *Süd- und Mittelamerika* (Frankfurt, 1965), vol. I, pp. 42–58, 174–5. A standard account, with ample detail, is S. Zavala, *La encomienda indiana* (Madrid, 1935). See also L. Bethell (ed.), *The Cambridge History of Latin America*, vol. I: *Colonial Latin America* (Cambridge, 1984).

22  See C. O. Sauer, *The Early Spanish Main* (Berkeley, 1966), pp. 200–12. This book gives a minute account of the liquidation of the islanders of Hispaniola, and we have followed its main points. Cf. W. M. Denevan, *The Native Population of the Americas in 1492* (Madison, Wis., 1976).

23  See Sauer, *The Early Spanish Main*, p. 204.

24  Ibid., p. 206.

25  Konetzke, *Entdecker und Eroberer*, p. 37.

26  Sauer, *The Early Spanish Main*, pp. 65–9.

27  Quoted in Sauer, *The Early Spanish Main*, p. 155. On these and similar demographic problems, see Konetzke, *Süd- und Mittelamerika*, vol. I, pp. 101–8.

28  Quoted in L. Hanke, *The Spanish Struggle for Justice in the Conquest of America* (Philadelphia, 1949), p. 17.

29  For guidance through the legal and theological debate, see the above-mentioned work by Hanke; M. Góngora, *Studies in the Colonial History of Spanish America* (Cambridge, 1975), pp. 33–66; Höffner, *Christentum und Menschenwürde*, pp. 183–297; and for a brief summary, Konetzke, *Süd- und Mittelamerika*, vol. I, pp. 175–7.

30  On Las Casas's biography, see L. Hanke, *Bartolomé de Las Casas Historian* (Gainsville, 1952), and Hanke's thorough *Bibliografía crítica* (Santiago de Chile, 1954). Cf. also the essay by Hans Magnus Enzensberger, 'Las Casas oder ein Rückblick in die Zukunft', in B. de las Casas, *Kurzgefaßter Bericht von der Verwüstung der Westindischen Länder* (Frankfurt, 1966).

31  B. de Las Casas, *Historia de las Indias* (Mexico City, 1951), with an excellent introduction by Lewis Hanke.

32  J. H. Parry, *The Spanish Seaborne Empire* (London, 1966), p. 143.

33  Voltaire, *Essai sur les mœurs et l'esprit des nations*, vol. II (Paris, 1963), p. 339.

34  See M. Mahn-Lot, 'Controverses autour de Bartolomé de Las Casas', *Annales*, 21 (1966), pp. 875–85, and the numerous works by Lewis Hanke, the chief authority on Las Casas.

35  'En estas ovejas mansas, y de las calidades susodichas por su Hacedor y Criador así dotadas, entraron los españoles, desde luego que las conocieron, como lobos e tigres y leones cruelísimos de muchos días hambrientos. Y otra cosa no han hecho de cuarenta años a esta parte, hasta hoy, e hoy en este día lo hacen, sino despedazallas, matallas, angustiallas, afligillas, atormentallas y destruillas por las estrañas y nuevas e varias e nunca otras tales vistas ni leídas ni oídas maneras de crueldad, de las cuales algunas pocas abajo se dirán, en tanto grado, que habiendo en la isla Española sobre tres cuentos de ánimas que vimos, no hay

hoy de los naturales de ella docientas personas.' Quoted in 'Brevísima relación de la destruición de las Indias', in B. de Las Casas, *Obras escogidas*, vol. V (Madrid, 1958), p. 136. See also the documentation in *Die neue Welt: Chroniken Lateinamerikas von Kolumbus bis zu den Unabhängigkeitskriegen*, ed. E. R. Monegal (Frankfurt, 1982).

36 B. de Las Casas, *Del único modo atraer a todos los pueblos a la verdadera religión* (Mexico City, 1942). On the 'just war' debate, see also E. Straub, *Das Bellum Justum des Hernán Cortés in Mexico* (Cologne, 1976).

37 The problem of slavery is dealt with in Book I of Aristotle's *Politics*: 'It is clear then that by nature some are free, others slaves, and that for these it is both just and expedient that they should serve as slaves' (Harmondsworth, 1981, p. 69). This sentence initiated a debate that lasted for centuries and was settled by international law only in the early nineteenth century. See D. B. Davis, *The Problem of Slavery in Western Culture* (Ithaca, 1966).

38 J. G. de Sepúlveda,*Tratado sobre las justas causas de la guerra contra los indios* (Mexico City, 1941).

39 Quoted in Höffner, *Christentum und Menschenwürde*, p. 170.

40 Ibid., p. 174.

41 On Vitoria, see Góngora, *Studies in the Colonial History of Spanish America*, pp. 56–8; also Höffner, *Christentum und Menschenwürde*, pp. 184–92.

42 See Góngora, *Studies in the Colonial History of Spanish America*, pp. 26–30.

43 G. C. Lichtenberg, *Ausgewählte Werke*, vol. I (Frankfurt, 1970), p. 227. The extent of Spanish guilt will no doubt always remain a matter of controversy. See the following comments: L. Hanke, 'More heat and some light on the Spanish struggle for justice in the conquest of America', *Hispanic American Historical Review*, 44 (1964), pp. 293–340, and B. Keen, 'The White Legend revisited: a reply to Professor Hanke's modest proposal', *Hispanic American Historical Review*, 51 (1971), pp. 336–55.

CHAPTER 4   MISSIONARY WORK AS A CULTURAL RELATIONSHIP: THE
FRENCH IN CANADA

1 A. and E. Ingstad, *The Discovery of a Norse Settlement in America* (Oslo, 1977).

2 On the discovery of Canada, see especially S. E. Morison, *The European Discovery of America: The northern voyages, A.D. 500–1600* (New York, 1971), pp. 339–463. See also B. G. Hoffmann, *From Cabot to Cartier: sources for a historical ethnography of northeastern North America* (Toronto, 1961).

3 On Cartier's biography, see C. La Roncière, *Jacques Cartier* (Paris, 1931), and J. P. Baxter, *Memoir of Jacques Cartier* (New York, 1906). The 450th anniversary of Cartier's voyage was marked by the publication of a large illustrated volume, *Le Monde de Jacques Cartier*, ed. F. Braudel (Paris, 1984).

4 See *A Collection of Documents Relating to Jacques Cartier and the Sieur de Roberval*, ed. H. P. Biggar (Ottawa, 1930), p. 42: 'descouvrir certaines ysles et

pays où l'on dit qu'il se doibt trouver grant quantité d'or et autres riches choses.'

5  Cf. Genesis 4: 12: 'When thou tillest the ground, it shall not henceforth yield unto thee her strength'; and 4: 16: 'And Cain went out from the presence of the Lord, and dwelt in the land of Nod, on the east of Eden.' Cartier's account is reprinted in *Les Français en Amérique pendant la première moitié du XVI^e siècle*, ed. C.-A. Julien (Paris, 1946), p. 87.

6  See *Les Français en Amérique*, ed. Julien, pp. 168–9. The botanical identity of this wondrous plant or tree remains controversial. Bruce G. Trigger suggests a white cedar (*Thuya occidentalis*); see *Le Monde de Jacques Cartier*, ed. Braudel, p. 269.

7  See *A Collection of Documents*, ed. Biggar, p. 70: 'il [le Roi] sçavoit bien qu'il n'y avoit point de mines d'or & d'argent, ny autre gain à esperer, que la conqueste d'infinies ames pour Dieu, & leur délivrance de la domination et tyrannie du Démon infernal, auquel elles sacrifioient jusqu'à leurs propres Enfans.'

8  C.-A. Julien, *Les Voyages de découvertes et les premiers établissements XV^e-XVI^e siècles* (Paris, 1948), pp. 138–41. Cf. *Le Monde de Jacques Cartier*, ed. Braudel, p. 273.

9  On Champlain's biography, see N. E. Dionne, *Champlain* (Toronto, 1963). Champlain's complete works have been edited in six volumes by H. P. Biggar: *The Works of Samuel Champlain* (Toronto, 1922–36).

10  The history of Canada in the seventeenth century is dealt with in a number of reliable works. I follow G. Lanctôt, *A History of Canada*, vol. I (Toronto, 1963); M. Trudel, *The Beginnings of New France, 1524–1663* (Toronto, 1973); S. Diamond, 'Le Canada français au XVII^e siècle: Une société préfabriquée', *Annales*, 16 (1961), pp. 317–54; also the survey (too brief on the seventeenth century) by U. Sautter, *Geschichte Kanadas: Das Werden einer Nation* (Stuttgart, 1972), and some chapters of the popularizing work by R. Cartier, *Europa erobert Amerika* (Munich, 1962). The two leading journals of Canadian history are the *Canadian Historical Review* and the *Revue de l'histoire de l'Amérique française*. Recently an outstanding body of pictorial documentation has been provided in A. Vachon, *Dreams of Empire: Canada before 1700* (Ottawa, 1982). A full history, down to the present day, is E. McInnis, *Canada: a political and social history* (New York, 1962).

11  *Voyages dv Sievr de Champlain*, in *Works*, vol. II (Toronto, 1925), pp. 46–7. The original runs in part: 'Tous ces peuples patissent tant, que quelquesfois ils sont contraincts de viure de certains coquillages, & manger leur[s] chiens & peaux dequoy ils se couurent contre le froid. Ie tiens que qui leur mōstreroit à viure, & leur enseigneroit le labourage des terres & autres choses, ils apprendroient fort bien: car il s'en trouue assez qui ont bon iugement & respondent à propos sur ce qu'on leur demande' (ibid., p. 46).

12  The trading company also called itself *Société des Cent-Associés*. See Trudel, *The Beginnings of New France*, pp. 163–80, and id., *La Seigneurie des Cent-Associés* (Montreal, 1973).

13  Trudel, *The Beginnings of New France*, p. 223.

14  Figures from R. C. Simmons, *The American Colonies: from settlement to independence* (London, 1976), p. 24. The article by Diamond (see n. 10 above) is

an interesting example of comparative analysis in social history.

15  The source material is assembled in *The Jesuit Relations and Allied Documents*, ed. R. G. Thwaites (73 vols, Cleveland, 1896–1901). See also E. Lauvrière, 'Relations des voyageurs français en Nouvelle-France au XVII$^e$ siècle', *Revue de l'histoire coloniale*, 16 (1923), pp. 288ff.; L. Pouliot, *Etude sur les relations des Jésuites* (Montreal, 1940).

16  On anthropology, see D. Jenness, *The Indians of Canada* (Ottawa, 1972). Problems of cultural contact are touched on in W. J. Eccles, *The Canadian Frontier, 1534–1760* (New York, 1969), and G. T. Hunt, *The Wars of the Iroquois* (Madison, Wis., 1960).

17  Father Le Jeune's Relation (1634), in *The Jesuit Relations*, vol. VI, ed. Thwaites, p. 233. The original runs: 'Ils s'entraiment les vns les autres, & s'accordent admirablement bien; vous ne voyez point de disputes, de querelles, d'inimitiez, de reproches parmy eux' (p. 232).

18  F. Parkman, *The Jesuits in North America* (Boston, 1898), p. 14.

19  Nomenclature is discussed by the missionary Father de Charlevoix in his *Histoire et description générale de la Nouvelle France*, vol. I (Paris, 1744), pp. 183–4: 'Mais leur véritable nom est YENDATS. Celui de Hurons est de la façon des François, qui voyant ces Barbares avec des cheveux coupés, fort courts, & relevés d'une maniere bizarre, & qui leur donnoient un air affreux, s'écrierent la premiere fois qu'ils les apperçurent, *Quelles Hures!*'

20  Father Brébeuf's Relation (1636), in *The Jesuit Relations*, vol. X, ed. Thwaites, p. 195. In the original: 'Persone n'ose leur contredire; ils sont continuellement en festins, qui se font par leur ordonnance. Il y a donc quelque apparence, que le Diable leur tient la main par fois, & s'ouure à eux pour quelque profit temporel, & pour leur damnation eternelle' (p. 194).

21  It has also been persuasively argued that the Iroquois obtained a better supply of weapons and munitions from the English and Dutch on the Hudson. See K. F. Otterbein, 'Hurons versus Iroquois', in *Ethnohistory* (1974).

22  See especially J. Höffner, *Christentum und Menschenwürde: Das Anliegen der spanischen Kolonialethik im Goldenen Zeitalter* (Trier, 1947), and a more recent study written from a legal standpoint: J. Fisch, *Die europäische Expansion und das Völkerrecht* (Wiesbaden, 1984).

23  The *Exercitia Spiritualia* appeared in 1548 in Rome.

24  See *The Spiritual Exercises of Saint Ignatius* (London, 1963).

25  Father Le Jeune's Relation (1635), in *The Jesuit Relations*, vol. VIII, ed. Thwaites, p. 177. 'Trois puissantes pensées consolent vn bon cœur, qui est dans les forests infinies de la Nouvelle France, ou parmy les Hurons. La premiere est, ie suis au lieu où Dieu m'a enuoyé, où il m'a mené comme par la main, où il est auec moy, & où ie ne cherche que luy seul. La deuxiéme est, ce que dit Dauid; selon la mesure des douleurs que ie souffre pour Dieu, ses Diuines consolations réjoüyssent mō ame. La troisiéme, que iamais on ne trouue ny Croix, ny cloux, ny espines, que si on regarde bien, on ne trouue I. C. au milieu' (p. 176).

26  The life of Francis Xavier and his conception of missionary work have been described in great detail in G. Schurhammer, *Francis Xavier: his life, his times* (Rome, 1973–82). In particular, it was Francis Xavier who made it obligatory for the Jesuit missionary to report regularly on his work. Hence, the Superior of

Quebec sent an annual report to the Provincial in Paris from 1632 onwards. These accounts were circulated more widely in a simplified form and served devotional purposes as well as missionary propaganda. See J. H. Kennedy, *Jesuit and Savage in New France* (New Haven, 1950), pp. 77–9.

27 There is an immense literature on the Jesuit state; not all of it is to be taken seriously, and much of it is controversial. See especially P. Hernández, *Organización social de las Doctrinas Guaraníes de la Compania de Jesús*, vol. I (Barcelona, 1913), and M. Fassbinder, *Der 'Jesuitenstaat' in Paraguay* (Halle, 1926). Also very useful is *Zwettler Kodex* 420, vol. I, ed. E. Becker-Donner (Vienna, 1959), which reproduces the account by the Jesuit Florian Paucke.

28 See M. Lescarbot, *The History of New France*, vol. I (Toronto, 1907), p. 47. Until the beginning of the nineteenth century, the existence of other races was most commonly explained by reference to Noah and the Flood. See U. Bitterli, *Die Entdeckung des schwarzen Afrikaners* (Zürich, 1980), pp. 107ff.

29 It is now assumed that the American continent was originally populated by migrants who crossed the land bridge (now flooded, forming the Bering Straits) 50,000 years ago and then pressed forward in repeated waves as far as the southern tip of America, reaching it about 11,000 BC. See P. Farb, *Man's Rise to Civilization* (New York, 1968).

30 See J.-F. Lafitau, *Mœurs des sauvages américains*, new edn, vol. I´(Paris, 1983), p. 55.

31 Father Brébeuf's Relation (1636), in *The Jesuit Relations*, vol. X, ed. Thwaites, p. 210: 'Ie ne pretends pas icy mettre nos Sauuages en parallele auec les Chinois, Iaponnois, & autres Nations parfaitement ciuilisées; mais seulement les tirer de la condition des bestes, où l'opinion de quelques-vns les a reduits.'

32 Father Lalemant's Relation (1640), in *The Jesuit Relations*, vol. XVII, ed. Thwaites, p. 127. 'Or apres tout, ce sont creatures raisonnables, capables du Paradis et de l'Enfer, racheptez du sang de IESUS-CHRIST, desquelles il est escrit: *Et alias oues habeo quæ non sunt ex hoc ouili, & illas oportet me adducere.*' (p. 126). Cf. John 10: 16: 'And other sheep I have, which are not of this fold: them also I must bring.'

33 Father Le Jeune's Relation (1634), in *The Jesuit Relations*, vol. VI, ed. Thwaites, pp. 229, 231. 'Pour l'esprit des Sauuages, il est de bône trempe, ie croy que les ames sont toutes de mesme estoc, & qu'elles ne different point substantiellemēt; c'est pourquoy ces barbares ayans vn corps bien fait, & les organes bien rangez & bien disposez, leur esprit doit operer auec facilité: la seule education & instruction leur māque, leur ame est vn sol tres bon de sa nature, mais chargé de toutes les malices qu'vne terre delaissée depuis la naissance du mōde peut porter. Ie compare volōtiers nos Sauuages auec quelques villageois, pource que les vns & les autres sont ordinairement sans instruction; encore nos Paysans sont-ils precipuez en ce point: & neantmoins ie n'ay veu personne iusques icy de ceux qui sont venus en ces contrées, qui ne confesse & qui n'aduoüe franchement que les Sauuages ont plus d'esprit que nos paysans ordinaires' (pp. 228, 230).

34 Ibid., p. 230: 'nos Sauuages sont heureux, car les deux tyrans qui donnent la gehenne & la torture à vn grand nombre de nos Europeans [sic], ne regnent point dans leurs grands bois, i'entends l'ambition & l'auarice.' Note the extraordinary

similarity to J.-J. Rousseau, *Discours sur l'origine de l'inégalité parmi les hommes* (Paris, 1954), p. 92: 'Tel est, en effet, la véritable cause de toutes ces différences; le sauvage vit en lui-même; l'homme sociable, toujours hors de lui, ne sait que vivre dans l'opinion des autres.'

35 On the relations between missionaries and fur-traders, see B. G. Trigger, 'The French presence in Huronia: the structure of Franco-Huron relations in the first half of the seventeenth century', *Canadian Historical Review*, 49 (1968), especially pp. 121–5.

36 Father Le Jeune's Relation (1633), in *The Jesuit Relations*, vol. V, ed. Thwaites, p. 107. 'Ou que le iugement des hommes est foible! les vns logēt la beauté où les autres ne voient que la laideur. Les dents les plus belles en France sont les plus blanches, aux Isles des Maldiues la blancheur des dents est vne difformité, ils se les rougissent pour estre belles: & dans la Cochinchine, si i'ay bonne memoire, ils les teignent en noir. Voyez qui a raison' (p. 106).

37 Father Le Jeune's Relation (1640), ibid., vol. XVIII, p. 83. 'Ceux qui nous ont parlé des siecles dorés, ne les embelissoient pas des mines du Perou, mais d'vne innocence preferable aux richesses de l'vn & de l'autre hemisphere' (p. 82).

38 Father Le Jeune's Relation, ibid., vol. VI, p. 144.

39 On the same cluster of problems in South America, see, *Die Neue Welt: Chroniken Lateinamerikas von Kolumbus bis zu den Unabhängigkeitskriegen*, ed. E. R. Monegal (Frankfurt, 1982), pp. 350ff.

40 See Trudel, *The Beginnings of New France*, pp. 150–62.

41 See Parkman, *The Jesuits in North America*, p. 156.

42 Father Brébeuf's Relation (1636), in *The Jesuit Relations*, vol. X, ed. Thwaites, p. 103. 'N'est-ce pas desia beaucoup de n'auoir dans le viure, le vestir & le coucher aucun attrait que la simple necessité? N'est-ce pas vne belle occasion de s'vnir à Dieu, quand il n'y a creature quelconque qui vous donne suiet de vous y attacher d'affection?' (p. 104). On the biography of Father Brébeuf, see F. Talbot, *Saint among the Hurons: The life of Brébeuf* (New York, 1949).

43 Charlevoix, *Histoire et description générale*, vol. I, p. 181.

44 Father Brébeuf's Relation (1636), in *The Jesuit Relations*, vol. X, ed. Thwaites, p. 91. 'La langue Huronne sera vostre sainct Thomas, & vostre Aristote, & tout habile homme que vous estes, & bien disant parmy des personnes doctes & capables, il vous faut resoudre d'estre assez long-temps muet parmy des Barbares; ce fera beaucoup pour vous, quand vous commencerez à begayer au bout de quelque temps' (pp. 90, 92).

45 Trudel, *The Beginnings of New France*, pp. 155–9.

46 Ibid., p. 159.

47 On the problem of communication, which can only be mentioned here in passing, see B. Malinowski, 'The problem of meaning in primitive languages', in *The Meaning of Meaning*, C. K. Ogden and I. A. Richards, 2nd edn (London, 1927), pp. 296–336; also, P. Masson, 'Interpretative Probleme in Prozessen interkultureller Verständigung', in *Grundfragen der Ethnologie*, ed. W. Schmid-Kowarzik, (Berlin, 1981). I would mention also an essay by the anthropologist Mark Münzel which uses the concept of God among the Tupinambá and Guaraní in South America to show how difficult it is in a concrete instance to produce a communicative consensus: see 'Juppiters wilder Bruder: Der Versuch der

Missionare, den Tupinambá und Guaraní einen christlichen Gott zu bringen', in *Mythen der neuen Welt: Zur Entdeckungsgeschichte Lateinamerikas*, ed. K.-H. Kohl (Berlin, 1982), pp. 101–9.

48  In China the missionaries adapted too fully to local customs and thus brought about the rites controversy and the condemnation of their practices by the Papal bull *Ex illa die* of 1715. See W. Franke, *China and the West* (Oxford, 1967), pp. 57–9; Etiemble, *Les Jésuites en Chine* (Paris, 1966).

49  The practice of sending Congolese to be educated as missionaries in Portugal began in 1506, though earlier there were similar training projects in the Congo itself. See G. Balandier, *Daily Life in the Kingdom of the Kongo from the Sixteenth to the Eighteenth Century* (London, 1968), pp. 42–63.

50  'Of the Caniballes', in *The Essayes of Michael, Lord of Montaigne*, vol. I, tr. John Florio (London, 1904), p. 244. The original runs: 'Ils sont sauvages, de mesme que nous appellons sauvages les fruicts que nature, de soy et de son progrez ordinaire, a produicts: là où, à la vérité, ce sont ceux que nous avons alterez par nostre artifice et detournez de l'ordre commun, que nous devrions appeller plutost sauvages. En ceuzx là sont vives et vigoureuses les vrayes et plus utiles et naturelles vertus et proprietez, lesquelles nous avons abastardies en ceux-cy, et les avons seulement accommodées au plaisir de nostre goust corrompu.' M. de Montaigne, *Essais*, ed. J. Plattard, vol II (Paris, 1946), pp. 92–3.

51  See Lanctôt, *A History of Canada*, vol. I, pp. 166ff.

52  See Trudel, *The Beginnings of New France*, p. 238.

53  Trigger, 'The French presence', p. 125.

54  Father Le Jeune's Relation (1635), in *The Jesuit Relations*, vol. VII, ed. Thwaites, p. 275. 'Il est bien vray que si ce peuple estoit curieux de sçauoir, comme sont toutes les nations policées, que quelques-vns d'entre nous ont vne assez grande cognoissance de leur lãgue, pour les instruire: mais comme ils font profession de viure, & non pas de sçauoir; leur plus grand soucy est de boire & de manger, & non pas de cognoistre. Quand vous leur parlez de nos veritez, ils vous écoutent paisiblement; mais au lieu de vous interroguer sur ce sujet, ils se iettent incontinent sur les moyens de trouuer dequoy viure, monstrans leur estomach tousiours vuide, & tousiours affamé. Que si on sçauoit haranguer comme eux, & qu'on se trouuast en leurs assemblées, ie croy qu'on y seroit bien puissant' (p. 274).

55  Letter from Father Lalemant to Richelieu (1640), in *The Jesuit Relations*, vol. XVII, ed. Thwaites, p. 221. 'On a annoncé l'Evangile à plus de dix mille sauvages, non tant en général, qu'à chaque famille, et presque à chaque personne en particulier: on en a baptisé dans les maladies extraordinaires qui sont survenues plus de mille, dont au moins plusieurs petits enfans s'en sont envolés au Ciel; et pour comble de bonheur, on a enduré force persecutions' (p. 220). There seems little point in trying to work out the total number of conversions or baptisms. On the basis of the Jesuits' narratives, Trudel, in *The Beginnings of New France*, p. 304, estimates that in Huronia in 1634–47 a total of around 3,000 conversions took place; over 1,000 Hurons were converted in the period of the great epidemics (1639–40).

56  See Parkman, *The Jesuits in North America*, p. 334, and Kennedy, *Jesuit and*

*Savage*, pp. 87–91.

57 Lanctôt, *History of Canada*, vol. I, p. 165; also Trigger, 'The French presence', p. 127.

58 See Parkman, *The Jesuits in New France*, p. 212.

59 Trigger, 'The French presence', p. 130.

60 Father Le Jeune's Relation (1635), in *The Jesuit Relations*, vol. VIII, ed. Thwaite, p. 123. 'Ces gens à mon aduis son[t] vrays Sorciers, qui ont accez au Diable. Les uns ne font que iuger du mal, & ce en diuerses facons, sçauoir est, par Pyromantie, par Hydromantie, Negromantie, par festins, par danses & chansons. Les autres s'efforcent de guerir le mal par souflemens, breuuages & autres singeries ridicules, qui n'ont aucune vertu ny efficacité naturelle. Mais les vns & les autres ne font rien sans grands presens, & sans bonnes recompenses' (p. 124).

61 See Parkman, *The Jesuits in New France*, pp. 177–8.

62 The two best-known works featuring Hurons are probably Louis-Armand de Lahontan's *Nouveaux voyages dans l'Amérique septentrionale* (Paris, 1703) and Voltaire's *L'Ingénu* (Paris, 1767). On them, see U. Bitterli, *Die 'Wilden' und die 'Zivilisierten'* (Munich, 1976), pp. 420–5, 411–15.

63 Relation of Father Paul Raguenau (1650), in *The Jesuit Relations*, vol. XXXV, ed. Thwaites, pp. 81, 83. 'Mais il fallut, à tous tant que nous estions, quitter cette ancienne demeure de saincte Marie; ces edifices, qui quoy que pauures, paroissoient des chef-d'oeuvres de l'art, aux yeux de nos pauures Sauuages; ces terres cultivées qui nous promettoient vne riche moisson. Il nous fallut abandonner ce lieu, que ie puis appeller nostre seconde Patrie, & nos delices innocentes; puis qu'il auoit esté le berceau de ce Christianisme, qu'il estoit le temple de Dieu, & la maison des serviteurs de Iesus-Christ, & crainte que nos ennemis, trop impies, ne profanassent ce lieu de saincteté, & n'en prissent leur avantage; nous y mismes le feu nous mesmes' (pp. 80, 82).

64 Kennedy, *Jesuit and Savage*, p. 160.

65 I rely here on the detailed analysis by Trigger, 'The French presence', pp. 130–3. See also id., 'Order and freedom in Huron society', *Anthropologica* (1963), pp. 151–69.

66 Champlain, afraid of being outnumbered by an Indian alliance, had already placed strict limits on the supply of weapons to them, and instructions to this effect were confirmed by Governor Montmagny. It was not the Hurons' lack of fighting spirit that led to their defeat, as is often alleged, but rather their distinctly inferior weapons. See Lanctôt, *History of Canada*, vol. I, p. 181.

CHAPTER 5   CULTURAL RELATIONSHIP AS 'HOLY EXPERIMENT': THE
ENGLISH IN PENNSYLVANIA

1 For a detailed account of this early voyage in its context, see S. E. Morison, *The European Discovery of America*, vol. I: *The Northern Voyages* (New York, 1971). Outstanding studies of the background and motives behind British expansion are D. B. Quinn, *Raleigh and the British Empire* (Harmondsworth, 1973), and A. L. Rowse, *The Expansion of Elizabethan England* (London, 1955).

2 This figure comes from S. E. Morison, *The Oxford History of the United*

*States*, vol. I (New York, 1972), p. 92.

3   Statistical details in R. C. Simmons, *The American Colonies: from settlement to independence* (London, 1976). Of the currently available studies of the British possessions in North America, this one packs the most factual information into the shortest space.

4. Figures from K. G. Davies, *The North Atlantic World in the Seventeenth Century* (Minneapolis, 1974), p. 97. On the demography of North America before independence, see also R. V. Wells, *The Population of the British Colonies in America before 1776* (Princeton, 1975).

5   See Simmons, *The American Colonies*, pp. 24 and 177.

6   See Davies, *The North Atlantic World*, p. 102.

7   Ibid., p. 170.

8   Ibid., p. 153.

9   On early travel narratives, see K. and J. Bakeless, *Explorers of the New World* (London, 1957). A rich selection of sources with editorial commentary is available in *The Discovery of North America*, ed. W. P. Cumming, R. A. Skelton and D. B. Quinn (London, 1971 and 1974); the second volume goes up to the outbreak of the Revolution.

10   These two individuals are the subjects of good monographs: P. L. Barbour, *The Three Worlds of Captain John Smith* (Cambridge, Mass., 1964), and B. Smith, *Bradford of Plymouth* (Philadelphia, 1951).

11   There is a series of historical accounts of Pennsylvania. The one by R. Proud, *The History of Pennsylvania in North America* (Philadelphia, 1797–8), is itself a major historical document. H. M. Jenkins (ed.), *Pennsylvania Colonial and Federal* (Philadelphia, 1903), is still important. A guide to early history is E. B. Bronner, *Penn's 'Holy Experiment': The Founding of Pennsylvania, 1681–1701* (New York, 1962). The most recent survey is P. S. Klein and A. Hoogenboom, *A History of Pennsylvania* (University Park, Pa., 1980). See also the relevant historical journals, especially the *Pennsylvania Magazine of History and Biography*.

12   The oldest biography that is still worth reading is S. M. Janney, *The Life of William Penn* (Philadelphia, 1852), which publishes some material that has since been lost. Also recommended are C. Peare, *William Penn* (Philadelphia, 1957) and M. M. Dunn, *William Penn: politics and conscience* (Princeton, 1967). Mary Maples Dunn, at present the leading authority on Penn, is also co-editor of *The Papers of William Penn* (University Park, Pa., 1981–). On Penn's relations with England, see J. E. Illick, *William Penn the Politician* (Philadelphia and New York, 1957).

13   At the time when Pennsylvania was founded there were an estimated 60,000 Quakers in England. Their rejection of ecclesiastical institutions, especially the mediating function of the priesthood, their refusal to take oaths and acknowledge the authority of the state, and finally their pacifism, caused them to be regarded as dangerous to the commonwealth and to suffer frequent persecution. Between 1660 and 1680 over 10,000 of them were imprisoned; several hundred of these died in captivity. Today the Society of Friends has 120,000 members in the United States alone. Its headquarters are at Philadelphia. See M. H. Bacon, *The Quiet Rebels: the story of the Quakers in America* (New York, 1969).

14   It has not yet been explained how the charter was secured with so little difficulty at a time when the English monarchy granted such privileges very sparingly. See Dunn, *William Penn*, p. 79. The text of the charter may be found in Penn's *Brief Account of Pennsylvania* (London, 1681).

15   The first passage runs in full: 'Charles the Second by the grace of god King of England Scotland France and Ireland Defend$^r$ of the Faith &c To all whom these presents shall come greeting Whereas our truste [sic] and well beloved subject William Penn Esquire sonne and heir$^e$ of S$^r$ William Penn deceased out of a comendable desire to enlarge our English Empire and promote such usefull comodities as may be of benefit to us and our dominions as also to reduce the Savage Natives by Gentle and just manners to the Love of civill Society and Christian Religion hath humbly besought leave of us to transport an ample Colony unto a certaine Country hereinafter described in the parte of America not yet cultivated and planted. And hath likewise humbly besought our Royall Ma$^{tie}$ to give grant and confirme all the said Country with certaine priviledges and Jurisdicions requisite for the good government and safety of the said Country and Colony to him and his heires for ever. Know ye therefore that wee favoring the petition and good purpose of the said William Penn [ . . . ]' Quoted in *The Papers of William Penn*, vol. II, ed. M. M. Dunn and R. S. Dunn (University Park, Pa., 1982), pp. 63–4.

16   The second passage runs (ibid., p. 71): 'And because in so remote a Country [ . . . ] the Incursions as well of the Savages themselves, as of other Enemies, Pirates & Robbers, may probably be feared: Therefore we have given, & for Us, Our Heirs & Successors doe give Power by these Presents unto the said William Penn, his Heirs, & Assigns, by themselves, or their Captains, or other their officers, to leavy, muster, & traine, all sorts of Men [ . . . ] to make war, & pursue the Enemyes & Robbers aforesaid, aswell by Sea, as by Land [ . . . ]'

17   Among the surviving documents in Penn's hand, the expression 'holy experiment' first occurs in a letter of 25 August 1681 to the English Quaker James Harrison: '[ . . . ] that an example may be Sett up to the nations. there may be room there, tho not here, for such an holy experiment' (ibid., p. 108).

18   The full text runs (ibid., p. 225): 'That all Persons living in this Province, who confess and acknowledge the One Almighty and Eternal God, to be the Creator, Upholder and Ruler of the World, and that hold themselves obliged in Conscience to live peaceably and justly in *Civil Society*, shall in no wayes be molested or prejudiced for their Religious Perswasion' (italics in original).

19   The best study of the Lenni Lenape is P. A. W. Wallace, *Indians in Pennsylvania* (Harrisburg, Pa., 1961). A well-known early account of these Indians is by the German missionary J. G. E. Heckewelder, *History, Manners and Customs of the Indian Nations who once inhabited Pennsylvania and the Neighbouring States* (Philadelphia, 1876). See also W. Lindig and M. Münzer, *Die Indianer: Kulturen und Geschichte der Indianer Nord-, Mittel- und Südamerikas* (Munich, 1976), pp. 57–71.

20   A. C. Myers, *William Penn, his own Account of the Lenni Lenape or Delaware Indians, 1683* (Moylan, Pa., 1937), pp. 48–9.

21   Franz Daniel Pastorius (1651–1720) led a group of German Quakers to Philadelphia in 1683 and founded Germantown (now in the south of the city), of

which he was the first mayor. The quotation comes from his *Umständige geographische Beschreibung der zu allerletzt erfundenen Provinz Pennsylvania* (Frankfurt and Leipzig, 1700), p. 28.

22  Ibid., p. 59.

23  C. A. Weslager, *The Delaware Indians: a history* (New Brunswick, N. J., 1972), p. 140.

24  *The Papers of William Penn*, vol. II, ed. Dunn and Dunn, p. 128.

25  Ibid.

26  The name 'Philadelphia', 'city of brotherly love', first occurs in a letter of Penn dated 28 October 1681. Penn's choice of name was probably inspired by a group of English pietists who in turn were indebted to the writings of Jacob Boehme.

27  '[ . . . ] wee have their good in our eye, equall w$^{th}$ our own Interest', *The Papers of William Penn*, vol. II, ed. Dunn and Dunn, p. 120.

28  Aristotle, *The Politics* (Harmondsworth, 1981), Book 1.

29  On George Fox's ideas concerning racial policies, see T. E. Drake, 'William Penn's experiment in race relations', in *Pennsylvania Magazine of History and Biography* (1944), pp. 377–8. Of Fox's own writings the most informative is his diary: see *The Journal of George Fox*, ed. J. L. Nickfalls (London, 1952), and also H. E. Wildes, *Voice of the Lord: a biography of George Fox* (Philadelphia, 1965).

30  2 Kings: 21–3. In his *Account of the Lenni Lenape*, Penn showed his concern to establish a similarity between the external appearance of the Indians and that of Europeans: ' [ . . . ] for I have seen as comely European-like faces among them of both, as on your side the Sea' (*Account*, p. 26). 'I find them of like Countenance and their Children of so lively Resemblance, that a man would think himself in Dukes-place or Berry-street in London, when he seeth them' (ibid., p. 45). These streets were in the centre of a Jewish quarter.

31  Ibid., p. 38. On the Puritan conception of missionary work, see A. T. Vaughan, *New England Frontier: Puritans and Indians, 1620–1675* (Boston, 1965), pp. 235–40.

32  These land transfer treaties are printed, sometimes in facsimile, in several publications. See Myers, *William Penn's Account of the Lenni Lenape*; Wallace, *Indians in Pennsylvania*; J. P. Boyd, *Indian Treaties Printed by Benjamin Franklin, 1736–1762* (Philadelphia, 1938).

33  See Myers, *William Penn's Account of the Lenni Lenape*, p. 72.

34  These instructions, dated 11 July 1681, are entitled *Certaine Conditions or Concessions agreed upon by William Penn Proprietary and Governor of the Province of Pennsylvania*, and contain twenty paragraphs. Paragraphs 12–15 deal with the Indian question. The crucial passage runs: 'That noe man shall by any wayes or meanes in word or Deed, affront or wrong any Indian, but he shall Incurr the Same Pennalty of the Law as if he had Comitted it against his Fellow Planter. [ . . . ] That the Indians shall have Liberty to doe all things Relateing to the Improvem$^t$ of their ground & provideing Sustenance for their Familyes, that any of the planters shall enjoy' (quoted in *The Papers of William Penn*, vol. II, ed. Dunn and Dunn, p. 100).

35  On the relation between morality and business sense among the Quakers,

see the path-breaking discussions of 'worldly asceticism' by Max Weber: *The Protestant Ethic and the Spirit of Capitalism* (London, 1930); 'Religious ethics and the world: economics', in M. Weber, *Economy and Society*, vol. II (New York, 1968), pp. 576–90. A good historical account of these interconnections is G. B. Nash, *Quakers and Politics* (Princeton, 1968).

36  The Quakers, incidentally, reacted similarly to the problem of negro slavery. Although they were among the first to advocate humane treatment of black slaves, they drew back before the economic risk involved in abolishing this institution. See D. B. Davis, *The Problem of Slavery in Western Culture* (Ithaca, 1966), pp. 303–26. Even Penn did not reject slavery: see J. E. Illick, *Colonial Pennsylvania: a history* (New York, 1976), p. 115.

37  For more details concerning this treaty, see S. P. Uhler, *Pennsylvania's Indian Relations to 1754* (Allentown, Pa., 1951), p. 28.

38  The painting is in the Pennsylvania Academy of the Fine Arts.

39  Isaiah 11: 6–9: 'The wolf also shall dwell with the lamb, and the leopard shall lie down with the kid; and the calf and the young lion and the fatling together; and a little child shall lead them.

'And the cow and the bear shall feed; their young ones shall lie down together: and the lion shall eat straw like the ox.

'And the sucking child shall play on the hole of the asp, and the weaned child shall put his hand on the cockatrice' den.

'They shall not hurt nor destroy in all my holy mountain: for the earth shall be full of the knowledge of the LORD, as the waters cover the sea.'

40  Quoted in C. H. Sipe, *The Indian Chiefs of Pennsylvania* (Butler, Pa., 1927), p. 60.

41  Voltaire, *Lettres philosophiques* (Paris, 1956), Quatrième Lettre: Sur les Quakers, p. 19: 'C'est le seul traité entre ces Peuples et les Chrétiens qui n'ait point été juré, et qui n'ait point été rompu.'

42  *The Papers of William Penn*, vol. II, ed. Dunn and Dunn, p. 121.

43  M. J. Vogel and J. V. Alviti, *Philadelphia: a city for all centuries* (Philadelphia, 1981), p. 7. On the founding of Philadelphia, see also *Narratives of Early Pennsylvania, West New Jersey, and Delaware, 1630–1707*, ed. A. C. Myers (New York, 1912).

44  *The Papers of William Penn*, vol. II, ed. Dunn and Dunn, pp. 87–8, 357–8, 383–4, 388–90.

45  This argument is plausibly advanced by D. J. Boorstin, *The Americans*, vol. I: *The Colonial Experience* (New York, 1958), pp. 40–54. The implications of the Quakers' pacifism for the development of political practice are dealt with in H. Wellenreuther, *Glaube und Politik in Pennsylvania, 1681–1776* (Cologne, 1972), pp. 322–56.

46  On the subsequent historical development, see J. E. Illick, *Colonial Pennsylvania* (New York, 1976), and Klein and Hoogenboom, *A History of Pennsylvania*.

47  Figures in Weslager, *The Delaware Indians*, p. 175, and Simmons, *The American Colonies*, p. 124.

48  This is evident from an accusatory letter sent in 1729 by the chief of the Lenni Lenape to the Governor of Pennsylvania, which runs in part: 'in time past

we Sold our interests to Wm. Penn (our Brother) [ . . . ] Late to ye great prejudice and Disquiett of us a people that has done and Still Desiers to do *to continue in peace and Love, and be as one Heart and Soule* with Wm. Penn and his People, the Land has been unjustly Sold whereby we are redused to great wants & hardships' (italics in original). Quoted from Weslager, *The Delaware Indians*, p. 186.

49   See Sipe, *Indian Chiefs*, pp. 18–26.
50   Estimated figures for 1760, from H. Deschamps, *Les Européens hors d'Europe de 1434 à 1815* (Paris, 1972), p. 72.
51   Cf. Tolstoy's story 'How much land does a man need?'
52   The substance of this speech was preserved by Conrad Weiser, an interpreter and forest-dweller of German extraction, whose house in Womelsdorf (Berks County, Pa.) may be visited at the present day. According to Weiser, the Iroquois ambassador was a diplomat named Canasatego, who addressed the Lenni Lenape as follows: 'We conquer'd You, we made Women of you, you know you are Women, and can no more sell Land than Women. Nor is it fitt you should have the Power of Selling Lands since you would abuse it. This land that you Claim is gone through Your Guts. You have been furnished with Cloaths and Meat and Drink by the Goods paid you for it, and now you want it again like Children as you are [ . . . ] And for all these reasons we charge You to remove instantly. We don't give you the liberty to think about it. You are Women; take the Advice of a Wise Man and remove immediately.' Quoted from Weslager, *The Delaware Indians*, p. 191. See also P. A. W. Wallace, *Conrad Weiser* (Philadelphia, 1945).
53   W. Churchill, *History of the English-speaking Peoples*, vol. III (London, 1957), p. 123.
54   Proud, *The History of Pennsylvania*, vol. II, p. 107. Italics in original.
55   Wallace, *Indians in Pennsylvania*, p. 141.
56   Boorstin, *The Americans*, vol. I, pp. 54–63.
57   A. F. C. Wallace, *King of the Delawares: Teedyuscung, 1700–1763* (Philadelphia, 1949), p. 17.

CHAPTER 6   THE 'CONTROLLED RELATIONSHIP': THE EUROPEANS IN CHINA

1   B. W. Diffie and G. D. Winius, *Foundations of the Portuguese Empire, 1415–1580* (Minneapolis, 1977), p. 380.
2   See *The Book of Ser Marco Polo the Venetian Concerning the Kingdoms and Marvels of the East*, tr. and ed. H. Yule, 3rd edn revised by H. Cordier (London, 1903).
3   On Columbus's notions about China, see S. E. Morison, *The European Discovery of America: the southern voyages, AD 1492–1616* (New York, 1974), pp. 26–31.
4   Quoted in E. Zechlin, 'Die Ankunft der Portugiesen in Indien, China und Japan als Problem der Universalgeschichte', *Historische Zeitschrift*, 157 (1937–8), p. 503. Zechlin also discusses the remarkable comparison drawn between the Chinese and the Germans, which may be found not only in Vasco da Gama but in

other Portuguese sources as well. See *A Journal of the First Voyage of Vasco da Gama*, ed. E. G. Ravenstein (London, 1898), and *The Book of Duarte Barbosa*, vol. II, ed. M. L. Dames (London, 1921).

5 For the precise dating of this voyage and the identification of its goal, see Zechlin, 'Die Ankunft der Portugiesen', pp. 509–13. Cf. A. Kammerer, *La Découverte de la Chine par les Portugais au XVI<sup>e</sup> siècle et la cartographie des portulans* (Leiden, 1944), pp. 8–47.

6 Quoted in T'ien-tsê Chang, *Sino-Portuguese Trade from 1514 to 1644* (Leiden, 1934), p. 36.

7 Quoted in Kammerer, *La Découverte de la Chine*, p. 14.

8 Quoted in W. Franke, *China and the West* (Oxford, 1967), p. 21.

9 On the history of the Ming dynasty, see W. Eberhard, *A History of China*, rev. edn (London, 1977), pp. 252–80; H. Franke and R. Trauzettel, *Das Chinesische Kaiserreich* (Frankfurt, 1968); also W. Franke, 'China 1368 bis 1780', in *Saeculum Weltgeschichte*, vol. VI (Freiburg, 1971), pp. 232–65, and the relevant articles in such specialist journals as the *Journal of Asian History* (Wiesbaden) and the *Journal of Asian Studies* (University of Michigan). On the problem of smuggling in particular, see Kwan-Wai So, *Japanese Piracy in Ming China during the 16th Century* (East Lansing, Mich., 1975).

10 Quoted from T'ien-tsê Chang, *Sino-Portuguese Trade*, p. 51. The term 'Folangchi' or 'Feringhi' probably goes back to the Muslim traders who visited Canton as early as the ninth century and returned periodically thereafter. See Kammerer, *La Découverte de la Chine*, pp. 54–5.

11 On the concept of 'barbarian' in Chinese usage, see J. K. Fairbank (ed.), *The Chinese World Order: traditional China's foreign relations* (Cambridge, Mass., 1968), pp. 36–7, and W. Bauer (ed.), *China und die Fremden* (Munich, 1980), pp. 8–11.

12 Gaspar da Cruz, 'Treatise in which the things of China are related at great length, with their particularities, as likewise of the kingdom of Ormuz', in *South China in the Sixteenth Century*, ed. C. R. Boxer (London, 1953), p. 191.

13 Ibid., pp. 190–1.

14 See D. F. Lach, *Asia in the Making of Europe*, vol. I (Chicago, 1965), pp. 733–4.

15 See T'ien-tsê Chang, *Sino-Portuguese Trade*, pp. 69–72.

16 C. R. Boxer, *Fidalgos in the Far East, 1550–1770* (Hong Kong, 1968). Boxer deserves the credit for pointing out the self-sufficient character of the Far Eastern trading region bounded by the Moluccas, Japan and China. On this topic, see his *The Christian Century in Japan* (Berkeley, 1951), likewise a standard work, which describes the early period of contacts between Portugal and Japan, particularly the considerable success of missionary work, and reveals numerous parallels to the situation in China. See also his *The Great Ship from Amacon: annals of Macao and the old Japan trade, 1555–1640* (Lisbon, 1959).

17 T'ien-tsê Chang, *Sino-Portuguese Trade*, pp. 72–5.

18 Quoted in J. M. Braga, *The Western Pioneers and their Discovery of Macao* (Macao, 1949), p. 85.

19 See T'ien-tsê Chang, *Sino-Portuguese Trade*, pp. 89–93.

20 See Braga, *The Western Pioneers*, p. 128.

21   See Kammerer, *La Découverte de la Chine*, pp. 121–2.

22   Quoted in *South China in the Sixteenth Century*, ed. Boxer, pp. xxxvi–vii. We have no exact information about the population of Macao at this period. For the year 1601 Boxer reckons 400 Portuguese households (*casadas*) averaging five persons each and the same number of Asian households (*jurubaças*); one should add the numerous slaves and domestic servants (roughly six persons per household) and all those persons stationed in Macao only temporarily. See Boxer, 'Macao as a religious and commercial entrepôt in the 16th and 17th centuries', *Acta Asiatica*, 26 (1974), pp. 64–90.

23   Diffie and Winius, *Foundations of the Portuguese Empire*, p. 389.

24   *The Travels and Controversies of Friar Domingo Navarrete, 1618–1686*, vol. II, ed. J. S. Cummins (Cambridge, 1962), pp. 269–70.

25   On the problem of self-government, see Boxer, *Fidalgos in the Far East*, pp. 8–10.

26   Kammerer, *La Découverte de la Chine*, p. 120. See likewise T'ien-tsê Chang, *Sino-Portuguese Trade*, p. 99.

27   See Franke, *China and the West*, p. 31.

28   Details of the goods handled in Macao may be found in J. H. van Linschoten, *Von allen Völckern, Insulen, Meerporten, fließenden Wassern und anderen Orten, so von Portugal aus lengst den Gestaden Aphrica bis in Ost-Indien und zu dem Landt China sampt anderen Insulen zu sehen seynd* (Frankfurt, 1613), pp. 69–70. See also *The Suma Oriental of Tomé Pires*, ed. A. Cortesão (London, 1944), pp. 123–6.

29   There is a minute description of such early encounters in the travel narrative of Martín de Rada, edited by C. R. Boxer. See *South China in the Sixteenth Century*, ed. Boxer, pp. 244–59. See also *The Travels of Peter Mundy in Europe and Asia, 1608–1667*, vol. III, ed. R. C. Temple (London, 1919), p. 171.

30   *The Travels and Controversies of Navarrete*, vol. II, ed. Cummins, p. 269.

31   A mixture of Portuguese and Chinese which in some places even outlasted Portuguese rule and was learnt by their Dutch and English successors. The derivation of the word is uncertain: some linguists trace it back to Chinese 'pei-chin' (to pay money). See E. C. Knowlton, 'Pidgin English and Portuguese', in *Historical, Archaeological and Linguistic Studies on Southern China*, ed. F. S. Drake (Hong Kong, 1967), p. 228. It is probable that only a handful of Portuguese could speak Chinese. Interpreters (*linguas*), mostly Chinese Christians, therefore had an important part to play in negotiations.

32   On this culinary transfer, see Braga, *The Western Pioneers*, pp. 135–8. Braga goes so far as to suggest that but for the introduction of European and American products and the corresponding modification of their eating habits, the Chinese could not have coped with the population explosion of the last few centuries.

33   Quoted from Lo-Shu Fu, *A Documentary Chronicle of Sino-Western Relations, 1644–1820*, vol. I (Tucson, 1966), p. 41.

34   *The Travels of Peter Mundy*, vol. III, ed. Temple, pp. 262–3. On English relations with China, see J. B. Eames, *The English in China* (London, 1909).

35   The history of Jesuit missions in China has often been recounted, though with emphasis on the eighteenth century as a particularly interesting period.

What follows is a limited selection from the work of prominent specialists. On the early period of the Portuguese mission, see G. Schurhammer, *Francis Xavier: his life, his times* (Rome, 1973–82), and 'Die Schätze der Jesuitenarchive in Macao und Peking', in *Die katholischen Missionen* (1929). See further the numerous works by J. Wicki; also the relevant chapter in W. Reinhard, *Geschichte der europäischen Expansion* (Stuttgart, 1983). See also L. S. J. Pfister, *Notices biographiques et bibliographiques sur les Jésuites de l'ancienne Mission de Chine* (repr. Nendeln, 1971); K. S. Latourette, *A History of Christian Missions in China* (London, 1929); J. Gernet, *China and the Christian Impact* (Cambridge, 1985).

36  Quoted from Boxer, *Fidalgos in the Far East*, p. 170. On the Jesuits' commercial role, see also Boxer, 'Macao as a religious and commercial entrepôt', pp. 71–2.

37  Boxer, *Fidalgos in the Far East*, p. 169.

38  T'ien-tsê Chang, *Sino-Portuguese Trade*, pp. 116–17.

39  These figures are taken from G. B. Sansom, *The Western World and Japan* (New York, 1965), p. 127, and Franke, *China and the West*, p. 35. On the history of Japan, which after expelling the Portuguese and beginning new trade relations with the Dutch likewise continued to operate a 'controlled relationship', see Boxer, *The Christian Century in Japan* and his *The Dutch Seaborne Empire* (London, 1965), pp. 237–8.

40  *Le Japon du XVIII^e siècle, vu par le botaniste suédois Ch.-P. Thunberg*, ed. C. Gaudon (Paris, 1966), pp. 223–4.

41  Quoted in Kammerer, *La Découverte de la Chine*, p. 136.

42  See C. R. Boxer, *Jan Compagnie in Japan, 1600–1850* (2nd edn, Tokyo, 1968), and his *The Dutch Seaborne Empire*.

43  Quoted in *The Travels and Controversies of Navarrete*, vol. II, ed. Cummins, p. 267.

44  *The Suma Oriental of Tomé Pires*, vol. I, ed. Cortesão, p. 123.

45  C. R. Boxer, 'Portuguese and Spanish projects for the conquest of southeast Asia, 1580–1600', *Journal of Asian History*, 3 (1969), p. 133.

46  *South China in the Sixteenth Century*, ed. Boxer, pp. 271–3.

47  Ibid., p. 138.

48  Ibid., pp. 141–2.

49  Ibid., pp. 288–9.

50  Ibid., p. 256.

51  Ibid., pp. 255–6.

52  Ibid., p. 115.

53  Ibid., pp. 213–14.

54  Ibid., p. 218.

55  Ibid., p. 217.

56  Ibid., p. 310.

57  Ibid., pp. 220–1.

58  D. F. Lach, *The Preface to Leibniz' Novissima Sinica: Commentary, Translation, Text* (Honolulu, 1957).

59  See the chapters on China in Voltaire, *Essai sur les mœurs et l'esprit des nations*, vol. I (Paris, 1963), pp. 205–26. There is an ample literature dealing

with the European cult of China, especially during the Enlightenment. The chief authority on this subject is Donald F. Lach: besides his *Asia in the Making of Europe* (cited above), see his 'Leibniz and China', *Journal of the History of Ideas*, 6 (1945), pp. 437–55. See also M. Devèze, *L'Europe et le monde à la fin du XVIIIᵉ siècle* (Paris, 1970), pp. 111–27; O. Franke, 'Leibniz und China', in *Zeitschrift der deutschen morgenländischen Gesellschaft* (1928); A. Reichwein, *China und Europa: Geistige und künstlerische Beziehungen im 18. Jahrhundert* (Berlin, 1923).

CHAPTER 7    CULTURAL CONTACT AS A SCIENTIFIC CHALLENGE: THE ENGLISH AND FRENCH IN THE SOUTH SEAS

1   G. Fernández de Oviedo, *Historia general y natural de las Indias*, vol. II (Madrid, 1959), p. 212.
2   A. Pigafetta, *Magellan's Voyage: a narrative account of the first navigation*, ed. R. A. Skelton (London, 1975), p. 56.
3   Ibid., p. 60. Magellan's first narrative was followed by a great number of accounts of Pacific voyages. See the full bibliography by E. Woldan, 'Die erd- und völkerkundlichen Quellenwerke über Ozeanien und Australien (1523–1873)', in *Wiener ethnologische Blätter (1974)*.
4   On the history of Pacific exploration, see the standard works by J. C. Beaglehole, *The Exploration of the Pacific* (London, 1946); J. A. Williamson, *Cook and the Opening of the Pacific* (London, 1946); O. H. K. Spate, *The Pacific since Magellan*, vol. I: *The Spanish Lake* (London, 1979), vol. II: *Monopolists and Freebooters* (London, 1983); H. Plischke, *Der stille Ozean* (Munich, 1959); id., 'Kulturgeschichtliche Grundlagen der Entdeckungserfolge der Seereisen am Ende des 18. Jahrhunderts', in *Petermanns geographische Mitteilungen* (1938).
5   See R. Konetzke, *Süd- und Mittelamerika*, vol. I (Frankfurt, 1965), pp. 331–2. On the Spanish phase of exploration, see also H. Wagner, *Spanish Voyages to the North-west Coast of America* (San Francisco, 1929); on the Dutch phase, A. Sharp, *The Voyages of Abel Janszoon Tasman* (Oxford, 1968). The French phase is dealt with in J. Dunmore, *French Explorers in the Pacific*, vol. I: *The Eighteenth Century* (Oxford, 1965), and P.-J. Charliat, *Le Temps des grands voiliers*, vol. III (Paris, 1952).
6   The problem of who first discovered Hawaii has been debated for many years. The debate is summarized in Spate, *The Pacific*, vol. I, pp. 106–9.
7   For the cartographic history of Terra Australis Incognita, see L. C. Wroth, *The Early Cartography of the Pacific* (New York, 1944); also J. H. Parry, *The Discovery of the Sea* (London, 1974); N. Broc, *La Géographie des philosophes: géographes et voyageurs français au XVIIIᵉ siècle* (Paris, 1974); G. Williams, 'Myth and reality: James Cook and the theoretical geography of northwest America', in *Captain James Cook and his Times*, ed. R. Fisher and H. Johnston (Vancouver, 1979), pp. 59–79.
8   J. Harris, *A Complete Collection of Voyages and Travels*, ed. J. Campbell (London, 1744–8).
9   C. de Brosses, *Histoire des navigations aux terres australes* (Paris, 1756).

10  A. Dalrymple, *An Historical Collection of the Several Voyages and Discoveries in the South Pacific Ocean*, vol. I (London, 1770), pp. xxiv, xxviii (italics in original). See H. T. Fry, *Alexander Dalrymple and the Expansion of British Trade* (London, 1970), pp. 94–135. On de Brosses and the French context, see Broc, *La Géographie des philosophes*, pp. 181–5, and Dunmore, *French Explorers*, vol. I, pp. 47–50.

11  See B. Willey, *The Eighteenth Century Background* (London, 1940), and D. J. Boorstin, *The Discoverers* (New York, 1983), pp. 278–80.

12  De Brosses, *Histoire des navigations*, p. 13.

13  Dalrymple, *An Historical Collection*, vol. I, p. x.

14  Quoted in *Bougainville et ses compagnons autour du monde*, ed. E. Taillemite, vol. I (Paris, 1977), p. 22: 'La connaissance de ces isles ou continent étant à peine ébauchée, il est très intéressant de la perfectionner.'

15  L.-A. Bougainville, *Voyage autour du monde*, ed. M. Hérubel (Paris, 1966), p. 180: 'Je tombe d'accord que l'on conçoit difficilement un si grand nombre d'îles basses et de terres presque noyées, sans supposer un continent qui soit voisin. Mais la géographie est une science de faits; on n'y peut rien donner dans son cabinet à l'esprit de système, sans risquer les plus grandes erreurs.' For Wallis, who reached Tahiti before Bougainville, see G. Robertson, *The Discovery of Tahiti: a journal of the second voyage of H.M.S. Dolphin round the world, under the command of Captain Wallis, R.N., in the years 1766, 1767 and 1768* (London, 1948).

16  *The Journals of Captain James Cook on his Voyages of Discovery*, ed. J. C. Beaglehole, vol. I: *The Voyages of the* Endeavour, *1768–1771* (Cambridge, 1968), p. cclxxxii.

17  Ibid., p. cclxxxiii.

18  Ibid., p. 290.

19  *Encyclopédie ou Dictionnaire raisonné des sciences, des arts et des métiers*, vol. XXXIII (Geneva, 1779), p. 117.

20  N. E. Restif de la Bretonne, *La Découverte australe par un homme volant* (Paris, 1781).

21  Quoted in *Bougainville*, vol. I, ed. Taillemite, p. 22.

22  *Voyage de La Pérouse autour du monde*, vol. I, ed. L. A. Milet-Mureau (Paris, 1797), p. 30.

23  *The Journals of Captain James Cook*, vol. I, ed. Beaglehole, p. cclxxxii.

24  See Broc, *La Géographie des philosophes*, pp. 290–1, and id., 'Voyages et géographie au XVIII<sup>e</sup> siècle', *Revue d'histoire des sciences*, 22 (1969), pp. 137–54.

25  See U. Bitterli, *Die 'Wilden' und die 'Zivilisierten'* (Munich, 1976), pp. 207–26.

26  G. Gusdorf, *Dieu, la nature et l'homme au siècle des lumières* (Paris, 1972), pp. 262ff.; A. O. Lovejoy, *The Great Chain of Being* (Cambridge, Mass., 1936).

27  *The Journals of Captain James Cook*, vol. I, ed. Beaglehole, p. ccxlii.

28  A. von Humboldt, *Kosmos* (Stuttgart, 1978), p. 268.

29  See G. Capus, *Les produits coloniaux d'origine végétale* (Paris, 1930).

30  See H. C. Cameron, *Sir Joseph Banks, K.B., P.R.S.: The Autocrat of the Philosophers* (London, 1952), pp. 64–72; also C. Lyte, *Sir Joseph Banks* (North

Pomfret, 1980).

31 The first mention of tea in Europe occurs in Giovanni Battista Ramusio's *Navigazioni e viaggi* (Venice, 1550). It was praised in 1615 by an agent of the East India Company in his letters from Japan. See C. R. Harler, *The Culture and Marketing of Tea* (London, 1964).

32 See Charliat, *Le Temps des grands voiliers*, vol. III, pp. 116–17; Broc, *La Géographie des philosophes*, p. 313.

33 *Byron's Journal of his Circumnavigation, 1764–1766*, ed. R. E. Gallagher (Cambridge, 1964), p. 4.

34 *The Journals of Captain James Cook*, vol. I, ed. Beaglehole, p. cclxxx.

35 *Voyage de La Pérouse*, vol. I, ed. Milet-Mureau, p. 53: 'Il prescrira à tous les gens des équipages, de vivre en bonne intelligence avec les naturels, [ . . . ] et il leur défendra, sous les peines les plus rigoureuses, de jamais employer la force pour enlever aux habitans ce que ceux-ci refuseraient de céder volontairement.'

36 *The Journals of Captain James Cook*, vol. I, ed. Beaglehole, p. 514. The text is by James Douglas, the President of the Royal Society.

37 *Voyage de La Pérouse*, vol. I, ed. Milet-Mureau, p. 54.

38 *The Journals of Captain James Cook*, ed. Beaglehole, vol. II: *The Voyage of the* Resolution *and* Adventure, *1772–1775* (Cambridge, 1969), p. clxviii.

39 *Voyage de La Pérouse*, vol. III, ed. Milet-Mureau, p. 198: 'il se flattait de les contenir sans effusion de sang, et il fut victime de son humanité.'

40 A good introduction to these themes is H. Baudet, *Paradise on Earth* (New Haven and London, 1965). See the following standard works: H. N. Fairchild, *The Noble Savage* (New York, 1928); B. Smith, *European Vision and the South Pacific, 1768–1850* (Oxford, 1960). See also K.-H. Kohl, *Entzauberter Blick: Das Bild vom Guten Wilden und die Erfahrung der Zivilisation* (Berlin, 1981); K. H. Börner, *Auf der Suche nach dem irdischen Paradies* (Frankfurt, 1964).

41 See J.-E. Martin-Allanic, *Bougainville navigateur de son temps* (Paris, 1964), p. 964.

42 There is a biography of Omai which records all the information about his European visit that can be found in English travel narratives and daily newspapers: E. H. McCormick, *Omai, Pacific Envoy* (Auckland, 1977).

43 G. Forster, *A Voyage Round the World*, ed. R. L. Kahn (Berlin, 1968), p. 182.

44 R. Hakluyt, *The Principal Navigations Voyages Traffiques & Discoveries of the English Nation*, vol. I (London, 1927), p. 238: 'Item every nation and region is to be considered advisedly, & not to provoke them by any disdaine, laughing, contempt, or such like, but to use them with prudent circumspection, with al gentlenes, and curtesie.'

45 Ibid.

46 See J. Stagl, 'Der wohl unterwiesene Passagier', in *Reisen und Reisebeschreibungen im 18. und 19. Jahrhundert als Quellen der Kulturbeziehungsforschung*, ed. B. I. Krasnobaev (Berlin, 1980); id., 'Vom Dialog zum Fragebogen', *Kölner Zeitschrift für Soziologie und Sozialpsychologie*, 31 (1979), pp. 611–38. See also M. T. Hodgen, *Early Anthropology in the Sixteenth and Seventeenth Centuries* (Philadelphia, 1964), pp. 162–206.

47 *Philosophical Transactions: giving some Account of the present Undertak-*

*ings, Studies, and Labours of the Ingenious in many considerable Parts of the World*, vol. I (London, 1665), p. 186.

48  B. Varenius, *Geographia Generalis in qua affectiones generales Telluris explicantur* (Amsterdam, 1650). This work by a German scholar who died prematurely exerted great influence in France and still more in England, where Isaac Newton prepared a new edition in 1672.

49  See Bitterli, *Die 'Wilden' und die 'Zivilisierten'*, p. 228.

50  *Voyage de La Pérouse*, vol. I, ed. Milet-Mureau, p. 185.

51  Ibid., pp. 182, 190.

52  J.-M. de Gérando, *Considérations sur les diverses méthodes à suivre dans l'observation des peuples sauvages* (Paris, 1800); reprinted in *Revue d'anthropologie*, VI, 2nd series (1883). Translated into English as J.-M de Gérando, *The Observation of Savage Peoples* (London, 1969). These instructions were probably composed for the expedition to Australia led by Nicolas Baudin (1800–3); see J. Poirier (ed.), *Ethnologie générale* (Paris, 1968), pp. 26–7.

53  Cf. the touching description of his difficulties in learning the native tongue given by the Austrian Jesuit missionary Florian Paucke, who was in Paraná around 1750: 'I found it wellnigh impossible to understand their language, of which I had hitherto learnt but little, although I often struggled with it until midnight. How often I shed tears and was overcome by deep sorrow because I could not retain the language as I wished' (*Zwettler Codex 420*, ed. E. Becker-Donner (Vienna, 1967), p. 289). The first dictionaries produced by missionaries in the Quechua language of Peru and the Montagnais language of Quebec appeared around 1600.

54  De Gérando, *The Observation of Savage Peoples*, p. 70. The original runs: 'Le principal objet sur lequel devrait donc se diriger aujourd'hui l'attention et le zèle d'un voyageur vraiment philosophe, serait de recueillir avec soins tous les moyens qui peuvent servir à pénétrer dans la pensée des peuples au milieu desquels il serait placé, et à s'expliquer la suite de leurs actions et de leurs rapports. Ce n'est pas seulement parce que cette étude est de toutes la plus importante en elle-même, c'est encore parce qu'elle doit servir de préliminaire et d'introduction à toutes les autres. Comment se flatter de bien observer un peuple qu'on ne sait pas comprendre et avec lequel on ne peut s'entretenir? Le premier moyen pour bien connaître les Sauvages, est de devenir en quelque sorte comme l'un d'entre eux; et c'est en apprenant leur langue qu'on deviendra leur concitoyen' (p. 159).

55  Ibid., p. 67.

56  J. G. Herder, *Auch eine Philosophie der Geschichte zur Bildung der Menschheit* (1774), in *Sämtliche Werke*, vol. V, ed. B. Suphan (Berlin, 1891), p. 509.

57  De Gérando, *The Observation of Savage Peoples*, pp. 103–4.

58  Ibid., p. 97. The original runs: 'Un voyageur philosophe porterait ses vues bien plus loin. Il verrait dans ce commerce un moyen de les conduire à la civilisation. En effet, ce n'est guère qu'avec notre secours qu'ils peuvent se civiliser, et le besoin seul peut les rapprocher de nous. Ainsi un premier échange facilitera les premières communications; ces communications serviront peut-être à inspirer au Sauvage quelques nouveaux désirs qui le rappelleront encore auprès

de nous. Toujours bien reçu, bien traité, témoin de notre bonheur, de notre richesse, en même temps que de notre supériorité, peut-être s'attachera-t-il à nous par la reconnaissance ou l'intérêt, formera-t-il avec nous quelque alliance, nous appellera-t-il au milieu de lui pour lui enseigner la route qui doit le conduire à l'état où nous sommes. Quelle joie! quelle conquête! s'il s'ouvrait pour nous quelque espérance d'exercer une douce et utile influence sur ces peuples abandonnés [ . . . ]' (p. 177).

59  See *Ethnologie générale*, ed. Poirier, pp. 22–9. On the history of ethnology, see also W. E. Mühlmann, *Geschichte der Anthropologie* (Frankfurt, 1968), pp. 48ff.

60  Since John Locke, the concept of trusteeship has played a leading part in British colonial policy. See E. Barker, *Ideas and Ideals of the British Empire* (London, 1940), and H. Gollwitzer, *Geschichte des weltpolitischen Denkens*, vol. I (Göttingen, 1972).

61  F. Péron, *Voyage des découvertes aux terres australes [ . . . ] sur les corvettes* Le Géographe, Le Naturaliste *et la goélette* La Casuarina *pendant les années 1800, 1801, 1802, 1803 et 1804* (Paris, 1807).

62  Forster, *A Voyage Round the World*, pp. 155–6.

63  I am grateful to Professor Niklaus Schweizer of the University of Hawaii for his kindness in supplying me with a copy and translation of this text. It is printed in German in *Die Entdeckung und Eroberung der Welt*, ed. U. Bitterli, vol. I (Munich, 1981), p. 244.

64  Cook's death has been investigated and recounted in numerous studies, some of them contentious. The sudden change in relations between the English and the Hawaiians may be attributed to several factors which are insignificant in themselves: the islanders were surprised by the sudden return of the English in order to repair a ship; a boat was stolen; and Cook was under a degree of nervous strain which sometimes made him react impetuously. See R. Hough, *The Murder of Captain Cook* (London, 1979); J. C. Beaglehole, *The Life of Captain James Cook* (London, 1974); and G. Kennedy, *The Death of Captain Cook* (London, 1978).

65  Thus, Heinrich Zimmermann, a German who accompanied Cook on his last voyage, was clearly disappointed by what he considered a much too mild response to the commander's murder. See his *Reise um die Welt mit Captain Cook* (Tübingen and Basle, 1978), pp. 110ff.

66  Cf. Hermann Melville in *Moby Dick* (Harmondsworth, 1972): 'For many years past the whale-ship has been the pioneer in ferreting out the remotest and least known parts of the earth' (p. 205).

67  I. Lee, *Captain Bligh's Second Voyage to the South Sea* (London, 1920), p. 87.

68  See K. R. Wernhart, 'Auswirkungen der Zivilisationstätigkeit und Missionierung in den Kulturen der Autochthonen am Beispiel der Gesellschaftsinseln', in *Europäisierung der Erde? Studien zur Einwirkung Europas auf die außereuropäische Welt*, ed. G. Klingenstein, H. Lutz and G. Stourzh (Vienna, 1980), pp. 120–46. See also the instructive foreword to J. Davies, *The History of the Tahitian Mission, 1799–1830*, ed. C. W. Newbury (Cambridge, 1961), and W. Wilson, *A Missionary Voyage to the Southern Pacific Ocean Performed in the*

*Years 1796, 1797, 1798 in the Ship* Duff, *Commanded by Capt. J. Wilson* (London, 1799).

69   *Journal of Voyages and Travels by the Rev. Daniel Tyerman and George Bennet, Esq.*, ed. J. Montgomery, vol. II (London, 1831), pp. 110–11.

70   See P. J. Hempenstall, 'Europäische Missionsgesellschaften und christlicher Einfluß in der deutschen Südsee: das Beispiel Neuguinea', in *Imperialismus und Kolonialmission: Kaiserliches Deutschland und koloniales Imperium*, ed. K. J. Bade (Wiesbaden, 1982), pp. 226–42; E. Dodge, *Islands and Empires: Western impact on the Pacific and East Asia* (Minneapolis, 1976), pp. 85–101.

71   A. von Chamisso, *Reise um die Welt* (Berlin, 1975), p. 230.

# Index

*Index by Gill Riordan*